CATBIRD

The Ballad of Barbi Prim

Barbara J. Ostfeld

To Marilen —
First time live —
written it that way!
Hurray!

Barbara

ERVA PRESS

**To contact Barbara for interviews, or to invite her to speak, write,
or participate in a book club discussion, visit catbirdbook.com.**

Although my memory is imperfect, this memoir does represent my best efforts
at accurate recollection. To protect privacy, however, I have changed the names
of almost all the people I mention here, except for those who have told me they
don't mind or those mentioned only in passing.

An earlier version of "Purim at HUC" was published in the Lilith Blog on
January 9, 2018 under the title "When I first chanted Megilah at 19, I was
harassed on the bima. I'm still not laughing, decades later."

An earlier version of "I Get a Tip about Tips" was published in the fall 2018 issue
of *The Reform Jewish Quarterly* under the title "Women Cantors and Dollars
in 1976."

Cover design: Joan Wong
Page design: Vaerden & Co.

Library of Congress Control Number: 2018964310

ISBN, print: 978-0-9980326-1-0
ISBN, ebook: 978-0-9980326-3-4
Printed in the United States of America
23   22   21   20   19   2   3   4   5   6   7   8   9   10

a collaboration with *Vaerden & Co., Publishers* | vaerden.com

For the first nests that held Hana and Tali,
and the Wings that flew them to mine

And for my ever-evolving Scott

When I was a little girl, I was fascinated by TV characters, like the obviously Jewish Gladys Kravitz on *Bewitched*. But I knew that she wasn't really a TV star because the stars looked like Samantha—blonde and sleek and charming. Plain women like Gladys were TV's comedic foils or gals Friday.

I knew I would grow up to be a Gladys. It was unfair. Wasn't I a smart girl who could sing rings around any of the Mouseketeers? Yes! Although I wasn't sure that was actually a good thing after my father told me at age eight that I inherited my singing voice from his cousin who was a chanteuse in a whorehouse in Lebanon. (Then he defined *chanteuse* and *whorehouse* and pointed to Lebanon on a map.)

What I was sure about—based on all the evidence—was that I was plump and plain and awkward, and so my fate was sealed.

Or at least it felt sealed for a long time, even though I did sing my way through a stained glass ceiling. Becoming a "first" in a previously all-male career, though, wasn't enough to free me from a quicksand made of fear and anxiety— and the belief that I deserved to go under because I wasn't wonderful enough to be rescued.

But then, well into middle age, I learned how to free myself, and in the process, I discovered what I had known before I learned to judge Gladys and Samantha—and myself.

Catbird is for all daughters—of any generation—and for anyone whose gifts or quirks are underappreciated.

— *Barbi Prim*

Contents

Barbi Prim, Herself

First, I know I am chunky. I have frizzled hair, and my mom cuts it to save money, even though we have money because my dad is a doctor. I have a really big nose, and I wear cat-eye glasses with sparkles in them. Mom makes my clothes, so I wear a style called "European." But I can really sing.

Because I want to wear high heels when I grow up, I wear oxfords—with white ankle socks, of course. Sometimes I wish I had store-bought clothes, a beauty parlor haircut, and fancy shoes, but I don't think I should ask for things like that.

Also, I have a hiding place. In temple the air smells like lemon polish, and when the ark is open something opens inside me too. When we read together during services, I feel strong and important. The cantor gives me solos. When I sing, I am not fat or near-sighted. I sing like a long sigh, like magic, like the hot glass I saw the man spinning in Colonial Williamsburg.

I want to wear a long black robe and sleeves that are like an angel's wings and a collar that puts your face in a painting.

And I want to stand right under the Eternal Light, and I want to hear the Civil Rights words so people can see me nod "yes" to Civil Rights. I want to sing songs with words like *thine* and *everlasting* in them.

I want to be a cantor who will give solos to kids who cry like I do when they don't get them.

I am eight years old.

Ditty

It would be pretentious
To say a star is born
Yet Ostfeld clan rejoices

1956, age 4

Sing Amy

("Once in Love with Amy")

Ori is three. I am going to be three too. We are going to Ori's party in the car.

I tell Mommy to turn on the radio. She says, "Say 'please.'"

I say "please" in a nice voice.

The Amy song plays on the radio. Then it's over and there is another song. But I want to hear Amy.

"Sing Amy, Mommy and Daddy!"

They sing it.

It is very short. "Sing it again."

I hear quiet. They look at each other. Then they sing.

It is over fast. "Sing Amy again."

Daddy says, "No more Amy."

I sing Amy. Mommy and Daddy look at each other again.

I say, "Now you sing Amy."

They sing.

Now they are making me sing Amy for Aunt Vera. I get kisses and hugs. Not from Daddy. Mommy cries.

They like it when I make my singing sound like radio singing. I can do that. I can make the notes last a long time. And I can make them shake.

Uncle Leo says, "Move to the music, darlin'! Put your arms out like this." He looks like he is pretending to be a bird.

"No." I won't sing now. Singing isn't silly like that.

We Don't Have Christmas

I don't want to ride in the grocery cart. It's cold and the wires hurt. And I want to push the handle and drop things in the cart by myself. Sometimes I can put something green and shiny in there to take home if Mommy doesn't see it too fast. But there is dirty snow on the white squares on the floor—more than on the red squares on the floor. I tried to clean it with my mitten last time, but Mommy said no.

It is nice to see piles and piles of boxes and cans like blocks. All the colors together are nice. Especially when the two colors next to each other are good colors, like green and golden. Golden is a color too.

We live in an apartment with Eda Neni because the NEW HOUSE is going up. There is a pantry where all the spices are in lines and rows, like when you play a game on a board. A grocery store is like that, only bigger and taller.

Sometimes Mommy takes the wrong can when she should take the next one in. The line gets crooked and the cans aren't next to each other, touching each other, the way I like.

Then you have to go to the next row in the store to see where the boxes are in a line.

There is a bad screechy sound coming from the bottom of our cart. The noise is hurting my ears, and the cart is not behaving properly.

Simon is napping the whole time, even if I poke him—only sometimes, only a little. Maybe he can't feel pokes in the snowsuit.

Now Mommy is at the money part where she is not happy. She drops things now. I put our new foods on the desk thing near the register. The clerk knows all the dollars and cents for everything. She is very important and wears a uniform with a hat that goes along with the uniform. When all the new foods are in bags, she winks at me and says, "Merry Christmas, little girl."

And I say, in a radio voice I like to make, "We don't have Christmas. We're Jewish."

This makes Mommy's mouth twist but in a smiling way.

neni: aunt (Hungarian)

When You Wish upon a Star

Jiminy Cricket is just the right color green, and I like his hat. He takes it off with a sweep that I like, and his knees are bendy for dancing and hopping. But what I like the most is he sings like melting Hershey's and the round chocolates with white dots—the ones where your tongue is happy and your teeth are swimming. Jiminy's eyes get bigger almost like he is alive and not a cartoon, which is paintings put together fast. He sings perfect sounds. Then the best part is when he closes up his face and you wait for him to sing ARE and then EXTREME and then THROUGH. Your tummy is fluttery and tight from waiting. And then at the end his voice flies up to the highest place—

The OO in TRUE sounds like it's shining like the star in the song.

And then when the song is over and the TV is off, and I might be crying, I sing the part about dreams coming TRUE.

I make my OO go to the same high place where Jiminy's OO goes. Because then the perfect feeling, like flying, comes again.

Brookfield Zoo

I wish the animals would be cleaner. I like their faces, but I don't think they care that their fur is all messy and has smears of things in it. When they're outside, it smells better. I like to get up close to see their faces, but then I see the little flies all around them too.

We visit Ziggy the elephant. Daddy says that Ziggy attacked his keeper once. I say that Ziggy is terrible, but Daddy says that elephants cannot be bad. They are meant to live in big spaces and should not have to live in closed spaces. He says that living in cages makes them not-elephants. Then I look at Ziggy's eyes, which are red and small. I try to feel sorry, but all I feel is happy that he can't get me or Daddy. I wonder if the children who are throwing peanuts for him know that he attacked his keeper. Maybe I will tell on Ziggy.

Mommy and Simon have moved ahead. We need to catch up or we will get lost. Daddy gets lost. Mommy never does.

We find Mommy right outside the kangaroo house.

"Hurry, Barbi!"

I run in with them. It smells so bad inside.

"Look," she says, "the kangaroos are having sexual intercourse!"

I look, and what I see is kangaroos playing piggyback. Then I see other mothers are all wheeling their kids out as quickly as they can. Mom pushes us closer to the railing to watch. I want to go out, too, where it doesn't smell. Simon is asking to be picked up. He's too big for that, now that Mommy is pregnant. Daddy doesn't pick us up.

Mommy says that we can get some ice cream. Right away we find a cart with a big umbrella. Daddy says we have to order for ourselves. I take Simon's hand and we line up. I order a chocolate-coated chocolate Good Humor, please. I hold out my dime. Simon starts to cry. He is too shy to order. Daddy says he has to order for himself or he can't have one. Simon cries harder. I start to cry too, because I want to have one, but I don't want to have one in front of Simon if he doesn't get to have one.

"I'll order his," I say.

"NO," says Daddy in a loud voice. Mommy steps up and orders Simon's in a soft voice. Simon hands over his dime and stops crying.

Daddy is very mad at Mommy.

"He has to grow up, Ruth."

I eat my Good Humor very fast and wipe the melted chocolate on my shirt. I look down and see big brown handprints on my front. And look, a fly. Now I am messy like the animals. I want to go home.

Mommy in the Bathtub

When Mommy takes a bath, she wants to talk and tells me to sit down. Mommy's breasts droop down, and her nipples look like strawberries. Sometimes my stomach hurts for a second if I look at her nipples and I think how I don't want mine to ever look like that. I ask about the blue lines on her legs and learn that they are veins. Very close veins.

I like talking to Mommy in the car, but not in the bathtub. In the car Mommy looks at the street, and I look out the window. I don't want to see the water in the bathtub get cloudy from the soap. I like when the water is clear, and people are wearing all their clothes.

Daddy in His Underwear

When Daddy comes home from the university, he takes off his suit and shirt and tie. Also his shoes and socks. Mostly this happens in spring and summertime, but sometimes in winter too.

By dinnertime Daddy is in his undershirt and underpants. They are white. Mommy, Simon, Sarah, and I are dressed. Simon and I wear our after-school clothes.

I don't look at Daddy, except his face. I don't want to see where his penis is, because sometimes it is showing and sometimes you can see pubic hairs sticking out. Even if I look away really fast, my stomach starts to hurt. So I look right at his eyes. Once he told me that it is important to look at peoples' eyes. Then they know you're paying attention and that you give a shit. When he said "shit," Mommy said, "ADRIAN!" When he says swear words, I get goose bumps. It is sort of neat and sort of scary.

Sarah wrinkles her nose at Daddy sometimes. She says that he smells. I don't smell it, but she's just a baby.

Mommy doesn't like when Daddy smokes a cigar in the living room. But one time she asked him to put it out, and he yelled something about his own house.

I like when Daddy is still wearing his shoes at my bedtime. Then I can hear him walking back and forth in my room while I am going to sleep. We call that "staying a couple of minutes."

Clark's Thumb

Mrs. Dean, my first-grade teacher, doesn't have a book for me today. She tells me to help Clark with his reading. I take Clark over to the window seat, which is a good spot for reading. You can see down to the stone wall and pretend that you could just jump right out to where the buses are.

Clark doesn't say much in class. He wore overalls on picture day, and Reuben made fun of him. Mrs. Dean made Reuben apologize.

I am feeling very important. Like a teacher.

Clark has beautiful eyes, very blue with no eyelashes. Well, he has eyelashes, but they are clear.

Anyway, I bet I can teach him to read today. Now. We hold the book together, and I point to the words.

"Sound them out, Clark."

He can't get started, so I give him the first letter.

"Ess," I say. "It has a ssss sound. You do it."

"Ssss," says Clark.

"Right," I tell him. "Now two e's. What sound do they make?"

Clark doesn't know.

"They sound like what they are," I tell him.

He looks down and shakes his head.

"Eeee," I say, loudly. Then I point at the e's.

Clark does not understand.

"Ssss. Eeee. See."

I feel my heart pounding. What if he never understands? If he never does, he won't be a reader. Clark HAS to understand! He has to! Right now!

I take Clark's finger to put under the e's, and accidentally my fingernail stabs his thumb.

"OH!" I half yell, "I'm sorry!"

I'm shaking a little and tears are coming to my eyes.

"'S a'right," Clark says. "Doesn't hurt."

But I see a spot of blood on his thumb.

"I hurt you! I didn't mean it. It was an accident," I cry. "Let's wash it and put a Band-Aid on it."

"No," says Clark. "Doesn't hurt."

He reaches to my face to catch a tear and rubs it on his thumb.

"Let's not do reading now, okay?" I ask.

"Okay," he says.

All day I can sort of feel his skin under my nail and can't stop thinking about it. I almost cry every time, but then I don't. I know one thing. I am never going to tell the two things. I stabbed Clark and he didn't learn how to read.

Reading

Mrs. Dean has to get out the step stool to reach the top cabinet in the cloakroom. Her shoes are tie-ups, but the laces have a fancy pattern, and there are lots of tiny holes in a curve on the front. They have high heels but not the skinny kind. I get a good look at them when Mrs. Dean is on the stool.

She picks a few books from the cabinet and hands them down to me. Then she steps down very slowly.

"I think you'll like these, Barbi. You're a good reader for a girl who should still be in kindergarten."

But they don't last long. And I want a fat book that looks grown-up and makes me important and that lasts longer.

I don't understand Mrs. Dean's hair. It is crinkly and close to Mrs. Dean's head but doesn't seem to be right on her head. It is brown, but not like other brown hair. If she wore a crown, maybe the hair would hold it up. Her hair looks strong like that. Mrs. Dean's hair is one good thing about going to school.

Another way school is good is because you always know when the snacks will come and when you should urinate. (We say "urinate" in my family because Dad is a doctor.)

Even if the snack is bad, you don't have to keep thinking about finding something better in the pantry or about what would be the BEST snack. Nancy eats the worst parts of her snack first, like the carrots, and saves the best parts, like the pudding, for last. I am going to do that too from now on. And you don't have to wonder if the dolls in the house corner are lonely. The dolls can't be waiting for you if it is not time to play in the house corner. At school you don't have to hate going outside to play, because recess will be over soon, and you can be happy about that.

The only bad thing is they never let me go to ART. I always have to go to MUSIC. I like the singing and the instruments, and especially when I sing one part of a round and the other kids sing the other part. That way the sounds are dancing with each other. But I still want to make an ashtray with a leaf pressed into it. I want mine to be that color between blue and green with a little more green. If I cry about needing to make an ashtray in art, they will let me go.

Daddy says that I am a good enough reader now that I can read any kind of book that isn't technical. I think he means like a science book about brains or how TVs work.

I try the books in their bedroom, and I can read them. I read a page in each one, and then I put them back. I don't like them. I look under their bed, like where I keep my library books.

There is one small, fat book, with a corner turned down at the beginning of chapter 4.

> I commenced to feel Alice by placing my hands one on each side of her waist, noting with cruel satisfaction the shiver that ran through her at their contact with her naked skin . . .

I get goose bumps reading the words. I feel funny and something sharp happens in my stomach. It might be a good feeling or it might be a feeling that comes because I am bad. I always like reading words, just like I always like milk chocolate squares. But not these words. I don't want to think about these words anymore.

Counting Time

Tonight Daddy has me stand on my bed in my nightgown for counting time. Sometimes he skips counting time and goes right to staying a couple of minutes. His shoes make sounds that are like counting but without the numbers. Step, step, step, step, turn. Step, step, step, step, turn.

When it's counting time, I know what will happen. It's what happens every night because I am not smart. I count my numbers for Daddy and the numbers line up in order until twelve. I say them fast but not too fast because that is cheating. I do not understand twelve. Twelve is where my stomach starts to hurt. Twelve does not make sense. Where does it come from? Fourteen comes from four, and fifteen comes from five. But I can't say the twelve at the right time and Daddy gets mad. Not the yelling mad but the quiet mad.

"Ruth!" he calls out to Mommy. "Your genetics are showing!"

"What are genetics?" I ask.

"Genes—g-e-n-e-s—are directions for making a person. Half of the rules come from the mother and half from the father."

"Do I have your reading genes?"

"Yes, I would say so."

"But I have Mommy's counting genes?"

"It certainly appears so."

"Could YOU say the numbers in line, Daddy? With me?"

"It's time for bed."

"Will you stay a couple of minutes?"

"Not tonight."

Permanent

Mom is giving me a Tonette Home Permanent. I am very happy. My hair never lies flat or looks good in ponytails. Hairstyles are important. Dad likes ponytails. When my hair is in ponytails, though, it looks like clumpy noodles that have dried up. Also, it is too short for ponytails, so a lot of it is hanging out and poofing around. A Tonette will make my hair look like Patty Miller's hair, which is perfect. She is the only other girl in my grade who has brown hair. Nancy's hair is squiggly, but it's blonde. A Tonette will be like magic. My hair will be perfect starting today.

First, Mom puts a towel on my shoulders after my bath. I am feeling very important, like an experiment person in science. She combs little patches of hair and tops them with little see-through papers. Then she winds the hair around these skinny pink rollers and snaps them shut. For the hair that's too short for wrapping up, she uses Lady Ellen pin curl clips. (She's used those before, and my hair comes out crooked.) My head feels tight, but it's okay because this will make my hair smooth like in the magazines. Mom looks nervous, like when she's got the candy thermometer in the saucepan or when she's looking at the knitting directions A LOT.

Now she tells me she's going to use the double applicator, and she squeezes a very smelly liquid all over my curlers. It stings my nose and I sneeze. I rub under my nose, and Mom says, "Don't disturb the rollers. Don't move your head around." I hold still and cough. I can't help it.

Mom says, "I don't know about this . . ."

I say, "It's okay, Mom, the smell will go away."

She still has that look, but she puts me under the hair dryer. It whooshes, and my head stings in a few places, but it's worth it to get smooth magazine hair. Maybe for Chanukah Mom will get me a Tonette doll, and we'll look the same. I know the one I want. She has red hair and a white blouse. Her jumper is lavender and purple and yellow and green and pink. There is even green rickrack for decoration. The best is her hair, which is long. I touched it, and it stretches halfway down her back. I really REALLY want this doll.

Mom says, "Don't jiggle or the curlers will come out."

I stop, but it's taking a long time, and my eyes are watering from the smell, which is worse from the heat. I cough again.

Mom is cooking supper but keeps checking to see if I'm dry.

Finally I'm dry. Mom lets me out from the dryer and unclips the rollers. My head feels all airy and cool. She unwinds them, and they make clicking sounds as they fall on the kitchen table. She pulls out the crinkled papers and takes out the pin curl clips.

Then she starts to put them away just so in the Lady Ellen box, but I say, "MOM! First I have to SEE!"

She doesn't say anything.

I go into the little bathroom behind the kitchen and step onto the stool to see myself in the mirror. I am the same Barbi. The Tonette didn't work. I look from every side—nothing is any different. There is no change. I am angry, but not at Mom. Her recipes always come out. And Tonette girls always are pretty, so it's not the Tonette inventors.

It's me. I am just not a Tonette girl. I'm not ever going to be a Tonette girl.

There is no such thing as magic.

Naming Barbi Prim

When Uncle Marvin comes for dinner, Mom is nervous. She says Marvin is a picky eater, like a child. He looks like Dad except handsomer. Will I turn out more like him or more like Dad?

I see how much we look alike, Dad and me. Relatives always say, "Barbi's the spitting image of Adrian." I know what it means even though it sounds very bad to say "spit." Simon doesn't look anything like Dad or like Uncle Marvin. That should mean that I am smarter than Simon, but Dad says that Simon is smarter than me and that boys show their intelligence later than girls. Like in high school. Simon can do arithmetic problems in his head on car trips. But I have a bigger vocabulary. Also people look in my eyes for not just a second, but for a little longer. This is what I have with some people. We look at each other and then we fit together like puzzle pieces. For more than a second. I have this with the looking-in-your-eye kind of people. Some teachers. My rabbis, my cantor, and my favorite relatives, especially Grandma.

Uncle Marvin calls Dad "Sonny," and Dad calls him "Map." This is because they had a made-up language when they were little and it had *p*'s after every vowel. I like the letter *p* but not because it sounds like *pee*, which is a word we don't say in my house because we don't use baby talk.

When we have company, Mom makes food from recipes in *Gourmet* magazine. She is very proud of being fancy and brings out the good china and the glasses that can make music if you wet your finger and go all around the rim. I get excited when we are going to have company. All the forks and spoons are lined up in perfect rows.

It's fun when Uncle Marvin comes because he makes jokes. Like he will say, "Why don't you get the CAT to clear the table?" And he says *cat* in a way that makes me laugh.

Uncle Marvin calls me "Barbi Prim" or sometimes "Zelda Prim." I know what prim is. It's like old ladies wearing bonnets in the movies. Zelda is a funny name because no one has a name that starts with *z*. Uncle Marvin signs his letters "Beowulf Schwartz." He smokes cigarettes and makes up jingles for commercials—like "Winston tastes good like a (clap, clap) cigarette should." I wonder if Uncle Marvin wrote that one. I have to remember to ask him.

I do like bonnets, so maybe Uncle Marvin has found the right nickname for me. It's kind of nice and kind of teasing. But he talks to me and thinks up jokes while he is looking at me. I always laugh but with my hand over my mouth, because my laugh might be too loud.

I like the word *prim*. It is almost like *princess* but plainer.

Central Facts about Plumpness and Singing

The central fact is that I am plump. It makes me feel like I'm by myself. The other girls at Edison School all seem to be blonde and skinny. All the other mothers have hairstyles. They seem to know each other and seem not to know my mother—or Harold Rosenman's mother, who is fatter than my mother, who is not actually fat. She just doesn't wear a girdle during the daytime.

Cindy Rosenman IS odd looking. And Harold walks funny, so we secretly call him "Storf," which means something, I think. His feet turn out. The Adelman kid is mean and spoiled. He is an only child. They have a pool in their backyard. When we went there, all I remember is that his mother's pubic hair was sticking right out of her bathing suit. I checked my mother's thighs as fast as I could, but in a way so no one would notice, and—whew—her pubic hair was all covered.

So all of this is Jewish somehow. I'm just not sure how.

When we go to temple on Friday night and on Sunday mornings for Sunday school, I don't worry. I am calm. No one in temple is making fun of me—or at least I don't think so. There are girls in temple who are beautiful and who dress like girls in magazines and whose mothers have hairstyles, but it doesn't feel like they are making fun of either my mother or of plump, messy me with the anklets. (I like that word, *anklets*, but not the kind of socks.)

Their fathers are different from my father too. My guess is that they pick their kids up when they come home from work and maybe swing them up in the air. Maybe they kiss them on the cheek. But those fathers wear pajamas and smell nice, like that George Washington cologne with the numbers on the bottle that Marcy Bácsi used to wear in Chicago.

One time I heard Abby Prinz's father say to her mother in a loud voice, "Doesn't Abby look pretty tonight, Shirley?"

Once Mom asked Dad if he was looking at my friend Regina's breasts. Regina got breasts really early.

At Edison, when Mrs. Musil, the music teacher, comes to our classrooms, I get excited. She lets me lead the DESCANT. At first I didn't know I was singing loud, not in the same way that I knew I was fat. That's just how the singing came out—I liked it. Well, *I* made my voice sound like that, because it sounded good, like the Vienna Choir Boys. Then I found out I was loud when the other kids covered their ears and made howling noises. But then Mrs. Musil asked me to audition for York High School's production of *South Pacific.*

Now I'm so excited I can hardly stand it. I practice and practice "Dites Moi." That means "Tell Me" in English. My French accent is perfect—my father taught me. Also, I ham it up A LOT. But I do not get the part.

It is hardly a wonder that Cantor Martin Rosen is my hero. To me he looks like Ben Casey, who is always fixing everyone's subdural hematomas on TV. Cantor Rosen gives me solos in Choraleers. He can't give me solos all the time—even though I pout and sometimes cry when he doesn't—because he has to be fair. Dad always asks if my solo will come at the beginning, middle, or the end of the service. I don't know that answer, but my stomach hurts when he asks.

In the temple people like my singing and don't tell me that it's too loud.

bácsi: uncle (Hungarian)

All the kids in the junior choir have been assigned to wear the same blouses or shirts from Marshall Field's and dark skirts or trousers for our service performances. I am not too happy, because in the fall Mom told me to choose between tap shoes and dress shoes. I chose tap shoes, needing all the help I could get in the tap department. This makes my junior choir outfit not quite right for tonight because I have to wear school shoes and the other girls are wearing dress-up shoes. But I think I look nice and dressed up— until a bunch of us go into the temple's downstairs bathroom right before services, and I see in the full-length mirror that the other girls' waists dent in. Mine is bulgy.

I tuck in my blouse so it will look crisp. That's another word I like. *Crisp.* I don't want to be a slob with my blouse just hanging there over the bulge. I want to be proper like the girls in olden times who walked with books on their heads. This is so they would learn good posture from their governesses. I don't have good posture. Mom says, "When you walk through a door, remind yourself to stand up straight." Now I think about good posture when I go through doors, but I don't have it. Standing up straight makes me feel like I'm showing off.

Is singing a solo like showing off? I think it is, but at least it's in temple, which is not like *The Mickey Mouse Club.*

After the service, at the oneg Shabbat, people approach me to tell me that my solo was lovely.

"What a lovely solo!"

I wonder if I would trade my voice for a waist and decide that I wouldn't.

When we come home from family services, I change into my pajamas and go down into our unfinished basement. I take a large pink ball, which I never paid any attention to before, and spend a very long time bouncing it up against the wall as hard as I can, trying to become thin this very evening. When it doesn't work, I give up on the pink ball. Does it work for other girls?

So I can't get skinny for now, but maybe I should practice my solo for Choraleers.

Hear my prayer, O hear my prayer.
Lead me that I go aright!
Only by Thy guiding flame,
Safe my footsteps in life's night.

Life's night? And shouldn't it be "save my footsteps"? What is
"*safe* my footsteps"? Mrs. Musil always makes me sing the harmony
in music and then looks at me gratefully and nods when we put it
all together. But the kids say I have a big mouth to match my nose.

Cleanse me and I shall be clean.
Thou alone canst make me pure.
Da da da da da da da
Brotherhood for all ensure.

I wish I could be in the Vienna Boys Choir and sing like an
angel. I try to make my voice sound like those boys, with that clear,
clean sound. Pure. The Choraleers at Oak Park Temple sing in a
messy way. There are no girls in the Vienna Boys Choir and no
Jews, and they all have floppy hair too. Dad says that I can sing as
well as those boys.

Cantor Rosen does NOT sing like those boys. He sings loudly
like a king—maybe like the King of Whales. Dad says there's no
such thing as the King of Whales. He says there's a Prince of Wales,
but Cantor Rosen sounds more like a king than a prince. His singing is so beautiful that it makes the back of my neck ache, just like
when I hear trumpets calling back and forth to each other with
overlapping echoes. And then the organ comes in through my feet,
and I want to "sing it, sister," like my dad says when he listens to
jazz. Then the rabbi talks about Civil Rights and the prophet Jeremiah and my dad nods, even though he really doesn't want to be in
temple. I feel proud and wish that we could always go to temple, not
just on Friday nights. I like that lemon smell, and we get ice cream
in Dixie cups at the oneg Shabbat.

Now I feel bad because I thought about dessert at the same time
as thinking about temple and Civil Rights. That is because I am

fat. Grandma says I'm not fat, but she is, and everyone in the whole family calls her "Chubbo," so how could a person trust her when she says that? Dad says that when she was young, people thought it was important to eat a lot to be healthy and not get disease. He's a doctor who studies diseases that hit lots of people, so he knows things like this. Now, everyone knows that being fat is bad for you. You can get a heart attack or a stroke if you get fat. But he says that I'm too young to worry about it. He's almost fat, but he cuts the fat off his meat, which he says is smart. I like that fat part, though.

Dad takes us to the ghetto for a family field trip to show us poor people. This makes us support Civil Rights, which we do anyway. Well, Simon and I do. Sarah is still pretty much a baby. I know that this is right and important. Some of the Negroes are pretty fat, though. Dad says they have even more heart attacks and strokes than white people. They don't get to have good health care or good food. I guess Dr. Nolan wouldn't go into the ghetto.

Dr. Nolan is my pediatrician, and Simon's and Sarah's. Every year Mom sends him a box of steaks for Christmas. This is because Dr. Nolan does not charge doctor fees for the three of us. We are the children of a doctor, so it is called a "courtesy." That is another word I like. It sounds like *curtsy*, which is something I wish we could do in front of the president.

Dr. Nolan is very nice and tells Sarah that he does not see a single elephant in her ears. When Mom asks him when I'm going to hit puberty, I can tell that he is a little sad for me. I'm not going to hit puberty anytime soon, if ever. Dad says Negro girls hit puberty sooner than white girls but he doesn't know why. It is a statistic.

In temple everyone is for Civil Rights. But not in school. They like Nixon. Cantor Rosen is for Civil Rights. I know because I asked him. Then I told him that the old cantor had us sing "May the Words" with a better tune. I feel good when I'm helping. But he said that this was the tune from now on. He said that his teacher said to sing it "with quiet enthusiasm." Then he gave me a solo. That was after we had tryouts for the solo. He was kind of quiet after I sang. I'm used to that. I may be fat, but I know I can sing.

I don't think it's the M&M'S. When Mom doesn't have a real dessert, she counts out M&M'S for us instead of dessert. Helen Sullivan told me that M&M'S make you fat. Dad said that's not true. He said it's eating too many calories that makes you fat.

Beauty and the Me

I don't look like the African queens in the Field Museum. I will never have hair that flies in ripples around my head, or breasts like on the clay goddesses in the glass cases. I just know.

I know that I will never stand on my toes and twirl in pink shoes with ribbons on the ankles. I will never have thighs that are smooth instead of jiggly or a neck that holds my head in a goddess position.

I am Barbi, whose mother tells her to stand up straight and whose nose is the first thing in the mirror and whose hair is all over the place and whose waist doesn't curve in and who can't catch a ball. I am a germ—that's what the boys say I am.

But I do know what is beautiful, and it is ballerinas and a full chorus with cello at the same time. And when it's dark in the sanctuary, with just the Eternal Light shining.

I will not be beautiful, but I will make sure that I can look at beautiful things all the time. On my desk is a glass rooster the size of a nickel. He has a green neck, a standing-up red comb, and dark purple wings. His tail is clear and ruffled at the edges. I sit him next to the little lipstick that the Fuller Brush Man gave me and right on top of a mirror that fell out of Chubbo's compact. Just a little bit off to the side is my ten-carat gold turquoise ring with the three stones. I put my white leather watch in a perfect circle around the ring. I open my music box, which is in the exact center of the dresser, but behind. I wind the little crank and listen to the sparkly sounds.

My dresser looks perfect just like this. From now on, I am always going to put things in exactly the right places, so they look perfect. The music I listen to is always going to be like little bells ringing. I am going to sing only music that makes me sigh, and read only books that have covers with birds or small leaves or flower petals. (It's perfect when books have gold edges.) It will be hard work, but I am starting now.

Brownies

I used to love Brownie meeting days. I loved wearing my uniform to school. On meeting days I looked more like the other girls. Well, I think my shoes didn't look like theirs. Mine are tie-up shoes, because Mom says that if I wear them, someday I will be able to wear high heels. They have support. Lois and Kathy and Patty and Helen and Mary all wear pumps. And they will probably get to wear high heels when they get older anyway. My opapa owned a dry goods store and sold shoes. He wouldn't sell a pair of shoes to someone if they didn't fit right, even when he was poor. Mom always tells me that story when she buys me shoes with laces. I guess the same goes for the thick socks too. No other girls in my class wear thick socks. Mom says that nylon doesn't breathe.

But from the ankles up on Brownie Day, I looked like the other girls. Except Patty Miller, the only one who is fat like me. And she's the only other one with brown hair. Her hair is always in a neat pageboy with a bow in it, and mine is always spreading out. Mom still makes my clothes. She says the seams in store-bought clothes are flimsy.

Mary Anderson's house is nice. We used to go right into her basement, which is finished. Ours isn't finished. It's still cement. We would each take a cup of juice and a cookie. Mrs. Anderson BUYS her cookies from the BAKERY. My mom would NEVER do that.

One day we all sat down to wait for the Brownie signal to be quiet. Helen told us that her mom had a baby growing in her tummy. I told her that the baby is not in her mother's tummy—it's in her mother's uterus. No one said anything. Patty Miller slid away from me just a little.

Then Mrs. Sullivan the troop leader said, "Barbi has said a private potty word that children are not allowed to say."

I knew she was wrong because I've known this word for a long time and it's a body part.

But since then I've been too embarrassed to go to Brownies, so I can't wear my uniform anymore.

My mother started a crafts group in our basement after that. She calls it "Edison Angels" after our school. Only a few girls come, like Sue Suconik, who is Jewish too. We learn to crochet and make puppets out of wooden dowels. Mom makes cookies with apricot filling and ground nuts. The girls keep coming even though they spit out the cookies. Kids don't like nuts or even apricots.

Helen is the first one in our grade to start menstruating. Today she tells us that she has her first monthly. She giggles when she says "monthly." Then the other girls giggle. I don't, and I think that she should have said, "got her first period." "Monthly" is a stupid way to say it. Then Helen looks at me and sees that I'm frowning. She tells me that my Brownie troop has sleepovers all the time but a few of the mothers didn't want to invite the sloppy Jewish girl with the loud mouth.

Dad said I had a big mouth once too, when I took a phone message and then asked him later if he called the man back. I had written the message very clearly.

When I get older I am going to talk like Julie Andrews, who has a perfect mouth.

Storefront Caroling

The other girls giggle as we climb into the department store display window. Neil and I are not giggling, because he is embarrassed to be the only boy and I have too much trouble climbing up.

We're wearing red choir robes, and we're supposed to stand in a semicircle around a crate with hay in it under Nancy's boy baby doll that has a washcloth on top of where its penis would be. When we get a sign from Mrs. Musil, we will sing Christmas carols and "Jingle Bells," which is not a Christmas carol. My robe doesn't fit. Neil's hair is still wet and you can see where the comb went. Simon's hair never looks like that. Neil's cheeks are staying red.

I have a solo—in "What Child Is This?" That is another reason why I'm not in a giggling mood. Some of the words are a problem. My solo is:

> This, this is Christ the King,
> Whom shepherds guard and angels sing.
> Haste, haste, to bring Him laud,
> The Babe, the Son of Mary.

I know *laud* means "compliments." The problem is some of the words are Christian words like *Christ* and *Mary* and probably *Babe* because of the capital *B* and then maybe also *Him* for the same reason. And I know that Jesus is NOT the son of God. So *Son*, too.

Before, because it was PRACTICE, I always sang all the words in my usual voice.

Now it's the real thing, in the real store window—like a service in temple. So it's like being in CHURCH. So I'm not going to sing Christian words, because it's praying non-Jewish prayers, which is against my religion, like bowing down.

It's the solo coming, and my stomach feels cold. Can I do this like a Jewess?

> This, this is MM the MM
> Whom shepherds guard and angels sing.
> Haste, haste to bring MM laud,
> The MM, the MM of MM-MM.

You Will Sing in the Opera

Rabbi Samuel Schwartz is the rabbi emeritus of Oak Park Temple. That means he is old and a saint, I think.

He sits in a fancy chair on the pulpit and says, "May the Lord bless you and keep you" at the end of services.

It's like a magic spell.

Rabbi Mervis frowns at the Choraleers when we are talking, but not Rabbi Schwartz. He just smiles and nods, even when our singing is messy, like it always is. You can tell that Rabbi Mervis is disappointed, because when we're done, his smile looks fake and he looks at Cantor Rosen like he's going to kill him later.

Not Rabbi Schwartz.

Last Friday night when I had a solo for Family Night, he put his hands on my cheeks and said, "You will sing in the opera!"

He didn't say it softly either.

I whispered back, in his ear, which had a lot of hair in it, "But I want to sing here."

When I looked at his face again he had tears in his eyes. I didn't know what to do. It was time to go to our seats, and all the other Choraleers had gone down to the choir row. I took one step back, and he just smiled at me. Then he nodded.

He's Hungarian, like my mother and like Omama and Opapa were. Like all the relatives who died in the concentration camps.

Maybe he doesn't really think I will grow up to be an opera singer. He's nice, so maybe he's just saying it to be nice. Mom says that people smile during my solos because I don't know that I'm pulling at my robe, making it slowly it come way up while I'm singing.

But I know I can sing. I bet he means it. Maybe those weren't tears. Maybe that's how emeritus eyes look.

Bless the Vogels, the Spieglers, the Walls, the Mays, and the Ostfelds

On TV, children kneel next to their beds and say nighttime prayers with their hands folded. Mom says that this is a Christian thing. Jews do not kneel. I know that. Jews do not fold their hands either. I know that NOW. We DO say the Sh'ma at night.

I learned this in Sunday school from Mrs. Siegel, who said my Hebrew name can be Bracha. It means "blessing." Mrs. Siegel likes me. I know it's because I pay attention to everything she says. I want to know all the right Jewish things to do so I can do them all the time. Bracha. It sounds bad, but at least now I have a Hebrew name.

Sh'ma: Hear (O Israel)—an important prayer that declares our belief in one God, and is the centerpiece of morning and evening services

Why didn't Mom give me one before? The other kids knew their Hebrew names.

I'm going to say the Sh'ma at night all the time and then bless my family like kids do on TV, on my knees with my hands folded. Praying in temple is just reading in a serious voice. Praying in bed is whispering, I think. Jews who are more Jewish than Mom probably do this, so I will too from now on.

When I learn the whole v'Awhavtaw, I will say the whole thing first in Hebrew and then in English like in services and then bless the Vogels, the Spieglers, the Walls, the Mays, and the Ostfelds for the night.

Then I will think about Hoss Cartwright or Ben Casey rescuing me from danger. And I will think of me being skinny with straight hair. And they will want to rescue me.

Other Fathers

Other fathers are so odd. They wear big aprons and stand at their grills smiling. They say things to try and make me giggle, like, "We're going to barbecue Barbi!"

I do not giggle. I run home. I know that it's a joke, but why are people's fathers joking with me? My dad hasn't ever talked to Missy or Pam or even to Sue. I don't think he's ever even said hi to them. Like if he got out of the car coming home from the university and one of my friends was standing right there by the car door and he had to walk right past her, he would not say hello.

Missy doesn't say hello to Dad either. She might be waiting for Dad to say hi first, thinking he's then going to mess up my hair and touch my nose with his finger and pick Sarah up from the grass to kiss her head. But nothing like that would happen because Dad just goes inside with his eyes down, and we are supposed to pretend like we don't see him. Until when he's ready, which we can always tell, because his eyes will be a little red and shiny, and even though he's in his underwear, he will look softer and smell kind of like the liquid that thermometers stand in. You can smell this when you go to the doctor.

So when other dads say, "We're going to barbecue Barbi," I just have to run home to where the dad is quiet and I know to look down too. And that way, no surprises.

I am not allowed to have friends play in the house if Dad is home, like now. Neither is Simon. Sarah is too little to have friends. I never ask anyway, though. Why would I have a friend come over with Dad home? Dad says he doesn't like other children.

I don't want to think about this anymore, but I need to know for sure. I go into the living room, which is not for children, but maybe it will be okay if I act grown up.

Dad is in his chair with the newspaper over his lap. That's good because I can't see his underwear.

So I say, "Excuse me, Dad." Like a grown-up. Then I ask him if he likes our cousins and he says, "Not particularly."

I ask him if he loves them and he says, "Not particularly."

"But you love us, right?"

"Yes," he says.

I think about this. Maybe if you are not pretty or skinny, only your parents love you. If you're like most of the girls in my class, your aunts and uncles love you too.

Aunt Vera loves me and Uncle Leo loves me. Dad says that Uncle Marvin is incapable of loving anyone but himself. But Uncle Marvin calls me "Barbi Prim" and that makes me feel like he notices that I'm different. It might be old-fashioned, but it's still nice to be prim. When he says "Barbi Prim," it feels like a magic wand is waving over my head and I feel tingly. There are four Barbaras in my grade at Edison School. There is only one Barbi Prim.

One Book

The new Oakbrook Center Mall has a bookstore, Kroch's and Brentano's. The main Kroch's and Brentano's is downtown, but I've never seen it.

We are going to the Oakbrook store now, and we each get to buy one new book. It's not Chanukah and it's not anyone's birthday, so this is very surprising.

I think that the car ride will be long, but it seems not too long. Mom puts Sarah in the middle so Simon won't bother me. This never works, because Sarah pokes Simon while looking straight ahead, pretending to be innocent. Then he whacks her and she cries. Then Dad says he'll knock our heads together. For a four-year-old, Sarah is pretty fearless. She knows Simon's going to hit her. I just leave him alone.

The car ride is too short for us to sing, although I'm in a good enough mood to start. Dad is quiet, though, so I'm not starting anything. I want my book. I already finished this week's library books. Miss Strand helps me pick out books. Sometimes she shakes her head at the books I pick out. She says, "You can make better choices than those, Barbara. These are for ordinary readers." I always put those back. I want her to like me.

The Oakbrook parking lot is full. Lots of people are shopping. I can tell that Dad is almost angry at being here. It looks a little like *The Jetsons* cartoon outside Oakbrook. There are lots of wide stairways and flat cement areas with big, smooth planters. Everything is even and new. The parking lot lights look like they're from the future. There are short cement pillars everywhere that connect to each other with chains. Some baby trees are here and there.

I wish I could go into the stores and look around, but I would never ask. I'd like to see the places where other girls buy clothes, but Mom doesn't go to those places.

I'm still very excited—very. I can feel the fluttering and tightness in my stomach. We find Kroch's and Brentano's just when I think Dad is about to get really mad. Once we go in, though, he goes to look at the books he likes, so it's okay.

Right away I love it here. It's very bright and new. Very clean— not like the library, where I sometimes don't like to sit because of all the people who've sat on the chairs and might have left some dirt behind. There are big squares of lights in the ceiling, so all the books look shiny. The children's section is big. I walk very slowly past the biography section, but there are no new books about Queen Elizabeth I. So now all I have to do is find Louisa May Alcott and

I'll be in the right area. I've already read *Little Women*, *Little Men*, *Jo's Boys*, *Rose in Bloom*, *Eight Cousins*, *A Garland for Girls*, and *An Old-Fashioned Girl*. But there will be other books by good authors nearby. And I find another Alcott book! *Good Wives*! This is going to be my new book!

I've found it very quickly, and everyone else is still looking. So I keep looking. All the books are so chunky, and the jackets are so glittery. One cover catches my eye. It's white with a red-haired girl on the cover. She's sitting in a wagon, looking determined. *Anne of Green Gables* by Lucy Maud Montgomery. Those are such ugly names, Lucy and Maud—fat names, like Barbara.

I read the first few pages. I must have it. I like the old-fashioned conversation.

The book says that Anne has grayish-green eyes. Dad says I have grayish-green eyes just like his father did. Anne and I are just alike. I am imagining myself an orphan. I read some more.

Mom calls us. Her voice is nervous. That must mean that Dad is ready to go. Now.

I bring my books to her and say, "Mom, I really love these books. May I please have them both? I'll do anything! Really!"

Dad is there too, and he says, "I said one book."

"Please, Dad! I need these!"

I am expecting Sarah and Simon to start asking for two books too, but they are both quiet.

"No," he says in the low, scary voice, and I start to cry. I am crying because I have to decide which one and I don't have any time.

I will choose Anne. Then in the car on the way home I can pretend that I'm an orphan. If Mom asks me to sing, I'm going to say no.

Ann Landers Rules against Me

We learned how to address envelopes in school, but I already knew. I write to Chubbo all the time. She lives in St. Louis, where I was born and where my dad was born. Chubbo likes letters and talking. Anything with words, I guess. She never hugs me or kisses my forehead.

I like words too. I like thinking of letters going from one mail-
box to another across the country. I like putting stamps on letters
so the sides match up perfectly. I am good at this.

When I write to Ann Landers, I know that I need two envelopes
and that one should be folded up. I need two stamps. It's strange to
write my own address on an envelope, but it's not strange to write
my letter. I have been thinking up this letter for a long time.

> Dear Ann Landers,
>
> Tell me what to do. My brother keeps beating me up.
> My parents don't stop him. Mom says that my words
> hurt Simon as much as he hurts me. Sometimes I
> won't set his place at the table but Mom makes me
> anyway so I put the fork in the spoon place.
>
> Sincerely,
> Barbi Ostfeld, Third Grade, Edison School

Chubbo's letters are fancy. Her writing paper is very thin and
has designs on all four edges. The envelopes match. She uses a
fountain pen and her capital letters have swirls. My handwriting is
good, but Miss Albright says my upstrokes are too pointy. My slant
is the second best in the class, but I can't relax my upstrokes.

After weeks and weeks, I get a typed letter inside a typed envelope. There is no stamp, just some wavy lines and numbers where
the stamp should be.

> Dear Barbi,
>
> Your mother is right. Little girls should not make fun
> of their brothers. If you are well behaved, he will stop
> hitting you in retaliation.
>
> Further, it is bad manners to set a table incorrectly.
> You know better.
>
> Sincerely,
> Ann Landers

I would like to tell Ann Landers that I have very good manners all the time except for with Simon. He has no manners with me or he wouldn't beat me up. I wouldn't make fun of him if he was nice to me. I planned on showing her letter to Simon because he would see that Ann Landers thought I was right. Then he would stop. Now I have to hide the letter.

Pattern and Material

Rickrack. My Passover dress is going to have rickrack on it. Mom thinks I will look good with an empire waist. This means a high waist. Maybe this will cover up my fatness. It will have no sleeves and it will have trim on it. I like things that are trimmed and not plain. I get to pick the material. This really means that I get to pick from some fabrics that Mom has already chosen. I pick a purple-and-blue-flowered print called "calico," like a cat. The flowers are tiny. This is a good choice. The fabric smells crisp, which is something else I like. *Crispness*—the word and the meaning. I will wear this for the Seder and when we go to Springfield for the weekend.

I'm lucky because my mother makes my clothes and they are unique. They aren't like the other kids' clothes, though. They flow more, which I don't like. I know that Mom is talented and has a skill, so I'm proud, but maybe this is another Jewish thing—having a mother who makes your clothes. Mom won't put any lacy ruffles on my collars or on my sleeves. She says they're "too fussy." I like the word *fussy*. It is a lot like the word *prim*. A prim girl would have ruffles on her dresses and a locket with a curl of hair in it.

I love the turquoise ring that Chubbo gave me. I look at it all the time. I'm going to ask her for a locket.

I love my hands because my fingers are skinny and I can play the piano a lot better than Mrs. Lingaas's other piano pupils. She says I have a feeling for the music. I wish Dad would come to the recitals. He just asks me later if I was the best. Then he tells people that I am the best pupil the teacher has. Other fathers come, and one even brought a flower.

Seder: Order—the ritual Passover meal

I would keep my eyes and my hands and my voice and my brain. The rest of me I might trade if I could.

We go to Springfield. It feels like an important trip because the places we are going to see are national historic landmarks. First we go to the Lincoln Tomb. We go around in a circle in a round lobby made of marble. It is quiet and serious, like in temple during the Kaddish, even though Abraham Lincoln died a hundred years ago. I'm looking at people and getting bored. I want to see the tomb because I've never seen a grave before and because it's a president's grave and I can say it to Mrs. Broud. (Miss Albright got married to a soldier. Now she's Mrs. Broud.) Even Marcia Brown hasn't been to Springfield yet, and she's teacher's pet.

There's an old, sad-looking man in a chair between the doorways. He calls me over, and I go because I am a polite girl; everyone says so. He might need something. Also he called ME. He takes my hand and says what a nice girl I am. I say thank you. Then I want to get back in line and not lose my place. But he doesn't let go of my hand and he undoes the buttons of my new dress with his other hand. I want to tell him that I don't even have breasts. I pull away hard but he is pulling harder. I don't yell because everyone is being so quiet. I look around for Mom but I don't see her. I look around for Simon, because he would kick the man in his testicles. I know he would, even though he's seven. But a policeman comes by. He is twirling his stick like a baton. He sees, and the old man lets me go, and I find Mom. Mom and the policeman talk, but just for one second.

Mom tells me, "Don't say anything to Dad or he will be mad at you."

"Okay," I say. I think I understand why he would be mad. He wouldn't want to get in a fight with some old guy. But Mom said "at you," not just "mad," so I must have done something wrong even when I was being polite. Maybe the dress was too nice for me or it made me look like I had breasts. Maybe I missed one when I was buttoning all the buttons? Had they all been closed? It was a little big and a bit long so I could grow into it.

I have to go to the bathroom. A girl comes in after me.

She says, "What did he do to you?"

"Nothing."

"Did your dad beat him up?"

"No. He is nonviolent," I say.

"My dad woulda creamed him," she says. "Show me where he touched you."

"No."

Dad doesn't talk to me the rest of the trip. He has that look on his face—the one where it looks like he's thinking, "How is it possible that a man like me has a daughter like YOU?" He doesn't talk to me even when we go to the Lincoln House, which I like much better than the tomb. We see Willie and Tad's room. Eddie Lincoln died while he was still a very little boy, and then Mary Todd got depressed because she loved him so much. She sat with him for fifty-two days in a row. Eddie was never by himself in the dark.

YMCA Camp

Mom doesn't like making pants on her sewing machine. She says it's too hard to get crotches to line up. Once she made Simon some plaid shorts for temple, but she had to rip out the crotch two times.

Mom almost always buys Simon's pants and shorts.

For camp Mom bought me two new pairs of shorts and matching tops. The outfits are the same but in different colors. One top is orange with swimming turtles on it, and the other one is green with swimming turtles on it. Dad says that their scientific name is *Chelonia mydas*. The shorts are from Sears. Now Mom wants me to learn how to iron them. The iron is heavy, plus noisy. I get to practice on Dad's handkerchiefs. Mom says not to iron the folds even though I want to. I want to make a perfect flat square. She says that ironing the folds will weaken the fabric in the folded parts.

When we get on the bus to go to camp, the kids start singing. "Ninety-nine bottles of beer on the wall, ninety-nine bottles of beer, take one down and pass it around, ninety-eight bottles of beer on the wall."

I hate that song right away, because the words are stupid and the melody is stupid.

When we get close to the camp, the kids start singing again. "We're here because we're here because we're here because we're here."

I hate that song even more, because it doesn't make any sense. So far the songs are making me start to worry about camp.

The other girls in my cabin all choose bottom bunks. I am glad and take a top bunk. Then I climb up and it hurts my feet so I feel even more worried about this whole thing. Mary Lynne, our counselor, tells us that we have to write a postcard home. I feel better and start to write, but the other girls are complaining. We are told that we have two minutes to write, so I make it short, even though I have so much to say.

"Dear Parents," I write in my best cursive, "We made it. (Late!) We have a NEW cabin. It's neat. I love everything! Barbi."

Quickly I address it. Dr. and Mrs. Adrian M. Ostfeld, 525 Park Avenue, Elmhurst, Ill.

That night after lights-out the counselor has us tell our names and a little bit about ourselves. I wait till last because I don't know what to say. All the girls tell where they go to church, so I say that I'm Jewish and where I go to temple. I say that I don't have a best friend and that I like to read and sing. Someone snorts and then others do too. It is not a nice sound, and I'm embarrassed.

Mary Lynne says, "Now stop it, girls. That's not nice."

But she doesn't sound mad. I bet she rolls her eyes. I want to go home.

In the morning the girls get dressed. I don't have to get dressed because I slept in my clothes. I don't want to get undressed in front of them.

As Candy and Ellen leave for the bathhouse, one of them says, "I know which one's the Jew."

I have to urinate, but I don't want to go with them. I wait. After they all leave, I start for the door and I realize that I'm going to wet my pants, and I do and I just cry. I stuff the wet orange shorts in my trunk and put on the green ones. I head for the mess hall and get a bit lost. I miss breakfast and have to find a counselor to tell me where to go.

I like making lanyards and I like rest time. I spend every rest time writing long letters home. Mom didn't let me bring books because I'm supposed to do what the other girls do and make friends.

We go on a long hike. It's very hot and I'm sweating. I have no one to walk with. One boy sprains his ankle and gets to ride on the truck. I ask if I can ride too but they say no. I cry a little and one girl points at me. I hate camp, and there are black flies. I have five bites on my legs and two on my arm. I think there are some on my back too.

The lake is very cold, and we have to tread water to pass our test. I don't care about the test. It's not like it's school. They make me try every day. They call out, "You can do it!" But I can't and I don't care. I just want to get out of the water. All of the girls in my bunk passed the test in the first few days. Just the little kids are in the water with me now.

Today Mary Lynne says, "Barbi, why don't you take a quick shower today? Won't that feel nice? Then you can change your clothes too."

"No, thank you."

"You really should, you know. Hygiene is important, particularly for growing girls."

"Well, Mary Lynne, I haven't started to menstruate yet, so it's really okay."

Mary Lynne sort of waves her hands at her sides and says, "Okay, okay," and backs away.

I knew before that YMCA stood for Young Men's Christian Association. And it's obvious from the songs we sing around the campfire that it's a Christian camp. All of the kids are Christian. I'm used to that—there are only a few Jews in my whole school. But none here at camp. So I'm wondering why my parents sent me to this camp. They make fun of me here—worse than at school.

I am a Jew. I am not going to the showers in a camp.

Mining

An abandoned garnet mine. I don't like the outdoors. I'd rather be indoors mostly always where there are no bugs and nothing to make you sweat. If I have to be outside, I'd rather not be hiking. Nothing is that beautiful. But an abandoned garnet mine sounds like jewels just waiting to be found. We are driving a long time, and I can't read in the car because I get sick. I look out the window and pretend that I have a long, curved blade. It is cutting down trees all over the world. Take that, you trees!

Other people's dads drive on family outings. My mom always drives. She always mows the lawn too, and barbecues. Dad never holds the door for her either. Or fixes anything. Mom fixes stuff.

We get there and get out of the car. I think it's going to be bad. Simon is already coming at me, and I don't see anything glimmering in the dirt. Then Dad finds one and calls us over. It looks black, and then he shows us the facets and I see them. It IS a jewel and I'm going to find some too. I look at the ground very hard and walk slowly. I've never looked harder. I'm going to find one before Simon does and before Mom does and before Dad finds another one. And then I DO!

I shriek and run to show it to Dad. He is impressed! He points it out to Mom, calling her Wenda-Gwenda—his pet name for her, which he almost never uses. I am VERY proud. Then I find lots of them and Simon does too. Dad is putting mine in his pockets. Sarah even finds some, but hers are sort of broken. I'm feeling good, so I don't make fun of hers, even though I could.

I show every single one to Dad. And then he is angry.

"ENOUGH!" he says in his angry voice.

And then he won't let me put any more in his pockets, so I have to leave a lot of them on the ground. I scatter them so no one will have it easy, finding them all at once. Now I'm sad, and it is ruined. We still have all that way to drive, too, and I can't read in the car because it makes me sick. Maybe we can get Dad to tell us how garnets are formed and he will get in a better mood. Mom wants us to sing in the car, but I just don't feel like it. It's all ruined.

Birds Calling Back to the Cantor

Consecration of new Sunday school kids is tonight, on the last night of Sukkot. Sarah has to go up to the bima, and she doesn't want to. She has to stand under the sukka with her class. She is wearing a dress that I used to have. It's too big on her. Uh-oh, she's about to cry. Mom takes her up and puts her in her spot. She won't smile for the camera, though. When she comes down, she puts her head against Mom's stomach. I'm not like that. I go up there sometimes just to look around and see what it's like from up there. It's nice.

Rabbi Mervis picks up the Torah, and Cantor Rosen takes up the lulav and etrog. Slowly we line up behind them, two by two. I won't stand next to a boy, but there are almost no boys and they are together, so I don't have to. I stand next to Regina. She's my friend, but there's too much air in her singing. It sounds like whispering. I don't tell her that, even when she has a solo. At least she can hold her part.

This is my favorite time.

Cantor Rosen sings, "Ana Adonai (Answer us, God)," and we sing, "Hoshia na (Save us, God)."

I feel the organ through my shoes. I close my eyes. The children's choir is walking slowly, in procession, when I open them. It is time to be serious. I feel very serious.

Cantor Rosen sings, "Ana Adonai," and we sing, "Hatz'licha na (Help us to prosper)."

And then it's like he's crying, "Ana Adonai," and we sing, "Aneinu, aneinu b'yom kor'einu! Aneinu, aneinu b'yom kor'einu! (Answer us, answer us today while we're calling!)"

What I love is that Cantor Rosen's voice is so low and sad. But strong too. And when we call back, our voices are high and chirpy like birds.

When I am a grown-up, I will wear a black robe and be in front of a procession. I will nod to people while I sing and be important.

Sukkot: Booths—the fall harvest feast ~ bima: platform—the elevated platform in a synagogue from which worship is led sukka: booth—a makeshift structure that symbolizes the frail huts the Israelites lived in during their forty years of wandering in the desert

lulav: a grouping of date palm, willow, and myrtle branches used in celebrating Sukkot ~ etrog: a citron used in celebrating Sukkot

People will call me "Cantor" like it's my name. Which is like "Doctor." Dad said I'm not smart enough to be a doctor, even though I got a 99 on the Iowa Tests last year in third grade and I read on a ninth-grade level. And last summer when the Elmhurst Library had the Climb-the-Cake Contest, my candle got all the way to the top layer, just like Sue Suconik's. I wonder if I'm smart enough to be a cantor.

Mrs. Lingaas keeps saying that my piano playing is actually very good and that I have real musical ability. It's hard to look at Mrs. Lingaas. Sometimes drool will come down the wrinkles on the side of her mouth. And she presses down your fingers on the keys. I only like her sometimes. Also her hair is crinkly. But Cantor Rosen plays the piano sometimes during Choraleers, so I should keep playing.

Now all the kids have to leave the sanctuary because it's time for the Kaddish. I don't mind. We get Dixie cup ice cream.

I get my little flat wood spoon and sit by myself at the oneg Shabbat so I can sing Cantor Rosen's part in my head. I know the whole thing.

Tinker Bell Gets Her Period

We are in the gym to see a filmstrip, and the principal talks to all the fifth-grade girls. I'm a year younger. I should be in fourth grade.

First, the principal, Miss Kimball, talks. She has a young face but white hair. She says *menstruation* wrong. She says it "men-STRAYtion." Also, she says it carefully, like maybe she never says it except once a year when she talks to fifth-grade girls who are ten or eleven, except for me. I'm still nine.

First she tells us all the other things a lady can say instead of that, and you can tell that she likes the other things better. Like "my aunt is coming to visit" or "I've got the painters in" or "I'm feeling delicate." I start to laugh, but then I stop because no one else is laughing or even smiling. This is like a secret. And then I find out that it is a REAL secret because we are supposed to hide the *You're a Young Lady Now* booklets on the way home from school because if boys see them, they will become overly interested. Which I don't believe. My mother never says she is delicate, and she only says Eda Neni is coming if Eda Neni is coming. When Mom has her period, she says, "I have my period. Barbi, would you bring me a tampon?"

The boys in our class are getting a talk from the gym teacher about taking showers and kinds of underwear. I hope I get to see the booklets they get. I'm interested—but not overly interested.

So I'm sort of listening. And looking at my booklet. The illustrated girls in it look like Cinderella and Princess Aurora in school clothes like Patty Miller wears. She's adopted and always has hair that's perfect, like in a magazine. The illustrated girls are looking in the mirror and thinking about lady-ness. Their mothers ask them things like "Do you want to use the pin belt or the clasp belt?" and tell them things like "Keep fresh as a daisy and shower or you'll develop an odor" and "It's so important to put on powder during those days." Also, "Don't sob in the mirror and be dramatic or eat fatty, rich foods during those days." And then one princess girl puts powder on her nose from her compact. Chubbo has a compact that is silver with flowers and ivy carved into it. She says it's sterling and that I will have it someday. I hope I don't have to wait till I get my period.

I think I will never figure out the five steps to using the clasp belt, so it's a good thing my period will never come. The fingers in the diagram look like Tinker Bell fingers with pointy nails.

Now comes the filmstrip.

Dad drew pictures of a uterus and fallopian tubes on the blackboard in the basement. So I already know that part and also about hormones. The lady in the filmstrip doesn't mention breast buds like Mom did when she asked Dr. Nolan when mine will make an appearance. I know those come before menstruation.

Now one of the princess girls is in the shower, and the voice says not to make the shower too hot or too cold. And then the princess girl is happily gliding on her bike. But she's not supposed to ride her horse because the horse would bounce her around. Then she's dancing with her boyfriend, and that's okay, but not when she starts showing her underpants when the boyfriend swings her around in the air. I guess when you're menstruating you can have delicate activity but not tomboy behavior like Cindy Seidmann next door. Dad says she could be a linebacker for the Bears.

In this filmstrip the girl stops wearing dungarees and braids and changes to flowing hair and ruffles. All of a sudden she looks like Tinker Bell without the bun, and she's sparkly, like Flora, Fauna, and Merryweather doing magic. And also she gets breasts fast, and her legs look like Miss America legs in a swimsuit. When Mom has her period, she eats Hershey's Kisses and sometimes wears her housecoat with the orange tulips on it all day. Then she says, "Maybe I will take an aspirin."

So Peter Pan got to fly to the second star on the right and doesn't have to grow up, which is supposed to be sad for Wendy. And Wendy does grow all the way up in the end. And also I guess Tinker Bell got her period. Because if you look at her body in her green pixie dress, you can see that her hormones did their job.

Just Some of the Bad Things about Gym

All day I think about gym. I think about tying my gym shoes, which I can't do from a crouch like other kids. I have to bend over, and that means I have to worry about someone seeing my buttocks. That's the first bad thing about gym.

Blubber is the next bad thing. I hate that word.

Whenever I run in gym, some boys yell, "Look at the blubber!"

I try not to run, but if I don't run toward the ball when it's coming toward me, they yell, "Move that blubber!"

The next bad thing is when teams are chosen for volleyball. Everyone in my grade knows who will be picked last. I line my toes up perfectly against the nearest black line on the gym floor, pretending to concentrate. I am not paying attention to the selection process.

A boy snorts when the team captain finally says my name in a tired voice. More like it's whispered. "Barbi."

Then I hear a thwack, and the ball is coming near me. I get out of its way. There is no point in going toward the ball. I can't catch. I can't throw. I can't run very fast. I get out of its way every time during every game.

Now the ball comes right at me. Fast. It hits me in the face. Hard. Am I falling?

Everyone's laughing.

I get up and think of a dragon. I think of fire coming out of my big nose. I am so angry that I jump in the air, and when I land, I trip.

Mrs. Broud is laughing now too.

I will hate gym forever.

Scrambled Eggs Committee

We are studying food groups, and I am in the protein category. I wanted carbohydrates, but that would have been embarrassing. The kids might guess how much I love spaghetti and dumplings, which is a lot. Kids are good at guessing embarrassing secrets.

Mrs. Broud divides us into committees, and I'm breakfast. So if I'm in the protein category, that means I'm going to be eggs, I think.

I'm right! And I am appointed chairman of the scrambled eggs committee.

A man from the *Elmhurst Press* comes right into our classroom. He asks questions, writes things in a notebook, and waves his camera around. When he walks over to our committee, Bobby is stirring the eggs in a glass bowl. It's his turn. But when the camera is about to shoot, I take the bowl from Bobby and announce that as chairman of the scrambled eggs committee, I should be the one stirring them in the picture.

When I see my picture in the paper, I look a lot shorter than the other committee members and a lot fatter. Still, I am smiling like a chairman. My picture is in the paper.

Vienna Choir Girl

I really want to be a Vienna Choir Boy—I mean girl. That's the music I want to sing. Music that goes higher and higher until it's so high that it IS God. I can sing that music, and I will. I want a robe too. Just like the choirboys wear. A long robe to my ankles. I will be all covered in rustling fabric. I want sleeves that flap and a fancy collar. I love costumes.

Then I will sing from inside the robe and no one will see me. They will just hear my voice.

Today I saw *Almost Angels* at the movies. Before, when I was little, I wanted to sing on *The Mickey Mouse Club* because I can sing better than those kids. But they are so pretty. If I get to wear a robe, it won't matter that I'm not pretty or that I'm fat.

The songs on *The Mickey Mouse Club* are stupid. Those girls' skirts stick out because there is netting underneath, and you can see their underpants, and sometimes they wear cowboy boots. The Vienna Choir Boys sing music that is better than opera. In opera the singing is fat and wobbly. Mom puts it on the radio every Sunday after we get back from Sunday school. But the Vienna Choir Boys sing like floating, like magic, like glass.

I can make my voice like that. And I'll stand in a high place, and if I cut my hair, no one will know that I'm a Vienna Choir Girl.

Barbara—Minus the Middle A

I love the Clancy Brothers and Tommy Makem. I hear them on *The Ed Sullivan Show* and make up harmony while they sing and pretend I am in the group.

When their act is over, a woman with perfect hair comes to the microphone. Some of her hair is in a big bun on top of her head, and some of it is down in a perfect flip. She is wearing a dress with a princess waist. Oh! Her name is Barbara. No, it's Barbra—so, minus a middle *a*. Dad says she's Jewish—"Look at that nose." I look and think, *Egyptian.* I think *Pharaoh's daughter.* She is so beautiful, but so not like Gidget. Well, her eyeliner is a little like Gidget's. Julie Andrews doesn't wear any.

Then she sings, and I like it, but I don't like it too. Her voice isn't like Julie Andrews's voice. It's big and raw, and she doesn't sound like a governess. Julie Andrews's voice is pure and clear, and you think of white gloves. Barbra Streisand's voice is loud and comes from her nose, which is big like mine. Her singing is like a whole play in one song, telling lots of stories. Her face tells stories while she sings. I stare at her nose, and at her eyes, like cats' eyes. When she sings, she isn't scared. She is loud and doesn't care that she isn't spit-spot clean like Mary Poppins. So I stare but decide not to change sides. I am going to sing like Julie Andrews.

I say I don't like Barbra Streisand. Inside I wish I were just a tiny bit like Barbra Streisand.

Children's Chorus of the Lyric Opera

Miss Taylor, my voice teacher, arranges for me to have an audition for the Children's Chorus of the Lyric Opera of Chicago. So right away Simon starts making fun of opera, screeching out high notes and holding his hands together as if his heart is broken, with a pitiful expression on his face. Little boys like to make fun of serious singing. I know because the boys in my class make fun of me when Mrs. Musil comes for music.

Mom calls Eda Neni to tell her about the tryout. I wonder if I'm good enough. I'm at the upper age, eleven, but I'm small—in height if not in weight. I am thinking about costumes. Long dresses with underskirts, petticoats, laced bodices, frilly caps. Shoes like little boots with buttons that have to be hooked. I think about props like baskets with rags, or trays with fake loaves of bread. Maybe I will carry these on stage. Or a handful of flowers. To be STREWN.

Mom drives me to the audition. I've auditioned for shows before—for Elmhurst Children's Theater and once for a York High School play. There was a part for a little girl who could sing. I don't remember the play, but they called back a girl from another school who was very cute and tiny. She looked like a pixie on stage. She sang loudly, but it wasn't pretty singing. I'm hoping that an OPERA company will want a girl who can sing really well. I can do that.

We are driving down the expressway, passing the sign for the Oak Park exit. That's where we get off for temple. The drive seems long.

One of Miss Taylor's other students is auditioning too. She has a big photograph of herself, and she's wearing makeup in it even though she's my age. She keeps it in a folder with some other papers that tell the story of her life, I think. I don't have papers or a picture. Once, her voice lesson was right before mine, and I could hear her singing "I'm Just a Girl Who Can't Say No." She sings *can't* like *cain't*. I hated her as soon as I heard her sing that song. What a stupid song. And she sang it with some fake accent. There was nothing nice or clear in her singing. She's tall, though. With really long, silky dark brown hair. Also, her mother waits for her—maybe every lesson. Her mother's here now at the Lyric Opera audition. Her mom is really dressed up.

My mom isn't dressed up, and I'm wearing school clothes—a maroon corduroy jumper that Mom made me and a white blouse. My anklets are not as white as my blouse, and my shoes are just brown with laces that I have to double knot. And two of the plastic tips on the laces are gone.

Mom looks at my hair and asks, "Did you wash it last night?"

"I don't think I did."

Now my face feels hot.

We wait for a long time. When my name is called, Mom has to stay and I get up to go with a woman with big hair in a gray suit who is carrying a clipboard. When she came in I was staring so hard at her lipstick, which is white, that I didn't hear what she said, so I'm just following her. The lights are bright and warm, and I can see a few people sitting in the middle of where the audience would be, and I have somehow appeared on the stage.

I feel small and plain and heavy in this golden palace.

A man in black glasses and a heavy sweater says, "Don't be nervous. We're just going to ask you to sing the National Anthem."

He smiles as if he just gave me a present. I don't smile because this is very serious. I won't sing high notes, so I know I have to start on a low note for this song. Not too low, though, because it goes lower.

"Oh-oh SAY . . ." So I sing it, and I remember to put my hand over my heart, which makes me get goose bumps.

I get in.

But I can't join. There are rehearsals during the week, and Mom can't take me. I think Dad doesn't want Mom to take away all that time from her other chores. But Mom plays in quartets and orchestras, so she might want to drive me anyway. She might understand.

I don't argue. I know better.

I go to the library. I ask Miss Strand about opera singers, and we go to the card catalog. She helps me look up biographies of opera singers. We find Jenny Lind, the Swedish Nightingale. Miss Strand looks right at me and asks me if I sing. I say yes, but I don't tell her any more facts. I just want to check out my book and go home.

Tune

She sings and learns
To oft judge lesser beings
Not worth the ground below

Carl Sandburg Junior High

No one has snapped my bra today. Usually it happens at passing time before or after lunch. But I'm never even wearing one. Mom won't let me wear a bra because she thinks it's ridiculous for girls to wear bras before they need them. This makes sense but leaves me with nothing to have snapped. The boys laugh hysterically at how pathetic it is that a junior high girl has no bra. I want to defend my mother, but mostly I just want a bra. There were days last week when everyone had to try snapping my back just to see if it was true.

It's not like I don't know where I stand in junior high. I eat lunch by myself. My only friends are at temple. I wonder if they have friends at their schools. My mom still makes all my clothes. My hair will not lie flat or flip up. I wear glasses.

But I was asked to sing some songs from *The Sound of Music* when the Board of Education was coming to visit for the day. In costume. My mother sewed a perfect Maria dirndl dress, with a flowery blue and white skirt, a crocheted lace and royal blue velvet bodice, and nice white puffy sleeves. Tiny pearl buttons too. I should've known not to wear it to school.

At least the French teacher likes me. Oh, and the English teacher.

But for today I've escaped the snapping.

On my way to English, I hear a loud hollow thump. In front of me a boy has fallen forward on his head. A crowd is gathering. He's a special ed kid with a head that's too big for his body, and he's hitting his head against the tile floor. For a second I'm frozen because I can't believe what I'm seeing. The boys are laughing and pointing at him. They're hooting at him. It's too horrible. I go to the boy, whose name I don't know. I'm afraid to touch him, but I scream at the circle of kids to go away, and I run for a teacher. The teacher takes the boy to the nurse, but the kids stay, pointing and imitating his head-banging.

I scream, "You're not worth the ground he walks on!"

But what I'm also thinking is, "You're not worth the ground I walk on!"

And I run to class.

Voice Lessons and the 'L'

I wake up on Saturdays with a feeling of dread. On Saturdays I take the bus and the 'L' to my voice lesson with Miss Taylor and to the Jack and Jill Players of Chicago. The part I hate is the bus and the 'L,' mostly the 'L.' It's noisy and dirty. There's always a man with no legs where I get off. He's on a dirty blanket that's on top of cardboard, and his hat is upside down on the ground. There's a little bit of money in it, and people are supposed to put in more, but I've never seen anyone do it. I'm too scared to get close enough to put some in too, but I always feel like I should. I want to look at his face, but I don't. I know going to the Loop isn't dangerous or my parents wouldn't let me go alone, but it feels dangerous.

Once Mom drove me, but it made Dad mad that she was gone all day. So she took me on the bus and the 'L' once so I would learn my way, and since then I've been going by myself. All during the day I think about stopping at Fannie May on my way home. I will buy exactly two green Mint Meltaways. I eat these slowly as I walk back to the 'L' station. Sometimes the man with no legs is gone. Where does he go?

First I warm up with Miss Taylor. She is fat with lots of white hair piled high on her head, and she wears powder. Also her eyelashes are spikey. She holds my fingers to her throat while she sings so I can feel that there is no tightness there. Then she holds my hand to her stomach while she sings so I can feel that it is very tight. That is her breath. She holds her breath underneath her tight dresses, on top of her high heels that she might be too old to wear. I breathe from my diaphragm too. Once she passed gas, but I pretended not to hear.

I sing exercises for half the time and then some art songs. She calls me "Bar-ba-ra," like Julie Andrews would.

Sometimes Miss Taylor gives me show tunes. I tell her that I will not sing "I Enjoy Being a Girl." I think it's idiotic. I will only sing serious songs. I will sing French or Italian songs or "Where'er You Walk."

Cantor Rosen told Mom to take me to Miss Taylor for voice lessons. He studies with her. I think it costs a lot of money.

After my voice lesson, I walk to the Jack and Jill Players Theater School. That name is so babyish. First we do improv. We pretend that we're playing tug-of-war. We have to do this in ensemble, so it's tricky. Or one of us will have to get up and pantomime a situation. I had to pretend to drag a stool from the window to the center of the room, sit down on it, look in a mirror, and cry at what I saw there. The other students applauded, so I felt good. Not even embarrassed. I wasn't acting a lot, though, except for the stool part.

I do get sad when I look in the mirror. I see my nose first. Chubbo says I have beautiful eyes, but that's what Grandpa told her, and she wasn't a pretty girl—I've seen pictures. My eyes are nice. I just wish they were spring green or cornflower blue, like the crayons. When I look in the mirror, I imagine myself thin, with long straight hair, a real waist, and thighs that don't jiggle. I wonder what it would be like to have "arresting" eyes, and then I think about Dorothy in *The Wizard of Oz*. When she's in the Emerald City beauty salon getting her hair done, right before she meets the Wizard, she asks if they can dye her eyes to match her gown. Even though she is such a pretty girl, Dorothy wants to trade her brown eyes for another color. Girls in books are sometimes "not quite pretty" or "just short of pretty." There are no girls who are "just not pretty plus chubby." Then the books say, "In the light, she was lovely" or "When she turned just so, she was charming." In the dark, I am invisible.

At Jack and Jill we mostly rehearse the musical we're about to
put on. Now it's *The Sound of Music*. Everyone gets a part. I get a big
part, although it isn't the one I wanted. I wanted to be Liesl. I want
to have the teenage girl part. But like always, a pretty, thin girl with
long blonde hair gets that kind of part. Kristin sings okay, but not
as well as I do. Just like always. The girl who gets the part of Maria
is pretty too, and older than me. Sandy is thirteen. She has a really
big voice, and she deserves the part. Her eyes are very far apart
and big. Also she has blonde hair like Julie Andrews in the movie. I
know she deserved the part of Maria. I get Mother Abbess. I won't
have any fancy costumes. Just a long black robe and a wimple. The
long robe is okay with me, but the wimple is tight. Jack, the owner
of the theater, who Dad says is a queer, told me, "Typecasting, dear-
est." I know, I know. Serious, stodgy, ugly Barb.

Trajectory

I learned the word *trajectory* from my script. It isn't in my lines.
The play is called *Rocket Ship to the Moon* by Rosemary G. Musil,
our music teacher.

I want to play the girl who goes to the moon with the boy, but
like always, I get cast as the housekeeper. She wears an apron. I
don't have a lot of lines, and I play someone old. Of course. When
you're plump, you don't get the pretty-girl parts. When you have a
big nose and twisty hair, you play grandmothers or old aunts. My
aunt Vera has twisty hair and a crooked nose. It's not like I think
I'm going to grow up and become a beauty.

But I love being on stage and I love rehearsals, even the waiting.
It makes me feel famous, and I'm going to be famous, even though
this is Elmhurst Children's Theatre. The singers on Dad's records
don't look like Brigitte Bardot. They're much chubbier, and they're
also black people. Opera singers are fat mostly too, and their eyeliner goes way beyond their actual eyes. I'm already taking singing
lessons, and my teacher, Miss Taylor, which she pronounces like tay-
LORE, not TAY-ler, said I could change my name to Ostefello. I am
never going to change my name. And that name sounds like a very

fake name. I'm learning some Italian art songs, and I brought home a German art song, but Mom said I couldn't sing that in her house. I'm really good at French songs because I can imitate Dad's French.

There is one part of the play that I really hate. I have to throw my arms around the boy who went to the moon, and say, "Jupiter, I thought I'd never see you again!"

Bobby, the boy who plays Jupiter, is in my class, and I just can't hug him. He's so cute and tall. All the girls like him. I'm so ugly and fat, everyone will laugh at me. And they'll tease me at school.

Bobby will make fun of me to his friends and say, "Can you believe I have to touch Ostfeld?"

So in rehearsal I say, "We can just skip over the hug part," and then say my line—"Jupiter, I thought I'd never see you again"—and I fake-wipe my eyes with my huge handkerchief like I'm supposed to do. (It's in the blocking.)

After the performance, which Dad, as usual, won't see, I'm going to take the handkerchief home with me. I'll put it under my pillow.

1964: Year of the Bike

Even though it's still hot on the front steps, I sit back down and pick up my book again. My heart is beating fast, and I want to go through the sprinkler. That's not unusual.

I look down at the cover of *A Tree Grows in Brooklyn*, feeling a little excited about myself. THAT'S what's unusual. I might even go through the sprinkler right now.

The book says that all the wonders of the world are in Shakespeare, and I don't know about that, but today's wonder is that I can ride a bike as of right now! Reading is how I have fun, but I didn't know about riding bikes. Now I do, and it's because of Sharon Mueller. I can still see her—she's riding away on her bike, almost to the Rubensteins' house already.

It's kind of a secret that I've never ridden a two-wheeler. No one ever wants to ride bikes with me—not enough to make me admit that I don't know how, anway. Until this minute, I was afraid of falling. Well, I'm still a little scared. In gym class, if I do sports or exercises, I will get hurt and be embarrassed. Why would I try to make my body do things it doesn't want to do, like climb ropes in gym or run or ride a bike? I wouldn't. But I might think about it again if it would be fun like the fun that girls have in books.

I see kids ride to the library with their books in a basket or to the dime store for penny candy or down the street to where the Good Humor man is parked. Until Sharon Mueller came over today, I just never thought about trying to learn to ride. I didn't think I could be a bike-riding girl.

When Simon was in kindergarten, he learned by himself on the Geneseo kids' bike, and now he rides everywhere. Even Sarah has a bike this summer, with training wheels. Mom and Dad never say anything about bikes to me. Maybe they don't want me to feel bad. I did feel a little bad, but I feel better now.

Sharon Mueller is one year ahead of me in school. She has a round face and big cheeks. She looks friendly all the time. Half an hour ago I was sitting on the front step reading *A Tree Grows in Brooklyn* and feeling hot. My shorts were sticking to my thighs, and I was making my new bad mosquito bite bleed. Then there was Sharon, putting down her kickstand and saying hi. She told me she was riding around and saw me just sitting here.

I was a little worried about anyone stopping to say hi to me because it could have been fake or for a reason I don't understand. But Sharon was smiling in a real way, so I said hi.

And Sharon said, "You can't ride a bike, Barbi, can you."

It wasn't a question. She knew.

So I said, "No, I don't know how."

And she said, "Yeah, but you can. I'll show you."

I said, "I'll fall down." And she said, "No, you won't."

Sharon started being in charge, like a young nice teacher. She showed me how to start—where the seat should be and how to keep the bike balanced—and then she pushed on the back fender and ran behind me on the sidewalk. Her bike was a little too tall for me, but it was close enough. She ran in back of me for a long time, breathing hard, and then she said, "Tell me when to let go." I felt bad because she had been running for so long and I was being a baby. So I said, "Let go," even though I didn't want her to. When I said, "Let go," she didn't just let go. She gave me a huge push from behind and yelled, "Pedal fast! You can do it!"

So I did pedal fast, and I did it! I was scared to stop, but I just put my shoe down, tap, tap, tap on the sidewalk until I could get off the seat and stand with both feet.

That was only half an hour ago! I'm still surprised that I can ride a bike!

I get up and go into the kitchen and tell Mom, and she says I can have a bike of my own. Tomorrow we're going to get a bike, and it will be new. Light green or maybe red?

I have stationery with tiny red rosebuds on it. The paper is see-through, and the envelopes match. The paper has a scent. It's supposed to be a rose scent. I use this paper and my school fountain pen to write to Chubbo a lot. Now I will write a letter to Sharon Mueller. But where does she live? Not around here. How will I find her to give her the letter?

Maybe after tomorrow, when I have my new light green or red bike, I'll find her the way she found me.

Sandra Kramov's Bat Mitzvah, and Dr. King

I go to one friend's Bat Mitzvah. Sandra Kramov. She's my age but a year behind me in school, like everyone else who's actually my age. Sandra has a funny speaking voice, high and in her nose with a kind of sharp edge to it. I like her well enough, but she isn't a close friend—although I'm glad that she invited me.

Sandra isn't on the bima for long and she doesn't sing, but she looks very grown up, and her parents are smiling. A lot. Maybe too much. They seem nervous. Sandra has her hair done. It makes her face look small.

As soon as the party starts, she takes off her shoes. That makes Mrs. Kramov mad, but by then Sandra doesn't care. I see her nylons running. That's why I'm not allowed to wear them. You wear them

bat mitzvah: daughter of the commandment—originally, the recognition that an adolescent girl or boy (bar mitzvah) had reached the age when she/he became subject to the laws of the Torah as an adult; today, also the term for the ceremony that commemorates this status

once, and they are ruined. Mom doesn't want to hear about all the other girls whose mothers let them wear nylons.

I am alone at a long kids' table, so I open and close the latch on my purse a few times. Snap, snap. I start to think. Would I have liked a Bat Mitzvah? I think yes because I could have maybe sung. I'm pretty sure that Cantor Rosen didn't let Sandra sing because of that catch in her voice. But I didn't want to learn Hebrew because Dad thinks it's antiquated. He says learning Hebrew is archaic, and that one time his father had taken him to a synagogue where there was mumbling and shuffling around, which does sound stupid. Dad said that there was no cantor and no choir and no organ—also that there were no kids there, only old men. *Archaic* is like old men with untrimmed fingernails in a yellow room. I might have gotten a new dress and shoes, though. Maybe a hairstyle.

People have started dancing, and I want to go home.

Rabbi Mervis talked about Sandra accepting the commandments and being newly responsible. Sandra nodded, but I could tell that she wasn't paying attention because she was looking at her new ring. She even twisted it so the amethyst faced her palm. Rabbi Mervis said, "Sandra?" and she looked at him and nodded fast and swallowed. I think she started to listen again.

Now she's dancing, with her shoes back on. I have forty-five minutes until Mom comes to pick me up. I look in my purse. There's a dime in case I need to make an emergency call, and a handkerchief. I wish I had lipstick—pink Yardley lipstick. My first choice would be London Luv Pink. It comes in a tube with baby blue and pink stripes going all around it. I'm too young to wear lipstick, Mom says.

I think I am responsible—more than Sandra. People trust me to babysit. I go back and forth to the Loop by myself. I get good grades. I have opinions about Civil Rights. I don't get in trouble. Sandra's parents take away some of the magazines she buys, and some books too. I'm allowed to read any books I want. I read *Lolita*, which I wish I hadn't because it comes into my mind sometimes. My mind isn't always responsible, which is why I like to read and why I wish I had a book now while I'm waiting. I feel like I'm just watching other kids a lot of the time. Watching is usually not good.

Watching my Sunday school friends is making me feel like a little kid. They look more grown up, and they know how to be at parties. Watching grown-ups isn't good either, because they can have too much alcohol and get loud or start to mispronounce words or say things I shouldn't hear. Listening can be as bad as watching. That's why reading is good.

When I'm in temple, I can watch almost anything and not worry about it being okay. It's quiet, and people say "shhh" to their kids or hold hands or look at other people's clothes. And I always have a book, with phrases like "Justice shall flow like waters" and "The earth is the Lord's" and "He that hath clean hands." I love all of these words, but I get a little twitchy when words like *brothers* and *mankind* and all the *he*'s start to add up. I understand that God is a male, but everyone isn't a male. What about everyone else? What about me?

Rabbi Mervis talks about Dr. King and how he nailed a list of demands on the door of City Hall downtown and how that was a religious act. He says that religion demands caring for the poor and not just coming to temple. He usually talks about one of the prophets in his sermons. Dad really likes that. We talk about it in the car going home—if Dad is in the mood. If he's not, we're all quiet.

Dad's going to take us to hear Dr. King at Elmhurst College. I can't believe Dr. King is coming to Elmhurst. His talk is part of his plan to integrate the suburbs.

There aren't any Negroes in Elmhurst. Once when Sarah was little, maybe three, we were in the car driving downtown, and she saw a little black girl playing in a yard, and she said, "Look, a baby maid!" Mom was very upset and had to do a lot of calm explaining. That story proves Dr. King's point about suburbs being all white.

If I had a Bat Mitzvah, in my speech I would talk about Dr. King and integration and going to march with him in the South when I'm in college. AND, I would wear London Luv Pink lipstick plus nylons and a bra.

1966 and I Understand Pink

I'm going into ninth grade wearing pink. Over the summer I grew out of all my junior high clothes, and Mom had to take me shopping for fabric for the skirts she's going to make. Then we went to Korvette's for actual store-bought school blouses. I picked a blouse for the first day of school. Pink. The skirt fabric is a pale pink too, houndstooth. The cotton-candy colored blouse zips in back, but otherwise it's completely plain. Mom doesn't like its seams.

I bought the *Seventeen* magazine August fashion issue and memorized the tips. I know all about checks and A-line skirts. (That's why Mom is making me my first A-line skirt. The skirt picture on the pattern packet looks a lot like the one on the magazine cover.) I'm starting at York High School and taking no chances. I am going to dress like the girls in *Seventeen*, even though I'm not turning fourteen until December.

I have brass incense burners in my room and candles. Also sealing wax and a stamp with my first initial for my letters to Gramballs—that's my new name for Chubbo. It's a tribute to her cockiness, and I do mean that. Simon and Sarah laugh when I refer to her as Gramballs. Even Dad laughs.

I made a haircut appointment for myself at the Pin-Up Salon, and even though the stylist was old, she gave me a good style and showed me how to tease the top of my hair with a long-handled comb.

Mom took me to Sears too, because she said that Korvette's is not known for the quality of its underwear. But I'm not complaining. She bought me two bras, a garter belt, two pairs of hose, and four pairs of underwear. Other girls were school shopping too and had their mothers wait outside the fitting rooms. I wanted to ask Mom to wait while I tried things on, but I didn't want to disappoint her.

Today is the first day of school, and I've checked everything off of the list I made. From setting my hair to putting on hose. I'm wearing my new shoes, Bass Weejuns, and I've filed my nails into ovals. Last night I painted them extra-frosted pink.

Mom goes to get the instamatic camera that she keeps in the

coat closet. She takes a first-day-of-high-school picture of me in the doorway. The cube flashes. For once I think it will turn out. For once I look okay. I walk to school, worrying only about finding my classrooms.

Drosophila, Frogs, and the Six-Day War

Dad "helped" me with the fruit fly experiment for Miss Henriksen's biology class. He got an A–. This is good. We're near the end of the second semester, and that grade will help wrap up my freshman year. Dad made me rewrite every sentence and look harder and longer at fruit fly eye color than anyone would want to. Maybe for one second I understood the idea, but now it's gone.

Miss Henriksen wrote, "Precise writing here."

No shit. Dad's a scientist.

Once when I was little, I said I wanted to be a doctor, and Dad said I wasn't smart enough because Mom had diluted his intelligence. There's some Mendelian genetics for you, I guess. Then when I said I would be a nurse, he said I was too smart for that, and that any gorngoot (an Ostfeld word) could be a nurse.

Maybe I could do Shakespeare and maybe live in London. I could wear long, pointy-bodiced gowns trimmed with seed pearls. Lace-edged sleeves. Rings on every finger.

I'd always do anything in a play just to be in a play, like when I had to fling my arms around a cute boy while dressed as his elderly housekeeper. This year I auditioned to be a frog among frogs in a play I will never understand, Aristophanes's *The Frogs*. And I had to write down my weight for all to see on the tryout sheet. I weigh 117, the same as Sue Suconik. Sue was never fat, like I used to be. We are also both five feet four inches tall.

I emphasized odd words in my audition lines to stand out, but I still got the same part as Sue and as every other freshman girl. *Brekekekèx-koàx-koáx.* Yes, I was a frog. We frogs had one scene, and the point was that we croaked with one voice. "Title role" my cloacal gland! (We dissected a frog in Miss Henriksen's class earlier this year.)

So I probably don't even have the talent to be a Shakespearean actress.

Today when I walk into biology, the whole class stands up and claps. I know why right away and start laughing. Yeah. The Six-Day War. We win. Weird that Israel gets applause now. I guess we're cooler than Arabs.

Somebody is always cooler or more talented or smarter. Today at York High School in my bio class, Israel is cool. Frogs, no way. Frogs wind up croaking in a chorus line—or croaked and splayed on a tray, stuck with pins. People swoon over pale blue eyes or sparkling green eyes. Does anyone care about brown eyes unless they are amber or golden or speckled with gray or something?

Here's a suggestion for you, fruit flies: For your eye color, go with vermillion. Given your lifespan, why not maximize your coolness? Who wouldn't want to be a winner or the smartest or to have eyes that put the *rrrr* in red?

Palms, Not Napalm

The phone rings first thing in the morning. My friend John Emerson tells me to report to the Episcopal church on Church Street at noon. There will be an action related to Palm Sunday. I have no idea what Palm Sunday is and call Joanne Pedersen. She laughs and asks her mother. According to Mrs. Pedersen, it marks Jesus's entrance into Jerusalem on a donkey. The palms come into it because they were strewn in his path as he entered. I know better than to ask Joanne to come with me. Protesting is not a subject I discuss with her. Only with John, who has red hair and blue eyes, whose mother goes to League of Women Voters meetings with my mother.

I don't know why I am going to this Episcopal church in the cold with some snow still left on the ground, but if John says go, I go, and there will be adventure. John and some guy pick me up in this guy's old and smelly car. John and I are too young to drive. When we stop at a stop sign, John screams, "Wait!" He leaps out of the car, as does the other guy, they fly toward each other in a parody of a loping run to the front of the car, kiss each other with tongues, and mock-run back to their seats. I am shocked but pretend not to care. I start wondering what it means that they kissed or if it only means that they are exuberant with some kind of Palm Sunday protest excitement. Maybe they're just stoned. That's it, probably.

We get to the church, where I see John's older friends, who live, I think, at People's House. I don't really know what People's House is all about, but I love the communistic name. It's where the activists gather and smoke marijuana and lie around talking at all hours. I've been there a few times, but not for long.

So on Palm Sunday I look around at the boys and see that their hair is longish. Some are ragged looking, but most of them just look like they might be from England. Their jackets look very worn, like they've been worn by previous generations. I see old-looking clothes that aren't in shop windows. There seem to be more than the usual number of people wearing glasses with heavy black frames.

I'm not dressed right. Why am I never dressed right? I'm wearing a pastel plaid A-line skirt with pantyhose. Most of the older women aren't even wearing pantyhose. The other girls are in earth-tone corduroy pants. A few have embroidered flowers on the legs of their pants. I set my hair last night so it would look good for today, but it's too fixed up or something. My hair never just hangs around my face like other girls' hair. It moves, but it doesn't sway or cascade. Nothing about me is just natural.

But I know my way around a protest all right. I pick up my sign, reading it. "Palms, Not Napalm." I think I get it. I've read about the Napalm Ladies. People should pray and stop supporting this war. How can we be burning little Asian kids with jellied poison?

I seize my palm branch but quickly feel a queasy pang of something. A Jew with a palm branch? I give the palm branch to a bearded guy in a tweedy-looking worker cap. Both the cap and the beard have seen better days. He winks at me, and I look away. *Don't wink, Older Creepy Guy,* I think. *This is serious.*

There are a lot of us in the street, and the police come, mainly to watch. They look stupid. People come out of the church and are sort of confused. They squint at us and gawk. We sing, but I don't know the songs until I've heard them for a bit. If Jesus comes into it, I don't sing. Some photos are taken, presumably by the *Elmhurst Press* photographers.

And then it's over and we go home. I'm sad. I take the cat up to my room along with some chocolate-covered almonds.

Monday after school Mom tells me that Uncle Marvin is furious with me. Apparently my picture was in the *Elmhurst Press* in connection with the Palms, Not Napalm protest. Marvin is incensed that my parents allow me to participate in a radical, hippie left-wing protest right in his backyard. Mom smiles. I don't grant my mother even the smallest acknowledgment. Instead I head upstairs for more chocolate almonds and Isaac Bashevis Singer. I reach for the cat, but she scoots away.

Contact Lenses, Torah Corps, and Chin Hair

We are returning to our bunk from chofesh (free time), practicing our new Hebrew words and deciding which white shirts we'll wear on Shabbat. These kids seem to know more words than I do. Words like *parasha* (weekly Torah reading) and *D'varim* (Deuteronomy or, literally, *words*). We've been hearing about footsteps in the sand from one of the rabbis here. It's so neat to learn this stuff. So when a guy is troubled and sees only his own footprints, he wonders where are God's, particularly in his time of need. After all, God has promised to be by our side, right? God comes to him in a dream to say that in such times the guy sees only one set of prints because God is CARRYING HIM IN HIS ARMS. I just love this!

Deb says, "Hey, you have one black hair right here in the middle of your chin!"

Everything stops. The words fly away and the wind blows in, filling up any outlines of feet in sand. I think I feel faint.

What could be worse than dark facial hair? I already spend tons of time worrying about managing the frizzing hair on my head, keeping my makeup fresh, hiding my sweat, my fatness (which could make a comeback any minute), my clothes, my huge nose.

If I have chin hair, I might as well lie down and die.

And I feel so good here, so at home and excited about what we're doing. This is Torah Corps: Torah study and Jewish folk singing in a camp setting with people who look something like me. How is it that I've never seen the chin hair?

I got contact lenses last year—finally, at fourteen. I know my vision's okay with regular glasses, but I've heard my parents say things from time to time about how even unattractive women who know how to take care of themselves can cut a decent figure. So the contacts had to be a pity present. Contact lenses are a big deal. Getting good at putting them in and taking them out took lots of practice, but I've got it down now. Losing one is disastrous— requiring a long wait for a replacement—not to mention expensive. They get oily and cloud your vision. Worse, people can tell if your lenses are smudgy. Also you blink a lot. But now that green lenses have entered my life, one thing is undeniable. I have green eyes. I am a girl with green eyes, not just greenish eyes. I am now pale with green eyes. If only I could imagine for a moment that the description ended there. My mind includes *oversized nose, bordering on overweight, clumsy, and stiff.*

So I wear lots of eye makeup now. Oh, and my ankles are narrow. Pale with green eyes and narrow ankles.

AND I've found clean-smelling perfume. Nothing cloying or fruity. I hate musk and sandalwood. I like green smells as well as green eyes. Grass, citrus, bergamot (whatever the fuck that is).

Verdant. I love that word.

So even with contact lenses, now I need a magnifying mirror? Like the ones in those mail order catalogs from Vermont?

I'm doing everything I can, but this chin hair escaped my notice. I'm not even fat this year. Now I have to add another thing to my list of grooming tasks. How many other people have seen that hair? Have boys seen it? Do people joke about it? Maybe Deb was the first to see it, the only one to see it. Maybe I got away with it. It's only one chin hair. Tweezers. Who might have tweezers? I know where Mom keeps hers at home.

Mom!

What is Mom going to say when I tell her that I want to observe kashrut from now on?

kashrut: cleanliness—the laws governing keeping a kosher kitchen

Coffeehouse Folk Singer

A very round man sings the Leonard Cohen song "Suzanne." I think it's the only song he knows. He sings it every Saturday night—that and nothing else ever. Sweetly, in tune, without hesitation, but never any other song. Poor man. I nod at him on my way to the main chair, in the center under the light.

My mind goes empty, and I am Joan Baez.

I sing, "Bad news, bad news to old England came." And then I sing, "Geordie will be hanged in a golden chain." Followed by "It was Mary Beaton and Mary Seton and Mary Carmichael and me." Of course I sing "A Hard Rain's A-Gonna Fall." Yes, I'm Bob Dylan too.

Joan Baez wouldn't be caught dead reading *Seventeen* magazine. I hide the copies I buy because I know this. Joan Baez is perfect— she doesn't need help with her makeup. I study *Seventeen*'s makeup rules until I'm an expert, even with Max Factor liquid eyeliner. That takes practice. I know exactly how to draw the line with my right hand while holding my lid still with my left. And I know that the line should start at the inner edge and should get a little bit thicker until it tapers into a wing just beyond the outer edge. The hard part is waiting for eyeliner to dry. I wear lots of mascara and Yardley slicker in Dicey Peach. I leave the rest of my face bare so its washable at any moment. (I've developed a face-washing technique that avoids contact with my eye makeup.) I hate the feeling of any goo on my face, so that's another reason not to wear foundation.

I had Mom make me several long skirts out of metallic fabric with a paisley pattern and insisted that she trim them with ribbons and braids. With these I wear one of my two peasant blouses. My favorite one has bell sleeves and a drawstring neck.

I let my hair be its wild, frizzy self. My nose makes its Semitic statement, proudly or not, but clearly.

My folk guitar skills are basic but adequate, learned from chord diagrams. Chord to chord, so slowly I thought at first the music would die, until they sped up and I could sing above them. That then was that. I played and played. Folk song and Child ballad after folk song and Child ballad. Even with all those years of piano and harpsichord lessons, I am a better guitarist.

To lighten the mood between ballads and protest songs, I sing,

> I wish I was a fascinating lady
> with my past kinda short,
> my future kinda shady.

People laugh generously. I have no idea if there is a deep meaning to this song, which I learned from my friend John Emerson.

I sit down. I drink a hot cider and feel triumphant. Yes, I'm a folk singer. Really. And I know more than one song. People clap, and my friends come to hear me. I sing in a dark coffeehouse with floors so dirty that it's hard to know if they're wood or linoleum. People smoke at small tables, and there's an actual haze. The chairs aren't comfortable, so it's weird that people stay for any length of time, but they do.

And the dark is good and the dirt is good and the haze is good and the hardness is good and the bad coffee (that I don't drink) is also supposed to be good somehow.

Oh, and most of the singing is bad.

Why do I love the dark and dirt and haze and cacophony and discomfort of this place? This must be as close as white people like me get to real life.

Moving to Connecticut

Torah Corps is over, and my life might as well be over too. We're moving from Elmhurst to fucking North Haven, Connecticut, which is nowhere. NOWHERE. I will start my junior year of high school in a new school, not knowing anyone, having zero friends. Goodbye, York High School. Goodbye, coffeehouse. Goodbye, Oak Park Temple and voices lessons in the city. Goodbye, Sue,

John, Jo, Deb, Regina, Luther, Bob, Keith, Jeff. I know I sound like a children's book, but it's all I can think. Goodbye. Goodbye, Baskin-Robbins, Hinsdale Health Museum (where you can see fetuses in jars), Elmhurst Public Library, Lizzadro Museum of Lapidary Art. Goodbye, backyard.

Dad is going from the University of Illinois to YALE. Big fucking deal. Yeah, I know Dad's work is important and that this is a huge promotion for him. I get that he needs recognition and wider funding for his research on the aging. But where will I buy my medieval music albums, and where will I walk with friends, if I even make any? Who will sit with me at lunch? Who will make me laugh? Who will be in the alto section of the chorus, if they even HAVE a chorus there? Will I get solos? Will the English teachers like me? After how long? Will there be advanced French with genuine idiomatic conversation? Will there be a decent theater group, a drama club? Will I get parts? What if I hate our new rabbi? What if I hate our new cantor? What if I don't know the music they sing in temple?

And now I have to introduce myself as WHO? Now I have to prove myself as WHOEVER I am.

Well, we did it. We moved into the ugliest, biggest, most modern house I have ever seen. Mom wants to paint the shutters orange, and if she does, I will die.

There are fluorescent lights in the kitchen. I look TERRIBLE in fluorescent light anywhere, in diners or at school. My skin looks so oily. I can see every pore on my nose, and it's not like I don't clean my pores every night. I use Phisohex antibacterial soap and rubbing alcohol. I wash my face between classes, but still I see the light glinting off my pimples, as if they were in a spotlight.

The only good thing is my room. It's on the first floor, and everyone else is upstairs. I have my own bathroom and a closet so large that I can hole up in it and write. In this closet I've put up my posters. There's SuperJew with his curly sidelocks. He's coming out of a phone booth and stripping off his ultra-Orthodox garb to reveal a blue skinsuit and tights. Instead of a capital *S* on his chest, there's a big shin. Next to him is Eugene McCarthy, who should have been president. I worked very hard on his campaign. On the opposite wall is Joan Baez, whose hair hangs in perfect sheets. Her legs are so skinny in her bell-bottoms. So I have my holy trinity right here in the closet. Jew, Gene, and Joan! I have medieval flower illustrations on the walls in there too. They give the closet a little formality.

Also in the closet is my record player and all of my early music records. I light candles and incense in there because Mom doesn't know and Dad's at work—as if I care.

I walk home from temple on our first Friday night. It's way over a mile and so long. It's also hot. I don't care. I've been dragged to Connecticut and away from everything I loved. I need to be alone. I don't even know where the bus stop is, and what do I say when I get there in a few days when school starts? Hi, my name is Barb? Like they're going to give a flying fuck. *I* don't even give a flying fuck.

Tonight I'm going to sleep in the closet with music playing and candles burning. It will be a funeral or a candlelight vigil for my LIFE.

Harpsichord

My parents buy me a harpsichord. They think it will improve my mood. The Yale student who built it from a Zuckermann kit needs to sell it, but he keeps running his hand over the slightly dusty strings near the tuning pins. His nose turns red while Mom writes out the check.

He gives me a small package of plectra (the picks that pluck the strings when you push the keys), a voicing knife for shaving them, a tuning fork, and a tuning hammer. Briefly, he demonstrates how to use them and shows me where he burned his name (in amateurish calligraphy) and the date on which he completed the harpsichord. I can't wait for him to leave.

I show little gratitude. Maybe none.

The piano bench is too high, but I make do. I roll chords. I play

shin: Hebrew letter for the s sound

the first pages of Hanon's *The Virtuoso Pianist*, smiling at the new sound.

And then I sing "When, Lovely Phyllis, Thou Art Kind" and "Ah! Cruel Nymph, You Give Despair" and "Amarilli, mia Bella."

I try some ornaments—vocal trills I've heard on recordings. I flatten out the vibrato and let the air flow through me, pretending I am a sopranino recorder. I wish I could sing for the Yale student.

Maybe then he wouldn't be crying like a girl over his lost harpsichord. It's mine now, buddy!

In My Own Hands

The safety razor is in my hand.

My copy of Michener's *The Source* is next to me on my bed.

This bed, by the way, is a fucking embarrassment. A canopy bed, for God's sake. French Colonial. COLONIAL! (Mom bought this bedroom set for me from Sears as a confirmation present.) I NEVER make this bed. And although I never wear anything that isn't fresh from the wash, my shirts and dresses and pants and sweaters and nightgowns and jeans and underwear are all over the floor. To Mom's eternal frustration, I do small washloads at night— my own, only. Like I give a shit about "economy" or "wasting hot water" or "efficiency."

This Saturday we're going to another group family session in the psych ward. We are supposed to feel close to the "other families who are going through something similar." This is bullshit. What I am going through is ANGER.

I don't even know who I am the angriest at, Mom or Dad. Dad is the villain, but Mom just let it happen. Why the fuck was it up to ME to get the guy formerly known as my FATHER committed to a psych ward? I'm fifteen! Mom said that Dad was still okay at work (which I found out was a lie). I talked to Simon, who agreed with me. But he warned me that Dad would kill me if I told.

Simon never says anything at these group meetings. Sarah looks down at the floor. Once a little boy said, "Adrian is acting like a doctor and not like a patient." I am furious that a little boy calls my dad "Adrian" and not "Dr. Ostfeld." I am furious that I can't be proud of him anymore, that we have to witness his humiliation in front of "other families who are going through something similar."

Last week I was asked if I had any concerns, and I said that I was worried about college. Later, in private, Dad told me in his new, even meaner voice that I was incredibly selfish and that I didn't have any feelings for him—and what kind of a daughter was I to put him in this situation and then not care about anyone but herself?

I figure he's right. I AM selfish—I know. Witness the laundry routine. I just don't want to take care of anyone. Sarah. Simon. I don't know. Mom is in fucking Oz. Yes, I'm selfish. I didn't want Dad to kill himself with pills or vodka or with pills AND vodka, but I really want him to die right now. He is not my father. I don't know him. He's ugly and cruel. Where is the dad who paced in our rooms at night and who told us serious truths? I mean, I know Mean Dad was in there but mostly in hiding. Pacing Dad never lied, though.

I made myself do it, and it was only last month. It felt like I was a grown-up for a day. I called Dad's secretary, and once I heard her voice, I couldn't stop crying for a long time. But she was nice. She waited, and when I stopped, she said, "Oh, sweetheart." Even though I'd only met her once at a Yale picnic, she called me sweetheart. I swallowed and asked my question. "Is my dad behaving normally at work?"

I heard her sigh while she picked out words, and she said, "Everyone knows he's taking pills from the pocket of his white coat. Everyone knows he's prescribing them for himself. And that he's drinking. I'm so sorry, sweetheart."

I found out from her that it takes two psychiatrists to make someone go to a psych ward against their will.

So I looked up "Psychiatry" in the Yale directory. Then I looked for Jewish names, because if you're Jewish and a psychiatrist, you're probably going to be nice to a Jewish kid who calls out of the blue asking for you to check out her dad—a department chair who's a fucking scientist. Unlikely, right? Well these guys did it. They listened to me, and they came to our house and told Dad that if he didn't check himself in, they would do something legal to make it happen.

After they left, Dad screamed at me until he was hoarse.

"You are SINGLE-HANDEDLY bringing me down! You are RUINING my career! You are a TRAITOR to the Ostfelds! My LIFE'S WORK will never be realized!"

So it's not surprising that the dad in the hospital is cheating. He tells us that he knows just what the psychiatrists are looking for. So he makes his bed and showers and shaves and dresses neatly. He talks to the other patients and is friendly to the staff. He diagnoses some of the patients who are really neurology cases and not psych patients. He says he knows that these behaviors will get him released more quickly. We say nothing to this.

But I want to scream, "Who the HELL are you, you fucking piss-poor excuse for a FATHER?!"

I fall asleep in English class. Mrs. Melillo asks me if everything is okay. She's nice. The boys think she's cute. I don't want anyone to know about Dad.

I cry for myself, and then I stop. What good does it do? I take the razor. It's been in my medicine cabinet. It's rusty and gross with dried-on shaving cream and probably leg hairs.

Where? Where should I cut?

I choose my knees. I hate my fat knees. I make a thin slice across my left knee. It stings but not much. Not enough. I slice my right knee. I blot the blood with tissue. Too soon, it clots. But if I bend my knees, the cuts open, and I can widen them a bit more with my fingers. That's better. They fill with blood over and over.

If Dad can become a secret monster over a matter of months, then I can take matters into my own hands. Again.

Night Sledding

A spray of gravel hits my bedroom window. I sigh. It's nearly 3:00 a.m., which means it's Anne and Moira. I pull back the curtain and see them squeezed between the overgrown rhododendron and the frost-edged glass. They're snorting with laughter, gesturing that I should join them. I have no choice. I pick up yesterday's clothes from the floor and then my coat.

Before I think twice, I'm stomping through the snow to where they're making snow angels as if they were five and not fifteen.

"No," I say.

"She said 'no,'" Anne says solemnly, grabbing my knee.

"No?" repeats Moira, yanking the bottom of my coat.

And I'm down. *They are so physical,* I think. I make a fucking snow angel and lumber to my feet.

"Sledding!" Moira hoots.

I love that they've captured me tonight, but I know my role. I'm the prissy friend who ends up going along.

"Where? Now? It's fucking freezing!"

We trudge up to the top of Homewood Avenue, towing the rusty sleds they've commandeered. Moira strides into the middle of the road, her shadow blue under the snow-trimmed streetlight. The surface of the road shines, and wet irregular flakes start falling. I defer the cold feeling and focus on the beauty of the snow against the night sky.

I sit behind Anne on the larger sled, and Moira flops down on the smaller one. We don't have gloves. Nobody wears gloves. I hunch against Anne and try not to squeeze her stomach with my hands. I can't remember having touched Anne before. She lives one house over, on the corner, with her weird, professorial, Danish dad and her tall, hippieish mom. Anne is beautiful. She puts actual kohl around her eyes and has perfect long, bouncy hair. Her siblings have odd names and slink around.

"That's it, Barrrb," she says, rolling the *r* to tease me.

Moira says, "Me first."

Moira is actually seldom first. Anne is quicker. Moira lives across the street. She's tall and horsey, even though her mother raises show poodles. She looks healthy enough to be on a Cream of Wheat box.

Anne shoves off with her gloveless hands, but Moira has jetted ahead of us. And we're going—fast! Fast! And the air around us seems less black, more blue, and clearer, and the flakes come harder and seem to swoop like squadrons of dive-bombing swallows. I keep thinking that we'll slow down, Anne and me, but we don't. Moira hollers below us, but Anne and I are concentrating. A jolt, and then we skid to a quick stop, all the way across Ridge Road.

"Groovy," Anne drawls, with her fingers in two peace signs.

I love winter tonight, and for that and for tonight, I love my neighbors as myself.

Calling Cantor Rosen from Grandma's House

Even though we've moved to Connecticut, when we visit Chubbo in Chicago she remembers that my favorite after-school snack, at least at her house, is fruit cocktail in heavy syrup with whipped cream. I don't remember when she started serving me fruit cocktail in her breakfast nook—in pink or lime-green Depression glass cups with stems. I am never going to have a breakfast nook. I feel trapped. It's too tidy, even for me. I love that Depression glass, though.

Wow. Grandma never gives up. She tells me that I inherited a need for God. This is such bullshit. I don't need God. It's just that I don't share this Ostfeld disdain for all things Jewish. I'm with Mom's family, the Vogels, and their deep Reform Jewish roots. I don't share this Ostfeldian loathing of observance. If I hear one more time from Dad or Grandma about Yiddish being low class or about women wearing furs in temple on the High Holidays in steamy St. Louis or about the piety of my great-grandparents being like a TRAIT to be passed down . . .

Still, Grandma and her nose remain actual members of Oak Park Temple in Chicago. This is because Mom and Dad put Grandpa's name on the yahrzeit list years ago when they joined the temple themselves. There's even a plaque with his name on it there, in the dark hallway that used to scare me when I was little. Grandma NEVER goes to temple now that we've moved away.

By the way, Gramballs, thanks for the nose. That IS an inherited trait.

So, since I'm visiting from Connecticut, I'm going to call Cantor Rosen at Oak Park Temple. It doesn't seem as scary to make a local call from Grandma's house as it would to make a long-distance call from Connecticut. Also, I'll have more guts if Grandma's in the room. I can be showing off to her a little. I'm going to ask him where he trained to be a cantor.

She has the temple directory, so I call.

"May I please speak to Cantor Rosen?"

"Barbi!" He chuckles his high-pitched chuckle. "It is so nice to hear from you!"

"Hi, Cantor! How are you?"

"I'm fine, Barbi! Are you continuing to sing?"

I tell him yes, that I sing a lot, and then I swallow and ask him my question. "So, where did you study to be a cantor? I'm thinking that I'd like to train to be a cantor when I get out of high school."

Cantor Rosen chuckles again, and I wait, holding my breath for the answer.

"Well, they'll never take you."

"Why not?"

"Becoss"—(he always says it that way)—"you're a girl. They don't take girls."

"Oh, well, what's the name anyway?"

"The School of Sacred Music at Hebrew Union College."

"Okay, well, I'm going to apply anyway, just in case. I think I'd like to do that. Be a cantor. Like you."

More chuckling—more like giggling—but softer now.

"Well, it's fine with me, Barbi. Where else are you applying?"

"Indiana. Eastman. Oberlin."

"Good! Listen, Barbi, I have to go teach. Stay in touch and let me know how it goes! It was great hearing from you!"

I hear a click, and the call ends.

Grandma asks, "How did it go, Barrrbi?" (Romanian r's.)

"Not that great, but I'm still going to apply. He doesn't think they'll admit a female student."

"Oh, vell . . ."

Did You Hear Me, Miss . . . ?

"Good morning, Hebrew Union College, registrar's desk, Miss Altshul."

"Hello, this is Barbara Ostfeld. I'm a senior in high school in North Haven, Connecticut, and I'm interested in applying to the School of Sacred Music. I'd like to request an application form."

"Hold on a minute. Just wait."

"Thank you."

"Now you're who?"

"My name is Barb Ostfeld. I'd like to apply to the cantorial school."

(Pause.) "I see. And how did you come to us?"

"The cantor of my current congregation went to JTS, so I called the cantor of my childhood congregation. He went to HUC."

"Who was that?"

"Cantor Rosen. Um, Martin Rosen from Oak Park Temple in Oak Park, Illinois."

"Well, hold on a minute. Just wait."

"Thank you."

"We've never had a request like this from a girl." (Silence.) "Did you hear me, Miss . . . ?"

"Um, yes. Ostfeld. Sorry—I did hear you."

"No girl has called up and asked for an application."

"Oh. Ah. Can I give you my address?"

"I'll take your address, but hold on."

"Thank you."

I hold while Miss Altshul consults someone or checks admissions requirements or finishes her grocery list—I have no idea.

The wait isn't long, but it's long enough to make me worry. My palms sweat and I think that my fate is hanging in the balance— that Miss Altshul, like Alice's Red Queen, will next either chop off my head or grant me freedom.

I hear a muffled sound from the phone and then her voice.

"Very well. Spell your name for me."

"O-S-T-F-E-L-D, Barbara." (Pause.) "Thank you, Miss Altshul."
"Hmm. Very well."

I let go of my breath and put the receiver down. This is happening. I will go to cantorial school. I wait for a trumpet fanfare, but there is nothing, other than the pounding of my heart.

"*Vergin, tutto amor*"

There is no phys ed requirement at the Hebrew Union College School of Sacred Music, and no math requirement either. I know. I looked at the school's tiny catalog. These are assets—huge assets.

I arrive for my audition at the Upper West Side address where the school is located. I like the building. It's old and shabby. A courtly man in a three-piece suit meets me in the lobby and introduces himself to me as Cantor Behrman.

We take an elevator up to the fourth floor and walk down a corridor into the audition room. It's a small, unimpressive classroom—less impressive than any high school classroom I've ever occupied—which surprises me. This is college! The piano is old and scratched up, so I'm guessing it's going to be out of tune. Even though this is a music school, it's no conservatory. But this shabbiness also relaxes me. This place isn't fancy or formal enough to scare me, even though I might be rejected because I'm a girl.

The other two cantors sitting here are dressed in black—shiny black, with shiny black yarmulkes. Two of them have hollows under their eyes. They look like supernatural characters out of Isaac Bashevis Singer—dybbuks maybe, except for the three-piece-suit guy. They look like they've seen horrors, or better days or something. I feel like I'm on a field trip to the Lower East Side.

I see them all look at the hemline of my dress. I know it's short, I know. I watched over Mom until I saw that she started hemming precisely where I'd put the first few pins. On another recent dress, she'd moved my pins down about an inch and a half, thinking I wouldn't notice. Who doesn't notice skirt lengths? But she did a good job on this one, keeping it just as short as I'd pinned it. It's light

dybbuk: the clinging soul of someone who has died but is unable to move on for one of many reasons

blue, with ribbing, baby doll sleeves, and buttons down the front.

My hair is separated into weak, snaky coils and does what it pleases down my back. Dad actually polished my shoes last night. Didn't say a word, but there they were, laid out on newspaper. My eye shadow matches my dress.

One of the dybbuks looks fierce, but I smile sweetly at him and then look down quickly.

"Please stand here, Miss Ostfeld," says Three-Piece, motioning toward a music stand that's barely upright. "Will you sing something for us?"

I feel quite prepared for the singing part. I've already been to Eastman and Oberlin, and for those auditions I memorized pieces from several periods and in several languages. I'm going to use the same material here. I hand a copy of my music to Three-Piece, who clearly will be my accompanist. I see him stifle a smile as he looks at my opening piece, the Neapolitan Baroque song "Vergin, tutto amor."

What's—? And then I get it. I've chosen a long prayer to the Virgin Mary for my cantorial school audition. *Fuck.*

He begins. He plays a bit stiffly but follows me well enough.

No one else has any facial expression, which is what I'm used to. I sing well, just like I had on the big stage at Eastman's Kilbourn Hall. I go right on, sticking to the script I prepared for my conservatory auditions, and announce a Debussy piece, "Beau Soir" and begin singing: "Lorsque au soleil couchant (When the sun goes to bed) . . ."

After this Cantor Three-Piece asks me if I know anything in Hebrew. I flash briefly back to the School of Sacred Music's catalog, which offers no guidance about auditions. It never occurred to me to prepare a piece from the Jewish world. I tell him that I do but that I haven't prepared anything. I wonder if they read my application essay. If they did, they should know that I grew up with my opapa's classical Reform background, with its absence of Bat Mitzvah and of learning Hebrew.

Three-Piece persists, asking me if I know the kiddush. "Sure,"

kiddush: blessing—specifically the wine blessing

I reply. He plays a flourish, and I begin, singing it through easily. The dybbuks seem surprised, which surprises me, since I've been singing the kiddush since I was seven.

Now I am feeling my oats, so I ask if they'd like me to play my piano selections. At this the hovering cantors lose their unearthly pallor and actually pink up. I assume from their reaction that few other candidates have demonstrated keyboard skills. The bench is from some other piano, but the instrument itself turns out to be in tune. I play two short Bach pieces—Inventions, numbers 4 and 8. Will my well-behaved fingers compensate for the fact that I can hardly distinguish between an aleph and a bet?

It's time for the interview, and my heart starts to thump. I feel like a pretender, even though this place looks like crap.

"Miss, uh, Ostfeld," one of the dybbuks starts, looking at my transcript on the desk in front of him to confirm my name. "Why is it that you really want to get into this school? You don't have any boyfriends at home?"

For a moment, I'm surprised. *I HAVE a boyfriend! What the hell does THAT have to do with cantorial school?* But I answer in full brown-nose mode.

"I'm not looking for dates, sir—Cantor. I want to be a cantor like my cantor, Martin Rosen."

They exchange glances, eyebrows lifted. There are small nods, and smaller blinks of assent.

Then they ask about my grades, and my French in particular.

I say that I've always gotten A's in French, to which Three-Piece says, "Your transcript says 3.8."

I'm stunned—caught out. "But it's a French 7 course," I say, fully aware that I'm choking. "It only has a few students in it. . . . They had to put it together for a few of us. . . . We couldn't be accommodated in the advanced—"

"Yes, yes," Three-Piece says mildly, waving his hand. *What a nice man*, I think.

Then he asks me to read some Hebrew. *Okay, I guess they haven't read my essay. I'm doomed.*

aleph, bet: the first two letters in the Hebrew alphabet

"I can't read Hebrew," I say softly, apologetically. "I was never taught. They weren't big on Bat Mitzvah in my temple."

"Here, let's see what you can do. Start here," he says, opening the *Union Prayer Book* and pointing to a passage. Equipped by my many years of Friday evening Shabbat services, I instantly recognize the prayer. I can say this prayer, but I am not reading it, not really.

I recite the prayer smoothly, from memory, with unanticipated accuracy. The dybbuks nod. I look down and make sure that my knees are still pressed together.

And then the audition is over. They thank me, and I thank them, imagining that once I've left the room they will cackle and then fly off to Lublin for tea in glasses.

When I go to leave, the door sticks. I press harder, twisting the knob farther. The door doesn't budge. I push my body against it. Nothing. Three-Piece asks if I need a hand, and I say that the door seems to be stuck.

He comes to help, and we push together. It jerks open, and I'm popped out into the hallway. It's crammed full of students. I'm face-to-face with the ones right in front of me, who have obviously been pressing up against the door, listening.

As I look at this small sea of men, they begin to part, lining the walls of the fourth-floor hallway. Some of them are abashed, having been caught eavesdropping, and some just smile and look away, and then back. It's quiet, which is surprising considering how many of them there are and how narrow the hallway is. But I can tell that it's a good quiet, a thoughtful quiet. I am at home in this quiet and in this press of skinny super-Jews—seminary students with long hair and frayed jeans. I am their younger sister.

One of them says, "We were just trying to hear the first woman cantor sing."

A great slippery bubble inflates in my chest and then tries to settle. I blink, expecting the hallway scene to vanish. I look again at this host of guys. Their many pairs of glasses reflect the fluorescent bulbs in the hallway ceiling.

My spine tingles, and I know I will somehow be that—the first woman cantor.

Dean Metsch Considers the Girl Who Would Be Cantor

I've passed my audition and faculty interviews and apparently my psychological evaluation. Now I sit across from the dean of the New York campus of Hebrew Union College. One more interview for me to pass.

The dean reminds me of my father. He's portly in the same way. You might say fat, but fat is such an undignified word for an academic guy like my dad who is all DOCTOR. My dad works very hard to seem humble, but he isn't—he's just weak. Dean Metsch is very self-assured, and he wants you to know that although he is a rabbi, an alumnus of HUC himself, he prefers that you call him "Dean Metsch" or "Dr. Metsch." It becomes clear almost right away that rabbi is the lowest of three title rungs on his academic ladder.

He asks me a lot of questions about Dad: How long has he been at Yale? What exactly is his title? Does he do much teaching in the medical school? How much of his work is research per se? What is his main area of study? Is he a first-generation American? Where are his parents from?

For some reason Dean Metsch is favorably impressed that Dad was brought up in the Ethical Culture movement. I guess it's right up there with Reform Judaism. The dean's eyebrows are the key to his state of mind, just as my dad's are. By the end of the interview, I know that I've passed inspection. Dean Metsch likes me—or rather, he's going to admit me because I'm respectable, I come from good stock, and I'll reflect well on HUC if I turn out to be the first woman cantor.

I probably remind him of his daughter.

Jesus and the North Haven Indians

I am voted Class Arguer by my fellow North Haven seniors. I do like arguing with teachers. My picture is taken for the yearbook. It's staged to look like I'm about to haul off and sock Mr. Keough, the principal. I've got my hand around his necktie. That's me. Class Arguer.

I'm a little bit famous in the halls these days also because word has gotten around that I was accepted to Hebrew Union College.

Although I'm thinking all the time about what it will be like at HUC, what's approaching first is my high school graduation. It's actually going to happen. Ah, the graduation ceremony. Perfect occasion for some protest action.

I meet with Mr. Keough.

He rises as I enter and says, "Miss Ostfeld," nodding.

I admire the courtesy of the gestures, especially since he knows what's coming. His secretary asked me many questions about my request for the appointment. I'm sure she is what's called "a treasure of a secretary."

Mr. Keough is prepared. He touches his fingertips together lightly and looks me in the eye with sincerity. It might even be real.

"How can I help you this afternoon, Miss Ostfeld?"

"I have two things to talk about."

"Yes."

"We cannot continue to call our North Haven High School football team the 'Indians.' What if we called them the 'Negroes' or the 'Jews'? It's embarrassing in 1970. It's backward. And the mascot is an actual 'RED' Indian! What if the North Haven Jews had a mascot with a hooked nose and thick glasses?"

Mr. Keough tries to contain his smirk. I hear my heart pounding. Even though I know I am in the right, my voice trembles and my vision blurs for a second. But the words come fast.

"Also, at graduation, the invocation cannot be made in Jesus's name. There is such a thing as the separation of church and state. If a minister is going to deliver some words, he can't do it in Jesus's name. A bunch of us will walk out if he does."

"Are those your two things, Miss Ostfeld?"

"Yes. Or maybe also the fact that the Quinnipiac Nation was here, right here, long before the white man."

"I can't help but notice that you're wearing trousers today."

"Excuse me?"

"Our new policy regarding girls and trousers?"

"Yes?"

"We've been most accommodating to student sensitivities here in North Haven."

"You mean in the pants department?"

"I believe that most students would acknowledge that our administration has been in the vanguard of—"

"Separation of church and state, Mr. Keough! Racial politics? The North Haven Negroes! I am not the only one ready to push forward!"

"Who else is aligned with these causes, Miss Ostfeld?"

"Lots of thinking people! Oh! You're asking for names?"

"Now, now."

Furious and wordless now, I start to cry and then have to leave out of embarrassment.

Not my finest moment.

When graduation day comes, a minister intones, "We welcome students, parents, teachers, members of the community, all who come here in peace. We welcome you in Jesus's name."

I rise and expect to feel my friends behind me.

Nothing. Nothing stirs the air. I step out of my row into the aisle on the lawn and start walking past the tightly packed rows of kids in robes, all of us sweating lightly. I feel deaf, so still is the air, so packed are my ears. I know that no one is following, and it changes nothing. I guess I probably knew it would come to this.

I think, *Jesus, it's you and me, baby. Neither one of us should be here today.*

Psalm

Cantorial school
Never again will be male
Though she pees alone

No Dorm, No Campus, No Lightning

When I think of GOING OFF TO COLLEGE, I think of bright autumn strolls between ivied buildings, stacks of alluringly shiny new books, and sharpened No. 2 pencils.

Hebrew Union College is one building. A single building on West 68th Street for both the rabbinic school and the cantorial school. I haven't seen any ivy.

I enter the building by tugging open its heavy double doors. The brass hasn't been polished since the founding of the college. I take the elevator to the bookstore on the fifth floor. This turns out to be a closet with a Dutch door and metal shelves piled with stacks of all kinds of books. There is one blinking fluorescent ceiling fixture. Fluorescent. A sighing white-haired woman sits heavily in her high-backed chair. She is put-upon and does not welcome me or even acknowledge my greeting. I tell her that I'm a new cantorial student. With reluctance, she hands me several paperbound folios and an octavo. After an additional sigh, she hands me a heavy, serious-looking book and informs me that the rest are on order. I'm too cowed to ask when they might arrive.

And so I begin my college career. One female cantorial student in this pungent, all-male environment. I say "pungent" because there actually is an odor. It's not a locker-room smell, because there's no locker room. It's a musty, old-book smell with a layer of steam heat, even now when the heat is off.

There's no gym and no dormitory, either. HUC is not a residential college. It's mostly graduate students who rent tiny apartments here and there, sometimes in clusters, but never all at the same address. To get here today from my tiny East 79th Street apartment, I had to take two busses. It took me forty minutes.

I leave the HUC building clutching my book, folders, and octavos, and wish that I had a shiny bag on my arm with a big seal advertising that I just bought books at the Hebrew Union College.

I adjust my armload of purchases and pass HUC's surface parking lot without reading the sign that lists its parking rules. I can't imagine ever driving a car in this city.

I keep my eyes on the brown-spotted sidewalk (*Oh, that's dog shit—in every size and color*), and I make my way to the bus stop at 68th and Broadway. Fall is not going to happen here. It's broiling and smelly now, and I've been told that it will be intense summer until one night sometime in November when it will instantly turn frigid and wet. As much as I hate this heat, I'm not hoping for rain—that's going to make the dog shit smell even worse.

As if to prove me right, the sky darkens with clouds and the rain begins. Here I am, smelling of Lily of the Valley and tugging down my short skirt as I run, trying to keep at least part of my waist-length hair dry. But I've survived registration, such as it was, and I have my books.

If any of the rabbinic scholars or cantorial professors were rattled by me just now, they didn't give themselves away. If the students wondered at today's infiltration of their ranks, I didn't perceive it. The only women I saw today were office workers.

There's no drumroll that announces my matriculation, but there IS thunder. I'm wet and I'm hot, but I haven't been struck by lightning—not God's or HUC's. And the REFORM MOVEMENT, which I also think of in caps, apparently isn't groaning and cracking and threatening to collapse on me.

Here I am. I've started seminary. Despite the hot rain, despite the smells, it's nice here. Classes officially begin tomorrow.

A New Sound

I sing carefully, trying to project modesty, to sound pure. I want my voice to have nothing to do with my body, that sluggish impediment to cleanliness. People want to hear a pure, clean tone, ruthlessly honed and polished. I will not be loud and dramatic, like I was in grade school, singing in a faux–opera voice that made my classmates howl or tell me to shut my trap.

My first assigned cantorial coach is flamboyant. He wants me to touch his tie and tell him what it is. I am unnerved by this, thinking that it's a ploy to get me to touch him. I do not want to be tricked by some cunning Yiddish composer. (I later learn from other students that he was going for the word *color*.) He raises his voice so as to inspire me. This gets under my skin. Dad would mock him for his ostentation.

I ask for a different coach and get a more paternal type. He clenches a pipe, unlit, between his teeth and calls me something nice-sounding in Yiddish. I remember him fondly from my audition. It's Three-Piece. He wears black, pinstriped, three-piece suits every day. He reminds me of my Austrian uncles, with their citrusy scents, their pocket watches, and their formality. I imagine that at home at night he wears full pajamas with piping and a bathrobe knotted at the waist.

We go along for a few weeks, quite uneventfully, until he says, "Open your mouth."

"What?" I ask.

"Your mouth is nearly closed when you sing. I don't know how the sound comes out."

"Oh," I reply, and open my mouth.

"That's it!" he cheers, popping the pipe back into his mouth.

Then he turns back to the piano, and I start over with my mouth open. A new sound comes out, and we both like it. It's a relief to let go of my jaw. I begin to be a singer. In a school full of singers, no one will make fun if I turn up my own volume. This is not an elementary classroom full of fourth-grade boys. My pipe-smoking teacher's command to open overrides my internal command to shut.

Now I remember why I used to sing so loud. It was joy about the sound.

First Year, New Life

I am in a first-year class of seven that quickly becomes a class of three: one guy my dad's age, one stoner in his late twenties, and me. Sheldon, Sheldon, and Barbara.

I arrive at HUC early and stay late, always attending chapel, never skipping class.

There are only old people in my apartment building. My studio apartment couldn't possibly fit a piano since I want a bed. A twin bed.

I make pasta, do my homework, and read. The old woman next door doesn't seem to leave her apartment. She might not even talk. The only sound that comes from behind my wall is the antiphonal meowing of her tabby cats. I imagine five of them, but there might only be two.

It's lonely when I'm not in school. And noisy with traffic, sirens, and mewing. I'm hemmed in by noise, by fear of mugging, and by inertia. At the end of each day, once I climb the five flights of stairs (maybe that's why my neighbor stays put), I can't think of a reason to go out again. To explore Germantown?

At HUC I know who I am, what class comes next, when chapel starts. I know the names of the custodians and who sits at what table in the lounge. Once a week in room 312 there is chorus. We are a TTBB chorus—tenor I, tenor II, baritone, bass: twenty-one tenors, baritones, and basses, and one seventeen-year-old alto. I've been asked to mouth the words.

I love chorus anyway. And as obedient as I try to be, though, sometimes I just have to sing.

On weekends, I babysit for Lazar's baby or Eddie's baby in their small Upper West Side apartments. I learn more about kashrut from them.

While babysitting, I dial the number left by Eddie's wife, Linda.

"Linda, I found a box of Milk Duds in your fleischig silverware drawer. What should I do?"

Linda laughs and tells me to hide it somewhere else and tell her where when they get home. I begin to understand why all of them

fleischig: meat related—designated for meat only

give their babies biblical names or modern Israeli names. Sarit. Noa. Liora. Names that sound like prayers or musical instruments. Names that sing themselves.

In student organization meetings, we're always lobbying for something. Judaic studies courses WITH the rabbinic students, upgraded music courses, advanced classes in pedagogy, a Bible class for God's sake! We don't make any progress, but occasionally we meet with the dean.

In our first-year music theory class, Rose Lischner demonstrates syncopated rhythms by having us skip around the classroom behind her. She calls us "kitty-cats." I cannot BELIEVE that THIS is college. I cannot BELIEVE that I turned down EASTMAN.

I'll have to remember to thank Mom, who made me study music theory on Saturday afternoons with Mrs. Lingaas, my piano teacher. Even when I was in fourth grade, I didn't have to skip to understand syncopation.

Miss Lischner, Dr. Judith Kaplan Eisenstein, who teaches Jewish music history, and I share the ladies' room on the third floor.

This is my life.

On my way to and from the first bus, I discover a Reform synagogue.

I need a teaching job, so I make an appointment with the rabbi.

He has long hair and tells me to call him Chuck. I can't. He is very welcoming and offers me a job teaching music in their religious school, which meets on Sunday.

I don't know how to teach, and I don't know many Hebrew songs. I only know what I learned at Torah Corps and in Choraleers. I have no sense of fitting these into a curriculum or of coordinating with anyone.

I try sarcasm.

"Hi, kids! It's time for music! Aren't you thrilled?"

Am I aiming for hipness?

"No? What a shock! Still that's what we're going to do. Sing Hebrew songs! Give me an *H*!"

Silence.

"Okay. Don't give me an *H*! Sing with me! Bim, bam, bim, bim, bim bam. Bim, bim, bim, bim, bim bam."

Silence.

I try begging. With a hint of sarcasm.

"Come on! It's just 'bim' and 'bam'! You can't do it? Repeat after me! Bim!"

Two of the nineteen kids reluctantly say "bim" in bored voices.

"That's the worst 'bim' I've ever heard!"

Not surprisingly the temple educator sends me a message asking to meet with me after school.

"Miss Ostfeld. At HUC, have you taken any courses in pedagogy?"

"Not yet. I think that's in the second-year curriculum. With Mr. Lister."

"What if you were to come back to teaching here once you've completed Mr. Lister's course?"

With the extra time on my hands, I learn to clean my apartment. I can't do anything about the roaches, other than not entering the kitchen or the bathroom at night, or leaving the lights off all the time. But I CAN clean everything every day.

First I dust. I use a ripped pair of underwear. I dust every day. Mom taught me that dusting comes before sweeping. So next I sweep with the little whisk broom that Mom gave me. After that I scrub the kitchen sink with the kitchen sponge she gave me. Then I do the counter where I eat. Nothing stays sticky in my apartment.

There are other sponges in the bathroom, obviously. I use one to scour the sink and another on the floor, which isn't much larger than the sink, although I hate being down on my knees. Still, it has to be done. Every day. And on Fridays I use a bit more detergent than on the other days. I'm preparing for Shabbat.

Preparing for Shabbat. This is new and wonderful.

I've learned to dress down on Fridays, in jeans and striped chunky sweaters, so I can dress up for Shabbat in a mod dress with a white collar and bib.

I can say a few words in Yiddish—words my classmates use

without thinking. I say these words to myself over and over to sound authentic. Bubkes. Boychik. Bissel.

I will be a part of this HUC family. Everything good happens in the building at 40 West 68th Street. When I'm not there, I am very lonely. In my mind, I hoard the communal moments in chapel, in chorus, in the student lounge. I collect them one by one.

Hebrew Tutor

I advance quickly in Hebrew. It feels like music to me. Mr. Moshief is astonished that I entered the school without knowing the alphabet. He gave me a primer on the first day of class and told me not to return until I knew it. I returned proudly the next day. Mr. Moshief likes me and I him. On days when I braid my hair and loop it up, he calls me "yalda perach." I show off for him in turn, displaying my linguistic ability. Now in my second year, he wants me to move up to a second-year rabbinic school Hebrew class. I'm not quite ready. I'm worried about keeping up. He assigns me a tutor, a rabbinic student whose apartment is a few blocks away from mine.

The tutor, I'm told, is a fourth-year student—in my mind, already a rabbi. He rings the buzzer, and I buzz him in. Several minutes later (it's five stories) he knocks, and I let him in. He greets me and asks to use the bathroom.

Moments later he emerges from the bathroom completely naked, tossing his balled up clothes on my floor. He proceeds awkwardly but quickly—with wide steps—to back me up against the wall. "Isn't this what you want?" he asks, seizing my crotch. "No!" I half yell.

And then my bell-bottoms are soaked and I think I've wet myself. I fling myself into the bathroom, half to save myself and half to get away from my shame. There's no lock, but he doesn't try to get in. He leaves after a few minutes—I hear the apartment door slam shut.

I hold my breath, waiting for some kind of ending, pressing my shoulder harder against the bathroom door.

Eventually I try to stop leaning into the door. I don't want to

bubkes: nada, zilch ~ boychik: sweet little guy ~ bissel: pinch of something ~ yalda perach: "flower girl," or maybe "hippie"

let go of the doorknob either, but I have to—I have to get out of my jeans and underwear. Finally, I let go and then peel them off. They're saturated—with blood. There's never been so much blood with my period, and it's never come on so suddenly. But I rarely get my period—this might be my fourth one ever—so I'm frightened, but maybe I should just be surprised. I don't know.

After removing the inevitable roaches from the tub with tissues, I shower and put on completely clean clothes.

I'll have to rinse out my bell-bottoms. They're the only ones I have, and I love them. But I can't bring myself to rinse out the bloody underwear, even though I worry that I won't have enough to last until I go to the laundromat the next time.

So I grab my apartment key, open my door, and look both ways down the hall. I go directly to the trash chute, pull open the door, and drop my underwear down. And I come right back in. The door locks behind me automatically as usual, but I lock the dead bolt too. I check it soon after. And then again. Three times.

The next day I tell Mr. Moshief that I would prefer to remain with my second-year cantorial class. He's perplexed, but he shrugs and gives me extra homework and some Israeli children's books to read for practice. Sheldon and Sheldon struggle along. There is only so much I am willing to do in the service of language as an art form.

In My Class, the Students Sit Down

I admit I'm nervous. Everyone here speaks of Hazzan Israel Alter in hushed tones. He's a genius. He's in his seventies, and they say he can't sing anymore, but his compositions capture the essence of the traditional liturgy. Although he's Orthodox and old school, he welcomes the dissonant accompaniments that others apply to his cantorial melodies. He's published many compositions, all with interesting modulations and perfect cantorial lines. Some of these are in our curriculum. He was among the best hazzanim of his generation. There are recordings—not that I've heard them. The rabbinic faculty members chat with him and look respectfully at him. So I'm not only nervous, I'm also feeling unworthy.

hazzan, hazzanim: cantor, cantors

Now that I am a second-year student, it's my turn to take his class in traditional synagogue chant. I don't know how he will receive me. There's never been a woman in his classroom. I wish I'd worn a longer skirt today. I take a long breath and open the door, which sticks. He is seated at his desk, and I am the first student to arrive. I wait just inside the door and try not to gape.

Then he says, "Nu, in my class the students do not stand."

I smile at him, and he raises his eyebrows. It's going to be okay. He will teach me.

He absently pats his head and adjusts his yarmulke—a tic of sorts.

"They are late," he says to me, indicating my absent classmates, Sheldon and Sheldon. I nod. "So we will begin."

Again he adjusts his yarmulke. He sees me watching intently and says, "Maminke made this for me. It is a little bit coming apart. The stitching."

I nod. It's shiny with age.

The cantor who taught us traditional nusach last year used to put on a kippah before beginning each class and remove it afterward. But Cantor Alter's yarmulke is not an accessory. I don't think I've known anyone like him before. Abruptly he sings a phrase for me from page 1.

> Shochein ad, marom, v'kadosh sh'mo
>
> שׁוֹכֵן עַד, מָרוֹם וְקָדוֹשׁ שְׁמוֹ
>
> (God lives forever, and holy is God's name)

The sound is a whisper, a ghost of a great voice, not to be ignored.

"Now you," he says.

I swallow, cough, and then sing.

"No," he says, "forget the notes." He sings again, throwing his arms out wide:

nu: Yiddish expression, somewhat ironic, that asks, "Isn't this obvious?" or "Need I say more?" or "Are you actually unconscious?" ~ maminke: my beloved mother

---

nusach: formula—the assigned scales for chanting the various prayers (but not Bible texts) in specific service sections according to day and time ~ kippah: dome—yarmulke (skullcap)

You who live forever, Your name is holy and exalted!

"Nu?" (Meaning I should try again.)

I do, and he frowns. "You are afraid. You have a voice—sing with it."

I try again and fail.

"You will work hard and remember the text. The text. If you are really thinking about the Holy One, you will forget to be afraid."

He makes a peculiar sound in the back of his throat and reaches up to adjust his yarmulke. My classmates come in and sit down. Class is starting.

Hell, No! We Won't Go!

On Fridays those few cantorial students who are undergrads, for whom the bachelor's in sacred music is a first college degree, take liberal arts classes. These are secular courses, but all are taught by the same Jewish (!!) teacher. Biology (without a lab), psychology, world literature. Teaching these classes is Renaissance man Marc Shiffman, a young composer of Jewish music. We see these various subjects through his lens. Mr. Shiffman is a good teacher and has a good command of these subjects, but he alone can't mitigate the little-red-schoolhouse atmosphere.

During today's student organization meeting, I look down the row of desks, absently counting my fellow students as I await the vote on the matter at hand.

One of the students is my father's age. He served in World War II, was once a successful lounge singer, and now sells ladies' shoes on the side. I have nothing in common with him, and his laugh grates on my nerves.

One of the students is a blonde fellow with a nose bigger than mine. He's a folk singer, a guitarist, a bit of a poser, scrawny. He wears color-coordinated scarves with his tie-dyed shirts. The musical things I have in common with him are eclipsed by the fact that I find him odious.

One of the students is a sullen rich kid from New Jersey who drives a red 1961 MG MGA and who between classes smokes pot on the roof of Hebrew Union College. He's nearly thirty, and although I've been on the roof with him, I don't hang out with him. I prefer the much happier cadre of rabbinical students.

One of the students is inseparable from his fiancée. She is not a student here but is somehow always in the student lounge waiting for him. This guy's voice is glorious, a marvel, deep and lovely, warm. The faculty members predict a great future for him in the American Reform cantorate.

And then there's Mitchell, the elfin kid, right out of high school like me, who's desperately in love with an older cantorial student, Sy Sherman, a fourth year. At every student organization meeting, Mitchell nominates Sy for whatever office is open.

One of the students, Lazar Nagy—the Hungarian concentration camp survivor—is artistic. On his book of Bach cantatas, he has fully realized the formal bust of Johann Sebastian—to reveal him sitting productively on a rococo chamber pot. Lazar is fantastic.

The vote is called, and I return to the present.

"All those in favor of demanding a parshat hashavua class in Hebrew, say 'Aye.'"

I call out aye with vigor.

"Ostfeld, will you be on the committee to meet about this with the dean?"

"AYE!" I answer, and there is friendly laughter.

I love being part of a student struggle. Any struggle.

Several cantorial students and many rabbinical students are here at Hebrew Union College for their 2-D deferments. As seminarians, they qualify for the ministerial student deferment. The most recent Vietnam draft lottery drawing was held in early August last year. A lottery drawing—an actual drawing of lots, like in the book of Esther! My schoolmates David, Eric, Steve, and Howard can now go to sleep each night without thinking about the round blue numbered capsules in the big glass cylinders. They don't have

parshat hashavua: weekly portion—Torah reading, week by week

to think for now about wizened old white guy hands pulling out their birthdays, one by one. David, Eric, Steve, and Howard can sleep now. These capsules no longer initiate the countdown to their yahrzeit dates.

And when these students worry about their less religious brothers, the ones not in seminary, there's always the respite offered up on the roof.

Congregation Habonim

Congregation Habonim, right around the block from Hebrew Union College, is a puzzlement—a Reform congregation that uses a Conservative prayer book. Until recently the sermons were delivered in German. The men are all older and courtly. The women are coiffed and powdered, and they hold their handkerchiefs in their hands all the time. Their dresses are old-fashioned, floral, made of rayon. The men bow slightly over my hand and say, "Gut Shabbes" in their German accents. They look mildly amused.

I'm a bit in love with all of them, wishing that my father had such a dignified and professorial demeanor. These men don't seem to mind my short skirts, my unruly hair, or even my Dr. Scholl's sandals. And they sure like my name, Ostfeld, and I love the way they say it. There are no other women my age in shul. I'm an HUC student and young; I get plenty of attention.

I'm always here early. I like the quiet and the familiar smell of lemon polish. I have a brief conversation with the cantor, Irwin Hirsch, and his wife, Marthe, the organist.

Then the rabbi comes in and snaps all the yet-to-flower tips off the gladiolus, saying in an undertone, "Hate zeese damn zings, hate 'em."

Oddly those are the parts I like best. All that pale green, waiting, racing against time. Will they bloom or dry out first?

Marthe plays softly until the very second the rabbi and the cantor mount the bima, and then, cheesily, she makes the music swell. I could do without that.

Habonim: (of) the Builders ~ Gut Shabbes: Good Sabbath ~ shul: synagogue

Irwin, the elderly cantor, can no longer sustain his longer notes. They wobble away from him. I don't care. No one cares or notices. What we hear is the sound of his soul—persistent, firm, and strong. Who cares about a few wavering notes or about the cheap electronic organ, faking its climaxes? Everything that's important is just as it should be, predictable, decorous, refined, holy. Holy are the starch and the rayon. Holy are the rows of shined shoes, punctuated by the one pair of Dr. Scholl's.

"Taaoof l'haaoodaaoos (It is good to give thanks to God)," warbles Cantor Hirsch. My ear is so used to the modern Israeli Hebrew taught at HUC that this nineteenth-century, German-accented, prayer-book Hebrew sounds almost comical to me.

"L'hagid ba-baoo-keyr (To tell God's praises in the morning) . . ." I purse my lips to get rid of my silly smile. I should be ashamed—making fun of their German pronunciations.

The usher pulls me aside. My guess is that he's bored and wants to chat in the lobby for a moment.

He wants to talk about picketing. We students are always on strike, and this fascinates him. Administration buildings are being seized, and protests are being staged all over the city. This usher, Mr. Loehmann, is one of my favorites. He is tall and wears some kind of cucumber-smelling aftershave.

He says, "All ze unrest out zere. Ve von't haf to vorry."

I say, "I'm sure we won't, Mr. Loehmann."

He pats his breast pocket and winks at me. I scrunch up my face in disbelief and say, "No way!" Sure enough, he shows me his Luger.

"Protests are chiltz play," Mr. Loehman says.

Taking care to dampen the sound of my Dr. Scholl's, I make my way back to my seat.

Lip-Synching with Tenors, Baritones, and Basses

My favorite class is chorus. The buzzing baritones, the piercing tenors singing "hallelujah." When I hear them together—the voices, the repeating psalm texts—I'm in a perfect place, much better than the one containing my voice alone. So when I was asked just to mouth the words, I was willing. I remember how to keep my big mouth shut. I can pretend that I've finally become a Vienna Choir Boy.

Outside the chorus room, my fellow students tell jokes I don't get, make sounds I can't imitate. The rickety Upper West Side elevator is either crowded with loud, heavy cantorial students or hissing with the fierce, private chatter of the slender rabbinical students. I am quiet, and I press my back against the rear wall of the elevator.

Still, I want to be a real comrade to the singing men. They are benevolent, raucous, brash, and kind. They hold crazy high C contests in classrooms between classes. For some of these men, everything seems to be about who can hit the highest note or whose stomach can hold the most chicken!

When it's my turn to sing in class, I know all the notes but can't spin the precise, florid patterns that my fellows are born to sing, the stuff that makes people in synagogue cry—the stuff that defines cantorial music. My teachers, the black-clad dybbuks, tell me that my voice needs to emote, to cry, to exult. So I change my facial expression, but I won't turn up the volume too high. I've been taught to open my mouth, but I don't do *fortissimo*. I am too embarrassed.

I see another singer who is embarrassed. Only three years older than me, Cliff is solemn, studious, and buttoned down. He sings with modesty, ashamed that his voice is pale in comparison to the others around him. I like this, and we speak. Cliff is deferential. He's never had a girlfriend. I flirt.

Cliff and I draw closer together. Spending time with him serves as an endorsement of my membership in the boys' club of the school. No one is threatened by our growing friendship.

Having been confronted in my HUC interviews about the possibility that I sought admission only because I was seeking a husband, I choose a man without ambition or stand-out talent—a smart man, although one held back by his tiny, haunted European parents and sickly, angry brother. Yes, this is Cliff.

We are, both of us, serious and intent on maintaining our seminary demeanor at all times and in all places. Our seminary selves are finer than our real selves. This is our secret as a couple. No one balks at our relationship.

The first woman cantor-to-be chooses low in the pecking order, although her choosing is not actually strategic.

Purim at Hebrew Union College

It's almost the spring of my second year at Hebrew Union College, and I'm studying cantillation. I love it. I feel clever when I get it right and adore picking up the little nuances that only the cognoscenti appreciate.

The faculty chair asks if I will chant an excerpt from Esther on Purim during the school-wide service. I demur a bit because I've mastered only one of the six systems of cantillation so far, and Esther is part of next year's curriculum. Still, I say yes, feeling sure that I can learn it, at least well enough to chant the assigned section, which is Esther 7:5-10. Only a few verses, with lots of "Hamans," so there will be lots of traditional noisemaking in the congregation to blot out his villainous name. I am excited.

I learn the system, with its odd melismas and strange ironic bursts of sound. Then I practice chanting the text over and over until I can do it from the fancy Purim scroll, which has no vowels or cantillation signs.

I'm not in the legally mandated zany Purim mood, though, since I'm taking this task very seriously. I'm new to the Hebrew of the book of Esther and new to this system of chanting. So much is still new to me. I'm self-conscious about being honored with a public reading on a day when everyone, students and faculty, will be in the chapel. At nineteen, I feel more like a Bat Mitzvah kid than a cantorial student.

When it's time, I get up for the reading. Very quickly I glance out at the rabbinical school congregation. As one would expect, the faces, mostly male, are red with drink, and merry after all the pranks and gags that have taken place so far. (On Purim we Jews are commanded to drink until we can't tell the difference between Mordecai, the hero, and Haman, the villain.)

cantillation: the ritual chanting of readings from the Hebrew Bible in synagogue services ~ Purim: an often raucous, Mardi Gras–like Jewish holiday that commemorates the saving of the Jewish people from Haman, who was planning to kill them all

I, on the other hand, haven't had a drop, and in my nervousness
I start my chanting in a smaller than usual voice—although it must
be said that the acoustics in the fifth-floor chapel are very encouraging. I'm fine, though, really fine.

And then, about four verses into my chanting, Dr. Samuel
Fischmann, the eminent Bible scholar, comes rushing up from his
seat in the congregation onto the bima, hurling himself toward me.
He is madly yanking loose his tie and wresting his arms out of the
sleeves of his jacket. I'm aware that this is theater, so I keep my eyes
on the scroll and keep reading, much to the amusement of the roar-
ing crowd.

I have been too focused on the accuracy of my chanting to think
about the words themselves, but when I chant, "'Does he mean,'
cried the king, 'to ravish the queen in my own palace?'" I suddenly
realize what the men before me are anticipating: that in this unfold-
ing pantomime, I am going to be the queen who is "ravished."

My face, like Haman's in verse 8b, blanches. Still, I persist with
my task.

But I know that these Bible scholars and students have just had
their way with me.

I look out at the laughing faces and, stone sober, I am unable to
tell the difference between friend and enemy.

Missing My Stop

It's Saturday night, and I'm on the 3 train heading uptown to
babysit Lazar and Gina's baby, Sarit. Since I'm always getting lost,
it doesn't rattle me too much when I miss my stop. I get off at 116th
Street, one stop too far, knowing what to do: walk a few blocks in
the opposite direction.

I climb the subway steps, careful as always not to touch the railing. The thought of contact with anything that's been touched by so
many hands has repelled me since my trips on the 'L.' I don't have
a free hand anyway. I've got two novels plus a pile of music to study
for my Monday nusach class.

At the top of the stairs, I look around for the street signs. I can't quite make out the nearest one, so I take a few steps toward it. Ah—no, it's the other way. I check the cross street and shift my books and purse to the other arm.

Someone grabs me from behind. For a moment, I think it's Lazar, joking around. But when a hand squeezes my breast, I realize what's happening. I try to scream, but just like in my nightmares, no sound comes out. Then a hand is clapped over my mouth and a thin blade is waved in front of my eyes. I hear my books fall and my music scattering. I think, *I have to pick those up—they'll get dirty!* But I'm being dragged into an alley, behind a wire fence. It's dark, but crushed cans and broken glass are reflecting what light there is. I smell urine. I'm dragging my feet and pushing to get away, but I know it's useless.

Now it's over now it's over now it's over and then it's actually over, except for the second boy but he is fast, and then they run away. I keep my eyes closed.

I don't think I can get up. I don't want to look around me because I know that there's dog shit—I can smell it, and maybe I've been lying in it, and that would be the worst. Then I try to get up, using only my fingertips for balance, but I can't get up without putting my whole hand down in the dirt. *I will wash. I will wash.*

I gag but I don't throw up. I stand there and touch my face and it's still me. Then I wait for a while. And a bit longer than that. I think of Lazar and Gina waiting for me.

I walk back to the sidewalk. One sheet of music is in the gutter, but I'm not going to touch it now. Everything else is gone. I walk to Lazar's. I don't have to ring the buzzer—they're at the door with anxious faces. They're shocked to see me looking the way I do. I tell them that I've been mugged and that I want to go home. They offer me water, and I say no. They offer to take me to the police station, and I say no, that I'll report it tomorrow. They believe me and call a cab for me. I feel bad because they can't afford cabs. I feel bad because now they can't go out.

When I get back to my apartment, I take off my clothes, crumple them into a ball, and put them near the door. I shower and put on clean clothes. I take my key, pick up the bundle of clothes, and stuff them down the incinerator chute in the hall. All night I read a book I've read before.

In the morning I take another shower. The thin cuts from their knives have left thin scabs on my stomach. There's almost no blood. There's hardly even a sting when over and over I scour them with rubbing alcohol.

I don't know what I'll say when I get there. I'm unprepared, but I go to nusach class.

An Usher Plots Revenge

I've been unabashedly emotional lately. The academic year is coming to an end, and I'm sad because so many of my friends are moving away and the school will feel so empty next year.

It's May, and everyone is gathered in the main sanctuary at HUC for the degree-granting ceremony for the class of 1972. Graduating rabbis, cantors, and educators are called up to the bima by group to receive their diplomas. I am one of the marshals. Really I'm just an usher. I pass out programs and get to sit on the bima wearing a carnation.

It's not that I'm not happy for my friends. I am. I look out at them from my seat above the congregation. I see the excitement on their faces. They've all found good cantorial positions. This is a powerful moment for them and for everyone here who is paying attention.

Lazar and Gina have come with Sarit. Frederick and Marsha Kaminsky have come with Liora, and Glen and Donna Bachmann with Noa. Yehoram and Monique Schwartz are here too.

Two of these grads have struggled to meet the academic requirements of Hebrew Union College. Two have breezed through.

I feel tears coming. I've babysat many times for the Kaminsky baby and for the Nagy baby and for the Bachmann baby. I know all of their parents well, even though they're so much older than I am. I think for a minute about each of them, sitting next to each other in the designated pew. Almost ritually I recall my most vivid memories about them.

Yehoram keeps Monique, his lovely French wife, locked up in their studio apartment while he's in class or working in his student congregation. Although he's unwittingly funny, pronouncing mitochondria as "mitt-oh-khon-dri-AH," as if it were a Hebrew word, it's hard to imagine him succeeding as a cantor. Everyone at school knows about Monique's isolation, but no one can reason with Yehoram. He is certain that Monique will fall victim to a crime. I wonder how she marks time or if she has a cat, since they don't have a baby.

During psychology class, as we were learning about traumatized children identifying with oppressors, Lazar broke out in a sweat and told us that when he was in the camps as a little boy, he and his friends pretended to be Nazi soldiers, who were so powerful and strong, and who looked so handsome in their bespoke uniforms. He didn't want to be like the skeletal waifs who were his people. And the class was silent as Lazar wept.

Frederick is one large cantor. He's known for once eating two chickens at lunch, and I always worry a little about the tiny, cranky elevator when I take it with him. Frederick is a kind man, though, usually smiling and often nodding agreeably.

Glen, a very precise and adept man, had the tenor solo in Rosenblatt's *Chassidic Half Kaddish* for cantor and male chorus. He chanted the solo line as if his light tenor were a laser beam, a magnificent contrast to the deep, low chorus. I got shivery during each performance.

Lazar's name is called. He puts Sarit on his shoulders on his way up to the bima. When Dean Metsch gives him his diploma, Sarit reaches for it too, and Lazar releases it into her grasp. Everyone smiles. Glen and Frederick follow suit, bringing Noa and Liora onto the bima in their arms. More smiles.

Then Dean Metsch ad libs: "Cantors might not be scholars, but they certainly are fertile."

I freeze. The thoughtless disrespect is staggering. Even cruel.

Instantly I remember Cantor Walter Dworkin having instructed us always to be wary "because da rabbi is da enema." (Yes, he meant "the enemy." That's just how it sounded with his accent.) But such a cutting joke—from a dean? During a degree-granting ceremony? In front of everyone?

A voice inside loudly announces a vow: *I will prove Dean Metsch wrong about our lack of scholarship. I will restore the dignity of HUC cantors.* I start to conceive of a plan. Fertile, my ass.

I sit quietly on the bima, wearing my white carnation, thinking hard.

Cocoon

Living alone in my apartment last winter, I would fold down the corner of the page in my paperback, drop it on the floor, and wait for sleep. Night after night, I would say, "No more, no more, no more." Repeating words soothed me when I was single, just as the God-bless prayers did when I was little.

But now Cliff and I are married, and repeating the daily tasks of married seminary student life keeps all my bad thoughts away.

I don't wear an apron like Cliff's mother does, but I make her Shabbat soup. First I chop an onion the way my mom taught me. Like Cliff's mom, I fry the chopped onions with some sliced carrots in the soup pot, a black-bottomed hand-me-down from my mother. When the onions are just brownish, I add the packet of Manische-witz Split Pea Soup mix and five cups of water, which I count and measure.

I rigorously perform my married seminary student tasks. The chicken, covered with kosher Wishbone Italian dressing, is baking at 350 degrees. The soup will simmer for an hour while I get the apartment ready for Shabbat.

This preparation is rhythmic and numbing—in other words, perfect.

Rosh Hashanah is coming up, and Cliff is at his temple office preparing. I should be worrying about Rosh Hashanah too: my Torah readings, rehearsals, and prayer book cues—also about dry-cleaning my white robe. But instead, I'm at home using Endust and Behold on my furniture and checking the soup and the chicken.

Rosh Hashanah: Head of the Year—the Jewish New Year, the anniversary of creation, the beginning of a ten-day period of self-examination

It's time to get a fresh dust rag. I keep mine in a corner of the bedroom closet. Old T-shirts, old towels, cut up. I spray a section of graying undershirt and head for the bookshelves.

I turn up the volume on WQXR. The Telemann Trumpet Trio makes me think about my wedding. Simon and his friends played this exact piece right before our backyard ceremony.

Again I replay the conversation I had last spring with Rabbi Block, a few weeks before he officiated at our wedding.

"Barb," he asked, "have you thought long and hard about marrying Cliff? I like Cliff. He's smart and serious. But you are something more. Wouldn't it make sense to wait a few years, to see how you evolve? Find out who you are becoming?"

I made myself smile at him. "I just want something ordinary. Let me fade in peace."

"Someone who says 'Let me fade in peace' is someone with a destiny! Don't you want to find it, unencumbered?"

I switch to Windex and yet another new rag for the glass coffee table, lift up a green vase, and rub beneath it. Mom taught me how to dust properly. I tell myself not to think any more about the wedding, but I can't shut it out.

The night before, we had Shabbat dinner at my parents' house. At the table, Mom's cousin Jerry elbowed Cliff, teasing him about his status as a blushing bridegroom. Cliff responded archly.

"Oh yeah right, I'm 'blushing'! Not even the construction workers near my parents' apartment in the Bronx make catcalls when BARB walks by. What groom would be breathless in anticipation of BARB?"

MY joke! That was MY joke! Or my version of a Joan Rivers joke. I'd told him this joke privately, self-deprecatingly! To Cliff and Cliff alone! How could he have used my own joke to humiliate me like that?

So I had left the house for a walk after that Shabbat dinner and stayed out for hours, hoping that Cliff would come after me with an apology. Or maybe that Dad would come to rescue me, as Ben Casey and Dr. Kildare did in my nightly childhood fantasies. But what was I thinking? Why would I have expected that from Dad, or even from Cliff, who had hardly even proposed? The neighborhood dogs barked in my wake. My feeble run for freedom went unnoticed except by dogs, and I slunk back home.

Walking down the makeshift aisle in my parents' backyard the next day, I ignored Mom's signals to stand up straight. I concentrated on the sound of my brother's cornet and on the sharp calls of his friends' answering trumpets sounding the Telemann trio.

Telemann's trio ends on WQXR, and I emerge from my reverie. I find that I've moved on to vacuuming the apartment. Actually, it's done. I yank out the cord and then splay the prongs as I always do.

My Bronx apartment is ready for Shabbat, now that I've changed the sheets on the sagging bed that Cliff and I inherited from Marsha and Frederick Kaminsky. I look around and register the clean. The ordinary satisfying clean of my just-short-of-ordinary life.

I smooth out the bedspread a second time. I pour cat crunchies lavishly into the cat dish and change the cat water.

Maybe this Sunday, after we finish teaching at our respective religious schools, Cliff and I will get take-out sandwiches, with pickles, from the kosher deli next door.

Cliff comes home, shouts hello, and goes straight to his upright piano. He begins with scales.

It's time for me to shower, shave my legs, and put on Shabbat makeup. Next my black dress and black pulpit shoes. I brush out my hair and pat it down. In the streak-free mirror, I see that I look as good as I can, dressed up, made up, elevated by one-and-a-half-inch block heels. It's time to light the Shabbat candles.

Cliff won't tell me that I look nice, but I don't expect romance. If I can't get catcalls in the Bronx, I can't expect candlelit dinners other than those prescribed by Jewish law.

After services tonight, Cliff and I will have sex. That's a commandment, so I observe it. At best I will feel nothing more than a tiny, promising sensation that never flowers.

But for now I've crossed everything off of my Friday list. Check, check, check. All is well.

In my blessedly confining cocoon—everything spelled out, few decisions to make, against a flat backdrop—I do the daily work of transforming myself into a cantor.

Student Pulpit

Students in the School of Sacred Music are required to audition and interview each spring in order to find student pulpits. You can always tell when someone has an audition. He'll be wearing a suit and, if he's conscientious, a white shirt that's actually pressed—not his customary ripped jeans or tie-dyed dashiki.

When I interview, I too dress up and wear a dress or a skirt that goes with my black jacket.

I pay special attention to my makeup for auditions, following my Shabbat makeup scheme. I start with Maybelline's Pearly Frost Blue eye shadow, which I apply beyond the lid nearly to my brow bone. I use L'Oreal's liquid black eyeliner, with which I am an expert. My mascara is by L'Oreal too. It's the best brand I've used, and I use a lot of it. It's all about layering—letting the first coat dry and applying a second. The only tricky part is removing any mistakes, but I do, every one, with a wet cotton swab. I don't think my lipstick should be too dark or too shiny. I love Clinique's Black Honey, but I have to be careful not to overdo it. I'm going for carefully turned out, not alluring.

The auditions make us feel as if we're on an assembly line. Every fifteen minutes one of us enters the seminary's chapel, hands music to Mr. Barasch, and introduces two songs, one of which is the kiddush. Then we wait half an hour in the student lounge until it's time to sit with groups of congregational officers in a classroom and answer questions like "What made you decide to become a cantor?" and "How would your classmates describe your personality?"

Congregational officers seem to like me, and for my third year I get offered a student pulpit in Clifton, New Jersey—an easy commute. I'm very lucky.

Several afternoons a week, I drive out to Beth Shalom to teach Bar and Bat Mitzvah students or to conduct the very small but enthusiastic junior choir. On Friday afternoons and Saturday mornings, I drive to Clifton to "do services." This means singing the same liturgical pieces every week while Phyllida, the organist, tries to play the accompaniment. Occasionally she's in sync with me, but most often not, and she usually plays with one hand, which I could do myself. She can't be fired, because she's a volunteer and a member of the congregation. I learn how to mask my embarrassment when Phyllida and I are performing different pieces of music simultaneously. It wouldn't do to roll my eyes, stop in the middle, or look angrily in the direction of the choir loft. That much I know, even as a student.

At an oneg Shabbat, I hear some talk about the rabbi's wife—and her bathing suit.

"What? Does she think she can take time off from being the rebbetzin when she's at a pool party?"

"I know! That was a bikini pretending to be a two-piece!"

"There were Bar Mitzvah students at the pool! What was she thinking?"

"My Jason is only ten, but he sure was looking!"

"Well, the men weren't exactly acting mature around her either!"

I sip my punch and think about having a chocolate chip cookie. They're homemade, and the baker has been generous with the chocolate. *Nope*, I think, and set myself a rule: I will never eat at an oneg Shabbat. What if a crumb settles on my blouse or if I have chocolate on my teeth? What if my lipstick wears off? Also, people will think that the student cantor can't control her appetite for sweets.

And what about my bathing suit? It has a khaki full-waisted bottom and a red calico top with ruffles. I've had it since sophomore year of high school. But yes, it's a two-piece.

I realize that I can't wear it—or any other bathing suit. What would people say about me? "The student cantor thinks she can pull off that swimsuit? Who is she kidding? The rabbi's wife could pull it off. Now there's someone who can wear a two-piece bathing suit!"

And it's decided. No swimwear for this student cantor, and no oneg treats.

rebbetzin: rabbi's wife

My Spot

When something perfect might happen, I like to hit the fast-forward arrows in my mind. I don't want to think too much about the perfect thing. The button works pretty well until the perfect thing gets close.

I've fast-forwarded over fantasies about being the first woman cantor, but now that the last winter break of my HUC career is almost here, I've worn down the mechanism. My anticipation of ordination is starting to grow.

Instead of excitement, though, what I'm feeling is suspense. It's about my spot.

I know it's arrogant, I know it's prideful, but I still have to admit that I'm thinking a lot about it—my spot in history. Sometimes those words bring me up short—but not as much as they probably should. Who am I to use the word *history* or even the word *spot*? How audacious. If I'm about to be a real member of the clergy, I'd better get a handle on this.

But my competitiveness is running high. Another woman in the cantorial school, Loretta, is pushing the faculty like crazy to be allowed to skip ahead and graduate this spring—at least alphabetically ahead of me—even though she entered a year after me. Sure, like most of my classmates but not me, she went to college before starting at HUC. She's even got a master's degree, so she's obviously more academically advanced than I am. But I don't think she's kind or principled. I don't think she's cantor material.

But it's not up to me, it's up to the faculty and administration, and even when my friends gossip to me about what they've heard from their faculty mentors, I don't say anything.

Today, like most days when I'm not at my student pulpit in Clifton, I eat lunch with my School of Sacred Music friends in the dark basement lounge—Bernie and Sam are here. Steve joins us and sits.

"So," Steve says, "what do you think?"

"About what?"

"Everett just let it slip to me—they're not letting Loretta graduate this year."

I hear Heather Harper in my head. She's singing Handel's "Rejoice Greatly, O Daughter of Zion."

I don't say it to anyone, but what I'm thinking is that the faculty and administration have decided that they prefer to have me—even at age twenty-two, even without another degree—in the role of First Woman Cantor.

Though I may be graduating with honors, I can see that my grade in humility would lower my average.

I can live with that.

Trumpets and Stairs

The first trumpet sound is piercing. I look at the rabbis lined up in front of me and at the cantors lined up behind me. Are they hearing it the way I hear it? Sharp and harsh and demanding?

And then I hear a rude whirring from the cameras and see them wheeling toward me. The bright lights over the bima challenge me to walk toward them, toward the ark and its winking gold tiles.

This is ordination at Temple Emanu-El of the City of New York, and there is media coverage today.

Sometimes it strikes me, like now, that I am the first woman to be ordained as a cantor.

It's a hot feeling, almost like a punishment.

But I'm also feeling proud in my long black robe and my pink-lined hood. Pink representing music, in this case. I wonder why that is. Is it an insult? Pink is a less-than color. Music is a less-than discipline. Cantors are less than rabbis.

Stop, I think. *This is the day of my ordination! Music is everything! Pink is heavenly and pure! Cantors sing Torah!*

When the time comes, President Gottschalk takes my elbow. Cantors everywhere hold their breath. We're good at breath control.

Will he walk me, a cantor, up to the fifth step, the highest? A spot reserved for rabbinic ordination?

Proceeding past the whirring cameras, he does.

Cantorial breaths everywhere are released without sound.

Orchids on Passaic Avenue

I must be bad-tempered. I spend a lot of time imagining that I live alone with my Siamese cat and my plants. I imagine how pleasant my life would be if the new apartment on Passaic Avenue held just Boint the cat and me—with lots of greenery.

Just as I head for home, the temple in the rearview mirror, it starts to rain. Lightly. I turn on the windshield wipers and think, of course. *Rain. Why not rain?* To the syncopated squeaking of the wipers, I imagine my constantly dripping worries being swished away.

After this week's Beth Shalom board meeting, the temple president plans to ask me to consider running the religious school, in addition to maintaining my cantorial duties. It will mean more money.

I've decided to say yes because I need the raise. This car has taken a lot of wear and tear, and it's going to need to be replaced soon. I drive into the city once a week on my day off to fill out the alto section in the School of Sacred Music chorus. On my way home, I usually have to put in a quart of oil.

Even now, more than five years after my admission, there are still only a few women at the school, and they're all sopranos. I'm not confident that my voice, which is lyrical rather than dramatic, actually helps the balance, but I look forward to this ensemble music-making all week long—and to seeing friends, and to working with the conductor, Max Gottheil.

As I get closer to home, I see a waterlogged sign on the south side of Passaic Avenue. Its hand lettering reads "Orchids," with an arrow pointing down a side street.

Orchids. I follow the marker to a large, somewhat shabby greenhouse. It's still drizzling, and I walk across a weedy gravel driveway to the door. No one answers my knock, but the door is ajar, so I walk in and call hello. I'm an ordained cantor and a respectable grown-up. I can be bold, and I want orchids.

The scent of bark and soil and hot greenness envelops me. Someone answers from the back. I can't hear the words, but the tone is friendly.

An old man in a work apron comes forward between rough tables covered with flats of homely green protrusions. I tell him that I've come to see his orchids. He shows me around.

Pointing at pots of scruffy nothings, he says, "Cattleyas. Most of the wild cattleya orchids grow in the rain forests of South America. They're epiphytes—they hang off trees. They need light but not direct sun. Some smell just awful, but some smell like fruit. Cattleyas need a temp drop at night too. Plus you've got to feed them if you want good blooms. Want to try?"

Do I want to try my hand at coaxing prom corsages out of shredded bark? Of course I do! I buy three orchids from the man in the apron. One looks totally dead, but the other two have buds. He gives me a mimeographed sheet of growing instructions.

It's pouring now. The mimeo sheet runs a bit. I drive the remaining two minutes to my apartment and feel myself smiling.

I pull onto our street and start looking for a parking spot. There! Fortunately, one life skill I've mastered is parallel parking. Could a flawless parking job be the high point of my day? No! I bought orchids!

I carry the box of orchids and the limp instruction sheet into my apartment. For a moment, I feel lost and wonder what to do next. Where should I put this wet box? On the table? Would it ruin the wood? On the counter? Is there room? Are the directions still legible, or have they bled away in the rain? Where should I put the wet instruction sheet? . . .

The panic rising is familiar, and I know what to do. I start by thinking only about placing the orchids themselves and not the box and not the paper.

I don't have a choice about exposure because there's just the one window. I position the orchids in their saucers on the sill. They don't look right. I shift the pots. The lost feeling comes back because soon I will have the plants perfectly situated, and then what will I do next?

My kitty happens to choose this moment to come out of the bedroom. She stretches, taking her time before coming toward me.

The cat. Yes, Boint helps kill the lost feeling, following me around as she does.

Cliff won't be home from adult ed until late. But I have a routine that helps with this unmoored feeling. It helps that I have to learn twelve Torah verses by Shabbat. Learning the passage is a chore, but a satisfying chore. Each step in the process is reassuring. Everything that repeats itself is reassuring. Feeding the cat, watering the plants, making the bed, cleaning the apartment, rehearsing music.

Sitting up in bed with my back against the wall, I chant a phrase from the pointed text, thinking hard. Again and again I chant it, looking at the words, thinking, *Affix, you words and trope signs. Affix!* Then I chant the same phrase from an unpointed text, without vowels, without signs. When I've got the phrase down, I proceed to the next phrase. Finally I've learned a sentence. Verse by verse I am soothed, filled up.

Having mastered some text, it's time to read for pleasure. My dessert—that's how I think of it. Fiction comes last. It helps crowd out the emptiness too. *I am crowding you out, Emptiness. And now I will have help from orchids.* I imagine that each bud will need my touch.

I picture myself in an even smaller apartment—Cliff-less, but with more windows, greenish light, that hot-grass smell, at least one orchid blooming. I envision a single bed, and at its foot, my one-woman cat. I can almost hear myself alone, chanting verses into the night.

The Scale in the Temple Office

It starts as a contest between the rabbi, the temple secretary, and the cantor. Stan, the rabbi, is a bit pudgy. Heidi looks fine. And I weigh in at about 165. This is the most I've ever weighed. At five feet five inches, it's not horrible, but my butt looks big even in my robe. We all decide to lose some weight. We take off our shoes and hit the scale in the bathroom off Stan's study. We plan to hit it again the following week. I buy a little calorie-counting book in the grocery checkout line and study it.

pointed: marked with vowels or cantillation signs

The next week I weigh 157, and the following week 153. Stan's numbers stay put. So do Heidi's. Soon my clothes are hanging loosely. I look good and feel incredibly triumphant. But at 135 the scale seems stuck. I spend two miserable weeks at 135. People tell me to stop dieting, but I'm thinking of little else. The weight comes off. I am someone new.

Not for the first time, I think back to high school and remember that Susan Suconik and I weighed 117 pounds in ninth grade. I was actually thin at that point, because I had grown a couple of inches during the summer. Longtime classmates walked past me without recognizing me. Now I am an inch taller than I was in ninth grade. I aim for 118 pounds.

The morning when the scale shows 130 is a wonderful morning, because I know that in my junior year of high school I weighed more than that, and I am now twenty-three. I look like other twenty-three-year-olds, even though I am a cantor and cloistered, raising orchids and not Cain.

I eat breakfast at 7:30 every day. I'm too hungry to stay in bed one minute longer. I eat lunch at noon on the dot, also because I can wait no longer. Whether or not Cliff is home, I eat dinner at 6 because there's no holding out. I go to bed early with my cat and my book because sleep keeps me from thinking about food.

Not that I let anyone see how much I've changed, though. I'm still wearing all my long, full-ish skirts, blousy tops, dark tights, and comfortable shoes.

Stan and Heidi have lost interest in the weight-loss contest, but I privately soldier on, alone and determined.

Then comes the glorious morn when the scale reads 120. Only two more pounds to go! I'm floating. I'm a nearly perfect girl. There's a swing in my step. My butt is hardly noticeable. My neck could be Audrey Hepburn's.

I decide to speed this thing up. I'll just do yogurt, and we'll be set. Yogurt—Dannon—three times a day. Six hundred calories. I allow only the lemon, vanilla, and coffee, since they each have two hundred calories. The others, the ones with fruit, have more.

And today it might happen. It does. There it is, 118.

It occurs to me, though, that this means there's no cushion. *I'll go down just one more pound, and then I'll have a margin of error. Okay. One more pound.* One more pound. One.

Because a woman's fat tells on her every second. Her fat broadcasts her lack of discipline. She is driven by pleasure. A woman whose appetite is on display cannot be pure. She is all about filling her body. A cantor who is virtuous is necessarily slender.

This is the new me, the new Barbi Prim—a true embodiment of self-control, chaste and upright. As far as my inherent fatness and my relentless appetite are concerned, well, these will be my secrets from now on.

And there's one more. Menstruation. It's every woman's secret anyway, or so we were told in fifth-grade health. My periods stopped months ago. They were never regular, and I haven't had them for all that long a time, so I barely notice the difference between menstruating every once in a while and never. I am light and nimble and unfettered. All I have to do to feel this way is eat very little.

My New Synagogue Home

Sixty cantors audition and interview for the position at Temple Beth-El of Great Neck, "the leading Reform congregation on the North Shore of Long Island"—or so every description of it claims. In the world of cantorial placement, Temple Beth-El of Great Neck is the plum job of the season.

Why wouldn't I interview? I decide to—along with every other cantor I know.

I've just lost a lot of weight and I look good. I'm twenty-three years old, though—much too young for such a heavy-duty gig—but something tells me to try for it.

After watching my classmates dress in somber suits and ties when auditioning for student pulpits, I have assembled an outfit that is analogous. Over a white blouse with a Peter Pan collar, I button every gold button on a black knit jacket. I choose from among several dark print, below-the-knee skirts. Chunky-heeled black pumps complete the look. For this audition I splurge on a pair of beige department store pantyhose. Usually I wear grocery store brands with color names like Natural 1 (orange), Natural 2 (mushroom), and Natural 3 (a kind of burgundy-beige).

I am overwhelmed by Beth-El's sanctuary. White, white, and white. A Louise Nevelson sculpture dominates the eastern wall. This is holy ground, and I have to calm my stomach as I walk up the many gold-carpeted steps to the bima, where I am to rehearse the audition pieces with the temple's organist.

Fortunately, the organist, Tom Williams, is kind and patient, with a fantastic laugh that I get out of him by being deliberately irreverent as we rehearse. The irreverence takes my fear level down a notch.

But fear can be a good thing in an audition. It can catapult you above ordinary singing and convince you that you need to sing for your future, for your convictions, for your life. This is how I sing for my audition at Temple Beth-El of Great Neck.

And then it's time for the interview. My heart slows. I'm not as afraid of talking as I am of singing, but I still think to pee prophylactically before "adjourning to the library." I release my breath as I sit to pee. I'm feeling cautiously optimistic—until I see red. It doesn't cause pain and hasn't marked my outer clothing, but it's here and must be managed. I don't have any tampons in my purse because I haven't bled in . . . six months? A year? No, not a year. But it's been a long time since I've seen red. Unfazed, I make a generous fan out of toilet paper and place it strategically. While still in the stall, I remind myself a few times in a whisper that I'm okay.

As frightened as I was of the sanctuary and its rich trappings, the cantorial search committee evokes in me nothing but a desire to charm. A very strong desire to charm.

The audition went well, and the interview is going well too. The committee members and I laugh and talk easily. My words come together as they nearly always do when I'm answering serious questions that appeal to me. I am passionate about prayer, about synagogue life, about liturgical music, about teaching, about working hard. Passionate but not doctrinaire. Also, I am not afraid of rich people. The congregants of Temple Beth-El are smart, successful, and beautiful, but I am not intimidated by them. Everything clicks into place.

I go home and wait in New Jersey. A few days pass. The call comes requesting a second interview. A bubble of excitement grows in my chest. I start thinking of pieces to sing and how I will introduce them.

When I'm offered the job, I think only of the joy—okay, and the pride. Imagine me standing behind the outsized blonde wood podium that proclaims in Hebrew and in English "Sing Unto the Lord a New Song!" Imagine me opening the Louise Nevelson ark and lifting a scarlet-wrapped, silver-clad Torah scroll! The many ranks of organ pipes gleam and ring above my head! This is as glorious a scene as any I pictured back when my only aspiration was to be a Vienna Choir Girl! Imagine the velvet-trimmed long black robe hiding my ugliness. It's almost as good a disguise as angel wings.

What's My Line?

What's My Line? returned to TV in syndication a number of years ago. I must have seen more of it than I remember because I understand its basic format. A contestant is questioned by celebrity panelists, who then try to guess the guest's occupation. The appeal of this game show is mostly its stars, of course, and their wittiness, but also the unlikeliness of the contestant's job.

A new congregant of mine appeared on this show many years ago. He likes to talk about it. He's a burly six-footer, handsome and dark. He manufactures powder puffs, and his line outfoxed the panelists. There was much laughter when he revealed the nature of his work. Powder puffs are big business.

I receive a call inviting me to appear as a contestant on *What's My Line?* Identifying a woman cantor would certainly require all the guessing skills Hollywood big shots could muster. If anyone

ever conjures up the image of a cantor, it's a bearded old guy holding a tattered prayer book and bobbing back and forth as he sings
nonsense through his oversized nose. At my age, the only thing I
have in common with this cantorial relic is the oversized nose. My
hair is waist length, and although I disguise, bind, and drape, I'm
clearly a woman. Clearly a game show winner.

I refuse. Politely, of course. I am too dignified to parlay my
ancient profession into laughter.

I brag about my piety to my colleagues, only to be met with
astonishment. "You turned down *What's My Line?* Are you crazy?
It would have been so much fun! It would have made the cantorate
look cool for once! What were you thinking?"

What was I thinking? This: that the laughter following the
denouement would have been mocking laughter—my ugliness and
stodginess having been on parade.

The thought of fun never crossed my mind.

Cliff and Sandy

Cliff, who's pursuing his master's in education, and Sandy, a rabbinical student, are enrolled in some of the same classes at Hebrew
Union College. Cliff talks about Sandy every day. I feel as if I know
her, he talks about her so much. To be fair, though, I bait him.

"What color is her hair?" I ask. "Is it longer than mine?"

Cliff is only a little bit taken aback by providing the answers.

I press harder on my bruises, goading him further. "Does she
have long legs?"

He draws his breath in between clenched teeth and then volunteers a description of her breasts.

The pain that results is oddly satisfying. I want him out.

I am spending even more time imagining myself alone in the
apartment. I want to throw out a lot of stuff and have a smaller bed.
I stiffen or even pull away when he touches me. I pretend to sleep. I
pretend to feel vindicated.

I ask him what they talk about, this smart, sexy rabbinic student with long legs and Cliff, with the Yiddish-speaking parents

who are unendingly kind to me—his mother breaking factory rules to sew me a wonderful gray polished cotton skirt. He doesn't reply.

So I begin to understand. They don't talk. She's a secret crush. I suggest that since she is ruining our marriage, he ought to at least explore the possibility of a relationship with her. I harp on this constantly, sounding quite reasonable in my cruelty.

Apparently he finally initiates a conversation. I wince at my callousness. This is all I need. I invite Sandy to lunch, to a small café under stairs, not half a block from the school. I move my undressed salad around on its plate. She tells me that she hardly knows who he is, and I tell her that she is all he talks about. Predictably she feels awful. She knows me by reputation, and now I am an object of pity. Oddly, I'm gratified by this. It suits my ends. Poor girl—married at nineteen, spurned at twenty-three.

A few weeks before we're scheduled to move to Great Neck, we give a goodbye party in our New Jersey apartment. I snipe at Cliff a few times. This is observed by one of my former professors, who draws me aside to say not only that I am being too hard on Cliff but also that were I ever to be free of him, that he, Max, would be standing in line as a suitor. Max, twenty years my senior, a successful composer and former lover of Leonard Bernstein.

I note that I am not at an impasse after all, and something small (and dark) inside me flowers.

Butter on Yom Kippur

Yom Kippur services really do end on a high note. Seven times the choir and I sing out that God is God. The shofar adds its mighty exclamation point.

And then I let out my breath. I did it. Note by note and word after word, I sang my first High Holidays at Temple Beth-El of Great Neck.

When the ark is closed and the organ's last pipe stops beating, I begin to cry. It's relief and happiness and a small concession to my fasting.

I turn from the ark and see Mrs. Baker stand at her aisle seat

Yom Kippur: Day of Atonement—a day of prayer, repentance, and fasting; the holiest day on the Jewish calendar

in the second row. The Bakers always sit on what I think of as "my side" of the congregation. Mrs. Baker is elegant, trim, and perfectly coiffed. Pointedly she begins to take the five steps up onto the bima. She seems to have words for me, but her face is closed like the ark.

Mrs. Baker smiles. "Why, Cantor! Shana tova! You look as though butter wouldn't melt in your mouth."

Exactly.

Zaydie's Unveiling

I don't know how to conduct an "Unveiling of a Monument or Marker." I've never seen one. We weren't taught about unveilings at Hebrew Union College. In truth, I've never heard the word *unveiling* in the context of synagogue life. It makes me think of a sculptor snapping the tarp off a new creation. A portrait artist reverently gathering up a silk sheet to reveal a recent commission. A magician whipping the tablecloth out from under elaborately laid place settings.

Now I'm going to remove cheesecloth from a headstone? And the cheesecloth is held in place by string? This is a Jewish thing?

Several pages in the 1961 Central Conference of American Rabbis Press edition of my *Rabbi's Manual* are dedicated to this ritual, so I can prepare on my own. Because it's summer, my new senior rabbi, Larry Rappaport, is on Martha's Vineyard. I can't consult him. I'm embarrassed to ask the assistant rabbi, Aaron Heilman, who went to school in Cincinnati and who seems to have known everything about everything since his infancy. (He's not much older than I am, but seems world weary.)

So I guess I should begin chanting, "I have set the Lord always before me."

Next, a few prayers, all of which begin with "O God."

Then, of course, "The Lord is my shepherd."

Ooh! A passage from Ecclesiastes! The "Turn! Turn! Turn!" section! I like that. People will find it soothing and familiar.

Then a prayer in which there are a lot of blank lines for names of the decedent. Our beloved X. Our beloved Y. Always beloved.

I see now that the manual does not mention death. Not even the grave is cited. It's all about eternal life and monuments and markers and living on forever.

In italics, my manual says, *"Covering is removed from monument by a member of the family."*

Okay, check. I'll ask Beloved's grandchild or grandchildren. That way they can have a simple role, and it won't be scary for them. I'll do it with them and smile at them. I'll thank them by name.

I make myself a note to get the names of any children present.

The preparation is going fine. I will be able to do this. Apparently, according to the temple executive director, I'll be doing a lot of unveilings. Maybe every week.

Then I'll chant the memorial prayer.

I make myself a note to obtain the Hebrew name of the decedent, but I learn I don't have to ask for this. A competent Jewish funeral home will always have someone give me the name in writing.

I will then need to ask for the Hebrew name of the decedent's mother. Traditionally a full Hebrew name is "[Hebrew name], son or daughter of [father's Hebrew name]." Most Reform Jewish officiants today also include the mother's name in the formula. Although I want to indicate by my request that this is the best way to honor a Beloved, I learn that the inquiry always embarrasses the Loved One. It's a little preachy to ask for more information in the name of equality for women. Still, I'm supposed to teach—and so I will, gently, in a soft voice.

Next I will lead the "Mourner's Kaddish."

The *Rabbi's Manual* tells me everything I need to know. I've been trained to chant prayer texts without sheet music, just from the Hebrew page. That's easy now.

So I am prepared to lead my first unveiling, and I decide to ride to the cemetery in the hearse so I won't have to find my way around. Afterward, the hearse driver, Salvatore, will drop me back off at the funeral home.

Sal likes to talk while he drives. He has the physiognomy of a twelve-year-old Bar Mitzvah student. I soon learn that his stature is his claim to fame. Until retirement he was a jockey. He raced horses! I'm impressed! Then he tells me about things that he did on the side for his "organization." Like delivering severed fingers in Lucite boxes. Sal is having a great time talking to me. I don't think many rabbis or cantors ride up front with him when he's on duty. Sal's conversation puts me in a suitable mood for conducting my first unveiling.

When we arrive in Babylon (yes, Babylon), the grandmother of the children whose names I now have, the wife of Beloved, tells her small grandchildren that now they must always be good because Zaydie will be watching them from heaven every minute. Little Brandon and Tiffany blanch, as do I. Where did Bubbie get this bit of Jewish wisdom? Not from Hebrew Union College.

Sheldon, the son of Beloved, Tiffany and Brandon's dad, affirms Bubbie's maxim with a nod.

I look away.

Toward the end of the actual unveiling, there is one glitch. A small one. Brandon and Tiffany have a hard time removing the cloth from the headstone. They wrestle with the string, which is tied very tightly to the stone. It doesn't budge. I assist to no avail. Fortunately, Salvatore has—oh!—a switchblade.

At this point, I'm pretty sure that Brandon and Tiffany will never forget the Day of Zaydie's Unveiling.

Sal's pig sticker makes quick work of the string, and I continue, in Hebrew, stifling my amusement.

No sooner have I intoned "Amen" than Sheldon grabs my arm to give me a vigorous handshake and a wink.

A wink? I look down and see that Sheldon, Son of Yitz, has pressed a meticulously folded hundred-dollar bill into my hand.

Thus I have been paid for my services.

I Get a Tip about Tips

Helga the Administrator calls me to her office. Her office is smack in the middle of the temple administration area. It has win-

zaydie: grandpa (Yiddish) ~ bubbie: grandma (Yiddish)

dows on three sides. Her sharp eyes see all, and there is much to see: A secretary at the copy machine pushing buttons, with another waiting behind her. Several volunteers collating flyers at a long table. A young woman sitting at the reception desk, comparing two lists and making check marks on one of them. In the rear to the left sits the bookkeeper, bejeweled glasses low on her nose and tethered to a bejeweled chain. Her ledgers, thick as phone books, are pale blue with smudgy edges. The clergy secretary is typing loudly under the fluorescents, head swiveling from copy to carriage.

"Here are some sample letters," Helga states without introduction. "What you've been writing isn't quite our style. So here are sample thank-yous and condolence notes. Here are birth, engagement, wedding, and acknowledging an honorarium. Please be less flowery in your letters. Now, you may rewrite these in your own words, but keep to the style and length. Our secretaries have enough to do as it is. Of course in special cases, handwritten is best."

I ask how I am to know when a case is special.

Helga explains that if I'm invited to lunch or dinner, a personal touch will be welcome. If an honorarium is unusually generous, I should put pen to paper.

I ask how much "generous" would be.

She sits back in her chair and answers with a question. "How much do you usually get?"

I'm not following. I tell her I don't know what she means.

Seeing that I'm perplexed, Helga snaps her chair forward and rubs the sides of her nose with both hands.

She says, "You'll never get as much as Larry, no matter how much effort you put in."

Seeing my blank face, she continues.

"You know, how, after every Bar Mitzvah, you get some cash?"

When I do not nod, she continues further.

"You probably already know that Larry gets the most. You and the assistant rabbi, well, it depends on how much time you've put in with the kid, how good the kid's speech is, how good the kid is on the bima. Let me know if you get a check made out to the temple.

Has that happened yet? We'll cash it for you and give you a check. Oh, if it's made out to a temple fund, like the Music Fund, you're sunk. It's ours. If—"

"Wait— I, uh, I got a hundred-dollar bill from a guy after his father's unveiling, but I'm not getting other, um, money."

Helga thrusts her chair back even farther and laces her fingers behind her head. She thinks for a long moment, and then she spells it out: My cantorial predecessors were family men, raising children, sending them to college.

Something connects in my memory, and I think back to my initial meeting with the temple president, when he offered me the cantorial position. The meeting wasn't much of a negotiation. The president simply named my salary in stentorian tones that did not allow for conversation. Fifteen thousand five hundred dollars.

Temple Beth-El is located on a main street of a wealthy New York suburb. It boasts fifteen hundred family members and about ninety B'nei Mitzvah per year. Even fresh from HUC, I knew that cantors of large congregations had higher salaries than this. The president could see that I was taken aback by the low number.

"We know it's not high," he said, "but you'll be able to pay your rent. The fathers of the Bar Mitzvah and Bat Mitzvah students will give you gifts."

Soon I learn from choir members, and from the organist, that my cantorial predecessors received fifty or a hundred dollars per student. Envelopes containing cash would turn up in their temple mail boxes the week following the service. Ninety students times either fifty or a hundred dollars. It would mean an additional $4,500 to $9,000 in earnings for me. I can't do math to save my life, but I can see what a difference that is on a $15,500 salary.

I guess the president wasn't trying to take advantage of me, not about this. He just didn't anticipate that instead of seeing see me as their cantor, B'nei Mitzvah fathers would see me as a woman wearing a long black robe. I am not what cantors look like, not to them.

But that's not the case with my male colleagues. In fact, sometimes nice older cantors call me to talk.

b'nei mitzvah: children of the commandment

"Hi, Barbara! It's Richard Abravanel."

"Hi, Dick! It's so nice to hear your voice!"

"Barb, I'm going to cut right to the chase because I only have a few minutes until my first student comes in. I've heard from some of our colleagues that Beth-El is underpaying you—by quite a bit."

"Um, I'm pretty sure that they're right, uh—"

"The last guy there, Neil, was earning in the mid-twenties. If you don't mind my asking, where did they start you? Your answer will stay with me."

"Fifteen five."

"It's a shanda! A congregation the size of Beth-El paying their cantor a student salary? And what do you have, eighty B'nei Mitzvah a year?"

"Ninety."

"Bavajadas de benadam! Neil was making at least ten thousand more, and he didn't teach the kids! Do you teach all of them, or do you have tutors to help you?"

"They let the tutors go. I teach all of them."

"Barbara, this is bad for everyone in the ACC. If congregations can pay women cantors that much less and get away with it, THEY WILL!"

It's true that the temple president didn't know I wouldn't be getting the gifts that all of my predecessors had been given. And it's true that the temple leaders were pretty progressive in hiring a woman as their cantor. But there's no way to deny it now: It's also true that they figured they could pay their woman cantor less.

Still, they won't have to defend themselves. I'm not going to say anything. I guess this is how it's going to start for us.

Divorce the First

"YOU. LOVE. HER! She's beautiful! Just leave tonight!"

Cliff and I have faced off in the hallway between the kitchen and the bedroom.

I've lost my composure now, and I won't let him think that he can keep talking about Sandy the rabbinic student! I won't watch

shanda: a disgrace or humiliation ～ *Bavajadas de benadam: The stupidity of some people* ～ *ACC: American Conference of Cantors*

him pretend to cup her breasts one more time! So I yell each word separately.

Since I'm shouting, it's odd that I'm alarmed by Cliff's sudden rush past me toward the kitchen. By his raw scream. I've seen him like this with his brother. I was afraid then, too, but not this afraid. He yanks open the middle drawer, and it flies out of its rollers. The contents spill onto the floor.

Have I not made this happen? Have I not WISHED for this precise thing to happen? Here it is. Now. Happening.

He grabs the kitchen scissors out of the debris and runs past me again. I follow him into the bedroom. He lunges so wildly toward my side of the bed that he trips and nearly falls. He jerks open my nightstand drawer and wrests my diaphragm from its case. He stabs it once in the exact center.

My brain slows itself down.

Oh, I think. *I need to leave now.* But my feet take a while to catch on. I step toward the hall.

Cliff seizes my upper arm. Would he really hurt me?

"Cliff," I say, suddenly calm. "Cliff. I need to get the laundry. Someone will dump it out on the floor. You know, that guy who always does . . . on Wednesdays."

How did I do that, lie like that? There's no laundry in the dryer.

But Cliff looks stunned for a moment and lets go of me. I walk down the hall and out of the apartment without closing the door, preserving the ruse, heading toward the laundry room, which is only steps away, but I continue down two flights of stairs and out the front door of the building in my stocking feet.

A woman is walking by with her dog. She's smoking a cigarette. I ask her for a quarter and head down the block to the pay phone. There go my pantyhose.

I call Aaron Heilman, the assistant rabbi. He is two years and two days older than me. His wife, Debra, is in law school. Aaron picks me up in his car.

I remember that Debra wears 7½'s—a whole size smaller.

I get a divorce.

Botanical Gardens

I take myself to the Bronx Botanical Gardens again. I alternate between pilgrimages to these gardens and the Met Cloisters in Fort Tryon Park.

The greenhouses are not crowded today, and I have the smells almost all to myself. No one will notice if I touch the *Mimosa pudica* and make its leaves shut up tight. I love tiny leaves. There's a wonderful array of miniature violets and other gesneriads under lights near the gift shop at the Botanical Gardens. I like the very littlest. They're hard to care for, though, because they dry out very quickly.

I love the rain forest displays in the greenhouses, especially the mist and the darkness. But I hurry through the desert pavilions. They're too hot, and even when the cacti are in bloom, they do not appeal to me. I like to hear the water dripping into pools, to smell the water. I curb my urge to touch the hanging plants, to examine the spores on the undersides of the fern fronds.

I don't have much money to spare, but I usually buy a little plant or at least a postcard on my way out. The purchase softens the leave-taking.

This is a hard trip to make. Half the time I get lost, and I don't like the drive to the Bronx. There are too many exits to watch for. I feel as if I don't deserve the beauty of this conservatory because I've come to it alone. Everyone else here is with someone. I must look odd. I feel odd. Is it cheating to come alone? When I see the Victorian glasswork, I tend to get dizzy, and it takes a moment for me to control it. It's the latticework that does this to me. I feel as if I'm being thrust up and down from within. It goes away fairly quickly. I just can't figure out why it happens.

After seeing the glass house, I'm more sad than before I came. And there's too much time until dinner, and I'm hungry. The yogurt is all I have to look forward to. Well, that and my book. I have no weddings tonight, and I don't really watch TV. Right now I am reading Singer's *The Slave*. I'm in love with Jacob's wife, Wanda.

There is too much time, and only one yogurt awaits me. I take a razor and look at myself in the mirror. I'm so calm. I hold the razor between my thumb and first finger and draw it lightly across my legs, right below my knees. No one will ever see. Maybe it stings and maybe it doesn't. I'm not sure. The blood runs, and I rinse it off. I cut again and rinse off. It's very pleasing to see the blood run down my legs, and now I'm sure it doesn't hurt. In fact, I feel nothing but an urge to sigh. I decide to stop. I wash the cuts with soap. Then I reopen them and wash them again. Still a few more minutes till dinner. I can wait.

I'm going to go to a psychiatrist. I need a psychiatrist.

This seems like a revelation, out of the blue, but I must have known it for a long time. My new position is doing something to me, even as I'm learning how to do it, to be a cantor of a large, programmatically complex, suburban congregation.

I eat my yogurt slowly, with my book propped open on the table, not thinking about tomorrow's work at the temple.

Analysand

I have read the preparatory materials about psychoanalysis, and I am ready.

When I was little I loved books about girls learning deportment. Proper turns of phrase, which fork for which course, at what age one's hair could be put up, for which occasion gloves were appropriate—every manner of politesse and decorum. I loved the words themselves too. Now I am an initiate into a new world of etiquette. I am to be an analysand. Despite the reasons that have brought me to the couch, this thrills me (and must be part of the problem).

My daily sessions begin at 7:50 a.m. The very first morning, I go to Dr. Glick's front door, ring the bell, and awaken his wife. Her voice sounds both annoyed and sleepy, and she doesn't open the door. I hear Dr. Glick's voice tell me to come to the side entrance. I feel myself turn hot with embarrassment.

I enter, and it is clear that I am to go directly to the couch. I do this quickly. I lie down and begin to apologize for appearing at the wrong door. I go on a bit.

"Why does this worry you so much?" he asks.

"I don't want to get anything wrong."

There is silence, and I wait for him to clarify. More silence, and it becomes obvious that I am to continue speaking.

"I want to get it right. I want to be a good patient."

Of course Dr. Glick says nothing.

My mind says, *I want you to like me. I want to you to be pleased with me.*

I force myself to say these things aloud. It's an effort, but I feel gratified. I must be doing well. He will like that.

Dr. Glick has curly light brown hair. He is not tall. I think his eyes are blue, but I haven't really looked at him directly enough or often enough to know for sure. He has a certain very controlled smile that must be reserved for patients. Yes, he's handsome. I wonder if he's looking at me. I wonder if he thinks I look nice enough or refined enough. I wish I'd seen his wife. I've read about transference. I'm not going to think about this right now.

I lie perfectly still, with my hands clasped over my waist. I wonder if I look fat like this.

Dr. Glick asks for some background. I tell him about committing my father to a psychiatric hospital. I tell him about Dad's subsequent demotion at Yale.

I tell him that Dad used to call me "O eldest child, firstborn of my loins." That he doesn't call me that anymore. I tell him about the tightrope of my work and my fear of falling. My fear that my rabbi will be angry with me.

"And you were worried that if you rang the wrong doorbell, I would be angry with you? That you would not be my favorite patient any longer?"

And thus begins my analysis.

Edith, Dorothy, and Joyce

Emeritus Rabbi Daniel Richard Goodman's wife, Edith, is clearly a woman on a mission. She takes me aside and asks me about my skin type.

"Your skin is lovely, darling," she gushes in her British accent of indeterminate origin. "Whatever do you use on it?"

"Oh, thank you, Mrs. Goodman. I don't use anything on it. I just wash it."

"Oh, you don't." She pauses, taken aback, and then regroups. "Even at your age, you must use skin care products and cosmetics! Let's go shopping! Such a treat."

Of course my skin is anything but lovely. It's uneven and spotty. I am into my third year of eating one grapefruit (or a cantaloupe, depending on the season) and two yogurts a day. I am aware that my hormones are seriously off—I haven't had a period in three years. I am likewise aware that my diet is not exactly a skin-care regimen. Neither is scrubbing my face five times daily and dousing it liberally with isopropyl alcohol.

Edith takes me to a little boutique salon on Middle Neck Road. Monsieur Louis takes a sea sponge and dips it oh-so-gently into a pot of salmon-colored paste, which he then massages into my skin. I begin to hope that I will emerge looking flawless. Edith is saying "lovely" and "brilliant" a lot. About the time Monsieur Louis starts applying black eyeliner, I realize that the salmon paste is foundation. After a "soupçon" of magenta blush, I am pronounced "jolie, non?" and am handed a mirror. I look like a bruised tangerine.

The prices of the many products are added up, and I cry poverty, which is not much of an exaggeration. I purchase a lipstick, and Edith drops me back at the temple, where no one says a word about my salmon transformation. Even my students are speechless, perhaps figuring that I've contracted a Levitical disease.

Two weeks later, when two wealthy middle-aged wives of board members offer to take me out for lunch and shopping, I start to pick up on the fact that I am a project. A congregational project. I think on this. I realize that some of my blouses were once dresses made by my mother when I was in high school. She has simply cut them down and hemmed them. As an ordination present, she bought me two pastel outfits—aqua and peach—at Sears. These were size 14, and I am now a 4. I pin the skirts on the inside of the waistbands.

I've bought a few items, but these are plain and multipurpose. When in doubt, I say to myself, *We wear robes on the bima, so how much could my wardrobe really matter?*

I find myself at Bloomingdale's with Joyce and Dorothy, who are both about my mother's age. They are sweet, well mannered, subtle, and incredibly well dressed. They pull things off racks and have me try them on. They do not invade the fitting rooms, which is great, because my underwear is pretty frowsy. They favor suits that I imagine are like the ones their husbands' secretaries wear in posh offices overlooking Manhattan—double breasted, with belts. Dorothy drapes scarves across my shoulders.

Joyce says, "Now that's the look we're going for," and Dorothy says, "Exactly so."

They look at me hopefully, penciled brows raised. I just can't do it. I can't afford any of these outfits. After all, I've recently negotiated my second contract, a two-year stretch with a five-hundred-dollar increase in the first year, no benefits (although I was later to learn that everyone else on staff had standard benefits—I just didn't know to ask for them), and was struggling to pay Great Neck rent. Their husbands' colleague, a multimillionaire, had negotiated with me over tea, served by his uniformed maid in his King's Point study. His driveway was the longest I have ever traveled.

Our shopping trip is a bust, like my negotiation session.

I wonder, *Are they paying? Are they going to just take these outfits to the cashier and whip out their credit cards?*

I figure not, since my budget-based protestations were not met with any offers to pay. I am humiliated, but I get the point. Suits.

I draw the line at scarves. Twenty-three-year-olds do not wear scarves.

My Strapless Dress Meets Joyce

The younger Steinhart daughter is getting married. Not only am I co-officiating, but I am also an invited guest. I have no date, but the party will be fancy, and I'm excited.

From the couch I tell Dr. Glick I'm not going to wear a suit.

Since I have to wear a robe to officiate, why shouldn't I wear a dress for the reception, like other women my age? Of course he doesn't answer. Is there a reason why I shouldn't just be a guest? Sit with people my age and dance if someone asks me? I skip past the silence.

"Yes, I know," I continue, as if I do know. "I am not a nun."

I tell Dr. Glick that I have a dress, chosen for me by a very fashion-conscious gay friend. Strapless, knee-length, and trendy—it will be just right. Turquoise chiffon with small black dots. And what woman cantor doesn't have black patent leather heels? I confess to Dr. Glick that I'm excited. I'm going to a party!

"Why, then, do you lie so still?" he asks.

"Doesn't everyone lie like this?"

No answer.

"I guess not," I say.

"Does my body need to be excited too?" And after a pause, I answer myself. "I'm guessing yes. But it isn't. It just isn't. I'm thinking about my dress and about the possibility that I'll be seated with people my age and maybe with some men my age. Am I supposed to shift my position? Unclasp my hands?"

I don't want to undo the couch-lying preparations I always make at the beginning of each session: I smooth down my long-ish skirt. I don't want it to hitch up. I check that my blouse—today one of the made-over dresses from high school—is properly tucked. I don't want it to ride up.

Lying flat and very still, locking myself more tightly into this position, I think I catch a whiff of dog shit. I can almost see broken bottles in my peripheral vision. I tell myself that this would be the time to bring up how I missed my stop.

No, I think. No. And a funny line comes to me instead.

Now I'm back on track.

And after another pause I say, "Well, maybe I do look sort of like the medieval effigies of Lady So-and-So in the Cloisters up in Fort Tryon Park."

And I start to recount the tale of my first York High School sock hop.

"Barbara Ann," "Hang On Sloopy," "Louie, Louie," and "Twist and Shout." I only knew one dance, the pony. After three dances, I was sweating and bedraggled, and beginning to notice that the other kids were varying their steps with what seemed like infinite creativity. I couldn't imagine how to make anything up, so I just kept ponying, heart thudding and sweat cascading. I had never heard this music before. I listened to Joan Baez and early music albums from Nonesuch Records. I wished I lived in times when people danced galliards or pavanes (not that Jews danced in Renaissance courts). So my ponying legs were simply pumping faster or more slowly, depending on the beat.

I feel myself wince as I tell this to Dr. Glick. I hate this memory. I wish I could tell what his face is doing or if he is even awake. I don't say this.

Weeks later I arrive at the Steinhart wedding. It's at the Pierre Hotel. I'm dazzled by the lights and dizzied by the scents coming from mounds of flowers.

Susan, the bride, is an acquaintance, and I'm inclined to like the kind-looking groom. I deliver the Sheva Brachot into their eyes. I will them to understand each word of the seven blessings. Joyce and her husband, Mike—the parents of the bride—wipe a few tears away.

And I feel as though I've given birth to the wedding moment, and simultaneously as though I am simply a mouthpiece, purchased, like the flowers, to enhance the occasion. What am I expecting?

I sit with people my own age. I talk, although the conversation is stilted.

"What do you do during the week when there are no services?"

"Did you go to school to become a cantor?"

"Do you sing opera too?"

I initiate some conversations, but these wind up being short. My cantorness makes my peers uncomfortable. Someone says "shit" and then blushes.

After a second, I say, "Shit is right."

There is no laughter. No one asks me to dance.

Sheva Brachot: Seven Blessings—the seven blessings chanted over wine at a Jewish wedding ceremony

But older people stop to chat and say sweet things. I pay attention to the toasts, the cake cutting, and other rituals. I clap and smile, smile and clap. As the popular music plays, music other young people like, I realize that it is completely unfamiliar. I listen only to classical music in the car. I am a creature of my own making. But my dress is great this time. Other women my age are wearing variations of it. The length is right, the neckline is right, fabric—all just right.

Ah, the final ritual. The photographer asks a few of us to get up from our chairs and to stand behind our tablemates. Flash, pop, and we are released.

I drive back to Great Neck thinking that the night passed well enough. I remove my mascara and examine my skin. "You are fine," I say to my clean face.

A month passes and Joyce comes toward me at an oneg Shabbat. She is smiling her gracious smile, which I return. I walk toward her and kiss her cheek.

"Shabbat shalom," we say.

"Barbara," she says in a hushed voice, "I have something to show you."

She beckons me to a curtained corner of the social hall. She pulls an envelope from her purse. In this envelope is a photograph of my table at the Pierre. I take it from her carefully, holding just the very edges of the print. I look and see myself. I let out my breath. I look nice.

"Oh, it turned out so nicely!" I say. I hold it out to her, although I hope she's giving it to me.

"Well, I just wanted to show you, and of course we'll have it retouched," she says, pushing it back to me. I look more closely, and then I see: My nipples are visible beneath the fabric.

I'm thunderstruck.

"We'll have it retouched for the album, but I thought you should know—about that dress. You might not want to— It might not be what you'd wear again to— Anyway, we thought we'd spare you any further embarrassment."

Embarrassment? Is that what I feel in my stomach? No, this is mortification!

The room starts to spin. Am I that shameless creature in Joyce's photo? I lose my grip on the picture, and in an awkward zigzag, it drops to the floor. I inhale slowly and think, *This is the inevitable consequence of wearing a party dress while being a cantor. I will NEVER let this happen again. I will never again show any skin.*

Glancing around to make sure that our exchange is private, Joyce picks up the photo and slips it back into the envelope and hands it to me, looking vastly relieved. I automatically say thank you to her without meeting her eyes.

Decorum

The oneg is over and I've greeted everyone in sight. My smile is gone and my cheeks are sore as I slowly make my way to the car. I'm deflated and thinking about the warm, fruity oil smell of the elevator in my apartment building. I tell myself to think instead about making a cup of tea once I'm inside. I conjure up an image of the book I'm reading and wait to feel anticipation.

Frieda, an elderly congregant, is walking toward her car even more slowly than I am. I join her and we smile at each other.

"So, Cantor, when are you going to move to the city? That's where the young people are. There's plenty of time to live in Great Neck once you're married with kids. What are you waiting for?"

Lots of people are put off by Frieda's abrupt manner, including me, sometimes. But she's usually right, and scarily shrewd.

We say good night and Shabbat shalom.

The railroad station is on my way home, so I pull into it and buy a *Times* from the kiosk. At home, I spread the real estate section out over my kitchen table. I shouldn't stay up late looking at the paper. I have a three B'nai Mitzvah tomorrow morning and, as mistress of ceremonies, it's important for me to be bushy-tailed.

But I suddenly and desperately want to live on the Upper West Side, near Lincoln Center. Not here in the suburbs where my congregants travel in packs with cubs, but I don't.

Thanks to Frieda, I have a mission. NOW I feel anticipation.

I'm imagining myself living in THE CITY. Five hundred twenty-five dollars a month will get me a studio apartment in this brownstone on West 84th Street between West End Avenue and Riverside Drive.

I circle the listing and reassemble the paper, which is now as limp as I am.

In the morning, I eat an entire grapefruit liberally sprinkled with Sweet'N Low, and head for the temple.

I spend the first part of the service adjusting my students' microphones whenever Larry looks my way. One of my students—the middle one, Jeff, a very small boy—whispers something in my ear before he begins his speech. I shake my head—I didn't hear him.

He repeats, "I'm not thanking my dad. I'm skipping that part."

The mic picks up Jeff's words, piercing the anxious silence of the congregation, and Jeff and I realize that everyone heard what he said. I don't know what to say or what to do. I look to Larry. *Save this. Save Jeff. Save ME!*

Larry smiles reassuringly and approaches the lectern. I don't hear what he says to the congregation because I'm talking at Jeff. At him.

"Jeff! This is not okay. Give the speech as you wrote it and smile."

The congregation laughs tentatively and then heartily. Larry is so damn good.

Jeff smiles as instructed, blinks back tears, and begins his speech. He thanks his dad at the end, and my stomach contracts.

I don't know what I should have said to him, but it shouldn't have been that. Jeff's newly divorced dad hasn't been paying any attention to him, and I know it. I also know that making him thank his dad was a knee-jerk reaction that had everything to do with maintaining appearances and nothing to do with Jeff's needs.

I try to comfort myself by deciding to tell Larry what I know about the family situation. Then he can decide on a next step, whatever it is.

I can hardly wait for the service to end. Sure I'm feeling bad for Jeff, but I'm eager to call the owner of the brownstone on West 84th.

When the landlady hears that I'm a cantor and that I work in Great Neck, she tells me to come right away if I want her apartment. I put the bad feelings out of my mind and head downtown as soon as I hang up.

I park at a meter on Broadway near 78th, considering myself lucky.

On my nine-block walk, I smell a batch of bagels baking at H&H Bagels. I hear a cornetist practicing an eight-bar phrase that's mostly triple tonguing. From an upper story of the building right next door, I hear a soprano singing Faure's *Vocalise-étude.* This city is going to keep me company.

I pass muster with the landlady and her kids, fill out a form, and sign a check for two months' rent.

Heading back to my car, I realize that I'm hungry, so I visit Zabar's. Even the circus-style orange lettering of the sign is appetizing. Any delicacy that can share a plate with a bagel is here. As soon as I go inside, I immediately have to suck back the saliva that floods my mouth. A few minutes later, I walk out the door with my naked espresso.

Of course there are two parking tickets under my windshield wiper. And fluorescent chalk marks on my tires.

I pour the dregs out of my cup and remember Jeff.

The bitterness of the memory replaces the aftertaste of my coffee.

Jeff tried to tell the whole truth on his Bar Mitzvah day, but I was so determined to preserve pulpit decorum that I muzzled him.

I drive away with my parking tickets, and a buzz in my ears that almost drowns out the movie music of the city.

Max Gottheil

When I'm not in Great Neck, the Upper West Side has all my attention. I think a lot about Max Gottheil, the School of Sacred

Music's new conductor-composer, who lives on West 72nd Street. I miss the retiring cantor-dybbuks, but Max and his American energy are refreshing. It feeds my soul to visit the school once a week, augmenting the choir's slowly burgeoning alto section.

Max and I start seeing each other, and the relationship is immediately outlandish. It would be—he's my former professor and twenty years older. Some days he does not want any company and is foul-tempered. Some days he is sweet and speaks kindly to me. He tells me about his years with Leonard Bernstein and about his friendships with Aaron Copland and Lukas Foss. I am utterly star-struck and falling in something resembling love. He tells me about growing up a sissy boy. I tell him about growing up befriending sissy boys in theater groups and chamber ensembles. He tells me about his visits to the Continental Baths, with its mouthwash dis-pensers and its particular vending machines. I tell him about my solitary pilgrimages to the Met Cloisters and describe the sense of refuge its garden and tapestries give me. These conversations are funny and sweet. Sometimes we have them over dinner on the roof of his apartment. When he's calm.

Max is difficult, everyone agrees. He's a demanding professor. He's got a terrible temper. But he can be charming even so. He likes me because I perform capably and have a good vocabulary. Words are important to him. He likes my voice, which he describes as unique in timbre. He composes liturgical pieces for me to sing and then drills me on them in private until I'm ready to cry. But when I finally get a phrase right, when my voice does what he wants it to do, and my breath manages to sustain the perfect level of vibrato, and I don't overenunciate, he's so happy that it's nearly worth it. He'll smile without parting his lips, and I'll feel it in my stomach.

Steven Perel, a fourth-year cantorial student, and I now rehearse endlessly with Max. We are preparing to perform Benjamin Brit-ten's "Canticle II: Abraham and Isaac," at HUC. I, as the alto, play Isaac; Steve, the tenor, is Abraham. And together, singing in unison, we are God.

There is some controversy regarding this performance. It's not a piece of Jewish music. It wasn't written by a Jewish composer. In fact, the text is from one of the Chester Mystery Plays, which are based on biblical and New Testament texts and date back to the early fifteenth century. They were performed on the streets of England by guild members and artisans on movable stages. Even though the story of the binding of Isaac is a Torah excerpt, this particular play makes it appear to foreshadow Jesus's crucifixion, and there are several references to the Trinity. Max fiddles with these and reworks some rhymes, so we'll escape outright censure from faculty and administration, but just barely.

I fall in love with the language right away.

> Alas! Father, is that your will,
> Your owne child for to spill
> Upon this hilles brink?

The piece is tricky and long, nearly twenty minutes. I practice until the phrases reside as units in my brain. But when Steve and I sing together and our voices collide or find each other at a perfect octave's distance, something sweeps through me. I imagine it passes through Steve and Max too. It's very nearly too much, so it's good that it doesn't happen often. But at its apex, I am afraid. Nothing so perfectly suspended can last, and I mustn't lose focus.

> Father, I am all ready
> To do your bidding most meekely,
> And to bear this wood full bayn am I,
> As you commanded me.

bayn: willing

The last two lines have to be sung on one breath. So difficult. I do it.

During the performance, I know I capture the sweetness and the dread of the best-loved child. I know Max is pleased.

I talk with Dr. Glick about needing to please Max. A lot. So, yes, I know that a forty-four-year-old homosexual man doesn't threaten me, that he's a daddy figure, that he's a safe choice for someone with low self-esteem. That I'm flattered by the attention of a composer of some renown, and so on.

I think I understand why Max is attracted to me. At 109 pounds, I don't overwhelm anyone with my femininity. He's asked me to shave my arms, so I'm pretty sleek all over. My hair is short. I get it cut when my rabbis do. I'm content with scant affection and separate sleeping arrangements, although I wish I were able to light up his eyes once in a while. Once he told me that I look adorably butch.

Is this anything close to love? We don't say love words. Interesting, though, that Max uses them extravagantly in his work. Love Songs for Sabbath. Songs of Godlove. He does wordplays on his name, Gottheil, like "God's health" or, better, "Yay, God!" Or even "Hey, God!" I remind him, as if he needed reminding, that some ancestor of his was pious as all get-out.

Max and I do some good talking. But no lovemaking, no kissing, no cuddling to speak of.

Then he shows me the first copy of his newly published High Holiday kids' service, *New Year's Service for Young People*. Flamboyantly, he flips to the dedication page, where I see "Dedicated to Cantor Barbara Ostfeld." Is this love? God's Health loves East Field? Healthy fields love the God of the east? One thing is sure: there is no godly health in our joint eastern field.

And one question that hasn't come up in our long conversations is this: With me as a girlfriend, does he still want to visit the baths?

Biblical Eyes

Max has invited me to the Dakota, the building where John Lennon and Yoko Ono live, on Christmas Eve, my birthday. My twenty-fourth birthday. I am determined to take this in stride, this invitation to Leonard Bernstein's Christmas fête. I will not be fazed. I will not worry about attending a Christmas party, although I have misgivings as a cantor. I will not think about my boyfriend having been Bernstein's lover during their time together in the New York Philharmonic.

I know that Max is worried about having invited me. He has as much as said so. "Lenny" will judge him on his date and wonder why he's brought a woman.

I plan every moment of my toilette and dressing. I am diligent. I will wear my red knit suit for Christmas Eve with the maestro. Red. Christmas. In the spirit. But then I think that the jacket is too formal, so I don the only real silk blouse I own and tie a narrow black velvet bow under the collar.

Alas, my effort to avoid overthinking this occasion was successful—and clearly misguided. I didn't envision the dressiness and dash of the Dakota, the abundance of silver, crystal, and astonishingly clever mistletoe-holly-ivy garnishes.

I am underdressed, my diligence thwarted.

The Bernsteins have servants. Why didn't I anticipate servants?

Their children are around. Felicia, Bernstein's fabulous wife, is here. Max greets them all by name, and they know him. Lauren Bacall is here, and people call her "Betty." Apparently she lives in the Dakota, too. I do not widen my eyes. I am still and smiling, as I have promised myself I would be. Then I see Mr. Bernstein tongue kiss a teenage waiter in front of his daughter Nina. My brain instantly decides that I must not have seen it.

The maestro sits at the piano and plays some carols. It's tom-foolery and it's amazing, and my mouth is utterly dry. Not that I sing carols.

I'm sitting with Max on a yellow silk sofa when the maestro walks in, greets Max, is introduced to me, and says, "You have biblical eyes." Then he is gone, making rounds as host. I don't know if I said a word. I understood what he meant, though: It was a blessing, for Max. And it was kind—acknowledging my profession. And what else do you say to an unlovely girl who can do no better than a high-strung, ill-tempered gay man nearly twice her age?

Is There Eros?

Max asks me to marry him. He says that we will both have other lovers and that we might have a single child together. He will buy the apartment unit next to his, break through a wall, and have enough space for a small family. I want to say yes, since I'm no prude, with all my reading. But I know I'd be jealous. I don't know what to think about this kind of compromise. A baby might make up for everything, though. What a special child Max and I would make.

The next time I'm at Hebrew Union College, I screw my courage to the sticking place and ask Professor Eric Werner if I could make an appointment to speak with him. NO ONE would ask for advice from Eric Werner! He's stern, gruff, pedantic, and arrogant. He lectures in a yelling voice. Yet he and Max are friends, and I know, somehow, that Dr. Werner likes me—not that he would ever indicate any liking for any student. So I don't know what possesses me.

He suggests that I visit him at his apartment in Washington Heights the following Shabbat afternoon. When I arrive, he says that his wife is not well, so we'll have to take a walk. We walk for a long time before I come to the point. I tell him that Max has asked me to marry him and that I'm conflicted about it.

We walk on for a few blocks, and then Dr. Werner says, "Is there eros?"

A perfect question. An ethical question, too, because it doesn't reveal that he knows Max is gay. He simply asks if there is a sufficient amount of physical attraction between us. He doesn't pontificate or advise. What's implicit is that we might be great partners in every other way—intellectually, musically (in terms of Jewish observance and background), socially. Yet instantly he identifies the only impasse, because even a twenty-year age gap can be addressed.

I leave Washington Heights with my decision made. The trip back to Great Neck takes a long time. I spend it looking at my reflection in the train window.

Dear Max

Dear Max,   5/30/78

Since you like things to be simple, without too
many adjectives or contrasting "flavors," I will make
my letter plain.

I do not want to see you anymore. You would be
crazy to want to see me again. I'm through vacillating.

This decision has nothing to do with Dr. Glick,
the psychoanalyst. It has a great deal to do with what
I have discovered about myself through analysis. As
you well know, nothing in your behavior precipitated
this decision. You and I simply have different goals,
worldviews, attitudes toward family, and lifestyles.

The difference in our ages is hardly small.

Your trip idea brought things to a head. Our
coasting has come to an impasse.

I could never have married you, and the coasting
wasn't good for either of us.

I write a letter because I would cry if I spoke to
you. Letters are final.

I'm sorry about Charlotte's wedding. You'll be fine
on your own.

Through you I have learned a tremendous amount.
I have grown up.

Barbara

I know that breaking up with Max is a sign of mental health—
that it signifies my ability to see myself as a woman deserving of a
true and romantic partnership. I've learned enough in analysis, and
spent enough money in the process, to recognize that I'm ready to
get better.

I will go forward without the drama of Max in my life. Living
without him will be like turning off the metronome with its driving, mechanical beat.

Gina Gets Her Period

On to work. Yes. It's Shabbat morning, and I am anxious. One of my three families is late. Sometimes an uncle will be late, or a favorite in-law, but not an entire Bat Mitzvah family. And not by half an hour.

Always, I meet with the families at 10:15 on the dot in the sanctuary to rehearse the Torah blessings and to go through the choreography of the Torah service. This is essential if decorum is to be maintained and the service is not to last into the afternoon and we are not doomed to dwell in the house of the Lord forever.

I've practiced with family number 1 and family number 3, but family number 2 is missing. Larry will be apoplectic if we start even one minute late.

I begin to worry about a car accident. This hasn't happened before, but statistically such a thing is possible.

Ah! The mother comes rushing in, flushed, with smeared eyeliner. As always, I am calm.

She takes me to a corner of the vast bima and whispers, "Gina got her, um, "friend" this morning. For the first time. You know. It was just awful, heavy and everything, and she's hysterical, and I, um, didn't know what to do."

Gina's mother bursts into tears for what I suspect, given the state of her eyeliner, is not the first time this morning.

"Okay," I say. "She's upset, and I'll go chat with her for a minute."

"No," says her mother. "She'll be humiliated if you say anything. Plus, I only had tampons, and she won't let me put one, um, you know."

"Okay," I say again. "I won't embarrass her. Just let me have a word. Where is she?"

"I'm right here," says Gina, approaching.

Gina is wide-eyed and a bit pasty looking. Her face is pinched. I take her with me into the Blue Room, which is what the assistant rabbis and I call the "robing room." This room is equipped with a bathroom and is directly in back of the sanctuary. It is VERY blue, royal blue, and decorated with white rattan furniture. Someone thought that plaid yellow and blue cushions would be just the thing. I've always hated it. Still, it has a private bathroom—clearly a blessing in moments like this. Not that it comes equipped with feminine products. But I do. I keep a small assortment in my purse. For student emergencies.

Okay, let's take a stab at this. "Gina, wow, you got your period on the actual day of your Bat Mitzvah. That's, like, a first! This will be a great story for your daughter someday. Believe me—you'll remember this all your life. So, look, here's what you do. Stick this to your underwear, and you'll be all set. Wash your face just to freshen up, and take your time. Deep breaths! Remember all the stuff about coming of age? You aced that! Perfect timing!"

Since we're so close to the sanctuary, I'm aware that Tom Williams, the organist, has been playing for several minutes already. Tom ascends to the loft and begins to play exactly ten minutes before the service begins. This morning I hear the music as if it were an alarm. But I am prepared to do battle with Larry over starting late.

"Two of my friends have it," she says.

"Just think how truly excellent it will be when you tell them your story," I say back. "They're going to be so impressed with your timing!"

Gina's timing makes an impression on me, too. It dawns on me with a jolt that my most recent period came the day of my audition in this very sanctuary five years ago. I haven't used a single feminine product since then.

I apply a mental fermata. My internal music stops for a moment. In this extended moment, I think.

I'm completely committed to upholding everything it means to be a cantor, so I've maintained regimented control over my body—for years now—by keeping to under a thousand calories a day.

A different thought breaks in. *I'm hungry, and there are almost three hours until my next yogurt.*

But the fermata holds, and I examine the facts.

I am slightly undernourished, maybe more than slightly. The

biblical "ways of women" have ceased with me. And in order to assess the worth of the work I'm doing this Shabbat morning with Gina, I need to consider the workings of my own body.

In the silence hovering over this moment, I see that the sacrifice of my cycles has not been in the service of God, Torah, or the people of Israel.

As my background music resumes, I apply a technique I've been learning in psychoanalysis. I focus—this time on the fact that I haven't had a period in almost five years—and then mentally zoom in on that. The sacrifice of my cycles—what has it meant? Have I made a blood sacrifice? On what altar?

I'm getting to an answer. It's as if I'm preparing to greet the answer. There's a crescendo that's beyond music. A swelling of understanding . . .

I've been wearing a habit. The habit of denying myself food. I've lived as if denial of appetite will suspend me in holiness. But this sacrifice has in fact been a rejection of the rawness, the earthiness, the bloodiness of physical existence. Do I really think that having a body taints my work? If Gina can come to grips with womanhood at twelve, I can too at twenty-eight.

The ways of women are holy. Women are made in God's image! Witness Gina, bleeding for the first time as she reads from the Torah for the first time. Bang! Gina comes of age today! She has done her first public mitzvah, she has gotten her period, and she has become my teacher. The whole Bat Mitzvah thing is a proof text for the existence of the Divine.

Meanwhile, Gina starts to smile a very small smile at me. It's good that she can't read my mind and therefore know that I've appropriated the enormity of her coming of age for myself.

Larry picks this moment, of course, to enter the Blue Room, jaw clenched, eyes blazing.

"There you are," he spits. He uncoils a bit when he sees Gina.

"May I speak with you?" I ask.

A few yards down the back hall, I say, "Gina just got her period for the first time, and her mother couldn't deal. It's handled, but it took a minute. And by the way, it's a whopper of a period. We'll have to start late. I'm sorry." No doubt the "whopper" description will stop him cold.

"Oh."

And here is the self-conscious pause I was hoping for. He reddens, his jaw tightens further, and then finally it relaxes.

"Okay," he says, his voice breaking just a bit.

We take our places on the bima, and Tom gives me the opening chords from the organ.

"Ma tovu ohalecha (How amazing are your tents)," I sing. Even if they opened late this morning, O Jacob.

The Breast in the Tent

It's Shabbat morning again, and the temple is full. I look out from my lectern. Underneath a pilling white blanket, a woman in the third pew on my right is nursing her baby. From what I can see, he's a big baby, perhaps three months. The woman, whose hair is especially dark, stares calmly, fixedly straight ahead, and has not even reached for a prayer book. She is sitting by herself, or maybe she is waiting for someone. I know what will happen, though, and I hear it before I see it.

Click, click, clickety, clickety. This is Larry frantically manhandling the toggle switch on his podium. At various usher stations across the sanctuary, little lights blink on and off in rapid succession. Blink, blink, blinkety, blinky. Within moments, a carnation-sporting usher appears discreetly to the far left of the severely angled bima, his back to the congregation, ready to receive a note or whispered instructions from the senior rabbi. Larry's face is slightly flushed, and his jaw, as usual, locked. I read his lips.

Remove the woman with the baby.

The hapless usher's brows lift, and I see his dismay. He's a doting grandfather himself and is not discomfited to see a young mother breastfeeding her infant, during worship or at any other time. He approaches the raven-haired madonna from the aisle closest to the wall and addresses her gently, soundlessly. She reddens, huffs out some air, and quickly gathers a large, floppy bag. Awkwardly, she hefts the baby, stands, and edges her way out of the pew.

In this moment, Larry does not see this woman as a Roma gypsy or a mother. He does not see her as a congregant or as a Jew. She is not even a human being to whom he might minister. He is aware of only one thing when he sees her in her pew with her infant: She is an irritant—something that distracts him from his work. Larry relies on his ability to extemporize. If he can't access his brain bank because it's screaming *breast*, he cannot sermonize.

The irritant must go.

I stand up here ready, my prayer book open. From the organ loft I hear the eight measures of the poundingly majestic introduction to Louis Lewandowski's setting of *Ma Tovu*. Black curls flying, the woman strides down the center aisle, from row three to the back. The *Ma Tovu* is in three-quarter time, but the woman's retreat is not a graceful waltz. It is a waltz of shame. Not that her breast is visible, but the baby is mewling, bereft, jostled—and her placid stare has been replaced by what I hope is a deliberately fierce look. I wish Larry could see that look. In my soul I will him to see that look. But the choir attacks, pouncing now on the words, "Ma tovu ohalecha Yaakov (How amazing are your tents, Jacob)."

This morning's stranger found no respite inside our tent. Her baby found no milk. When it comes time for me to sing my solo, I close my eyes so I don't have to look at the words sitting so righteously before me on the white, white page.

"Adonai, I love the place where You dwell."

With my eyes tightly shut against the text and my ears closed to the toggle switch, I send out my voice. I send it wrapped as a gift in silk scarves to the Roma woman with her enviable breasts. Attached to my voice is a deep note of apology. I hope that somehow it reaches her.

Reindeer Games

Elliot's Bar Mitzvah is today. He's "got a single"—meaning he doesn't have to share the date with any other students, which in his

case is good, because he's by no means a Hebrew scholar. He could
be, but he makes it clear that assuming responsibility for a bunch
of commandments is not on his agenda. Elliot has made a few other
things clear, such as: The Hebrew language, which links us to our
people over space and time, is mumbo jumbo to be discarded at
noon on Bar Mitzvah Day. And: The service is a showcase for his
cuteness. Fortunately I don't encounter too many Elliots. And he's
not at fault, really. He's just a product of his parents' attitudes. I
warrant they'll resign their temple membership the moment the
younger sister becomes bat mitzvah.

It's December 22. I finish up my short choir rehearsal behind
the sanctuary and steel myself for the dry run with Elliot and family. I stop for a second in the robing room. For the millionth time,
I confirm that I am never dressed quite right. Not that anyone will
know once I don my robe, but I'm wearing my Laura Ashley portrait
collar white blouse and a Black Watch mid-calf-length plaid jumper.
The women who are attending the ceremony will be bedecked in
jacketed sheaths and skinny silk suits. The jewels will be out today.
And there will be too much conflicting perfume in the air. Even if
I were to become wealthy for some reason, there's no way I would
dress like they do. Of course I like jewelry, but not big jewelry. One
of these days, I'll have to give some thought to growing up my look.
Not today. Elliot is growing up today.

I cross the empty bima and the sanctuary, heading toward the
lobby to fetch the family for the run-through. In the center of the
lobby, I catch a glimpse of the florist's display table and stop dead.
On it sits a miniature old-fashioned sleigh trimmed with twinkling
lights. In the sleigh are tiny, cunningly wrapped presents. I blink.
Then I blink again. *Larry will lose consciousness when he sees this.* I
decide to postpone the family's dry run and fetch him. If I warn him
in advance, the damage can be contained.

I find him and tell him about the Christmas display in our
synagogue lobby. His jaw tightens, and his face starts to redden.
"You're fucking kidding," he says without a trace of humor in his
voice. "No," I say softly.

He starts for the lobby at a good clip. Fortunately for the thickening crowd, Donald Freedman, the building superintendent, is already on the scene. Larry makes a vicious grab for the sleigh, but Donald is quick. He wrests it from Larry's grasp and suggests that the whole display simply be taken down. Larry was ready to smash it to smithereens—like Abraham smashing his father's idols in the midrash, or like Moses slamming down the tablets when he observed God's people worshipping a golden calf.

I beat a hasty exit to the sanctuary and orient the family to the Torah service. I'm happy to see that the sanctuary is still empty. I have the family to myself.

"Shabbat Shalom, everyone! The Temple Beth-El family is delighted to celebrate with you as Elliot becomes a bar mitzvah during our Shabbat service this morning. Let's go over the details of the Torah service so everything goes smoothly. First—"

"Such a mensch he looks in that suit!"

"Where did you buy it, dahling?"

I continue, "When you hear the choir start to sing 'Ein Kamocha'—"

"Rhonda, you've got lipstick on your teeth."

I try again. "If I could just have everyone's attention for just a few more minutes—"

"This is the girl cantor I was telling you about!"

"They got a girl for a cantor?"

Running Beside You

Wind me up, and I will chant memorial prayers. Wind me up again, and I will escort a congregational family all the way to what feels like the last exit on the Southern State Parkway, off of which many Beth-El burials take place. Our congregation is so large that funerals are frequent. Rabbis always lead the funeral services and give the eulogies, and I always chant the same two prayers at the prescribed times. And generally, unless the family is prominent, I conduct the burial ceremonies—by myself. This is because the cantor is the most dispensable person on the clergy staff and it takes

midrash: narrative—the kind of rabbinical stories that explain or comment on Torah text nearly an hour most mornings to drive out to the Jewish cemeteries in West Babylon. Longer if you drive with the hearse at thirty miles an hour. And then even longer coming back, depending on the traffic. West Babylon. Aptly named.

So I don't get emotional at 94 percent of all funerals. Even if I know the decedent, my sadness is in check. Death is often the kindest visitor, even among loving family members and close friends. I can help to ease family members into the gentle caress of the funeral rituals—the words, the melodies, the welcome quiet, the orchestrated solace. It can feel good to guide people quietly into the mourning process.

Of course I've also experienced the other 6 percent of all funerals, like this one—tragic and overflowing with anguished souls. These are scary because even as officiants, we are mourning too.

Most of us have practiced methods of dodging our feelings. My methods involve talking very emphatically in my own ear. *I will just look at my book and chant when the time comes. Then I will sit down and not listen anymore. I will cry later, after the service is over.*

The chapel of Temple Beth-El is full, of course. I don't need to look at the congregation to know that. I feel the pulse of many souls. People are standing in the aisles, amid a certain kind of quiet. Usually I meet with the family before the funeral, but not this time. I decide they would prefer privacy. The truth, though, is that I don't want to see them. I simply wait in the chapel, near the bima, until it is time. I take my seat with my finger pressing tightly against the next text I will chant, concentrating with all my heart. At the rabbi's nod, I walk to my lectern and look at that text. To distract myself—and to demonstrate to myself that I am in control—I make it blur and come into focus, blur and come into focus.

I sing, and as I begin, I feel people crying. This is normal. I am a stone. Even if I sing softly, so as not to break in on anyone's pain, they cry. Even if I whisper a name in the hope that no one will recognize it as lost to the living, still it is heard, and they cry.

I can't trick them into holding back their tears so I can play my goddamn part. No one told me how much this would hurt.

I soften the final notes, as if I'm pressing the damper pedal on a piano. I keep my head low, so as not to see anyone, as I walk back to my seat on the bima. The rabbi reads the psalms and other passages and begins his eulogy. I will not listen. *I will not listen.*

Struggling to maintain control, I again make the page in my manual blur and come into focus, blur and come into focus. I remember my best trick, the one that always works if I'm in danger of crying. I visualize this passage from the *Union Prayer Book* "Service for Sabbath Eve I":

> O Lord, open our eyes that we may see and welcome all truth, whether shining from the annals of ancient revelations or reaching us through the seers of our own time. . . .

I wait for the imagined words to do their magic. Did it work? Have I escaped the need to cry?

Then the sound of Larry's eulogy intrudes.

"She will always be there, running beside you."

His voice breaks. Damn him.

She was nine years old. A runner. Up every morning before the sun to sprint around the track.

It is time now for me to chant El Malei Rachamim for a child. For a searing second I hate everyone who never told me what this would be like.

I send out my voice as gently as I can. I don't want to be heard at all in front of a casket this small. But if my singing must be audible, then let it be a lullaby.

What Dr. Glick Might Say

I position my wedge of cantaloupe and begin breakfast. My tea is still too hot. Outside my window I can just about see the scraggly forsythias in the park across the street. They're starting to turn yellow. Spring. I want spring.

And it comes to me that I also want a new kitten. But as soon as I start thinking about getting one, I stop. I'm out of the apartment

El Malei Rachamim: God Full of Compassion—the prayer for the deceased chanted at a funeral

all day, and many evenings too—for choir rehearsal or meetings. A cat would be lonely.

I think of what Dr. Glick might say—if he ever said anything. The Dr. Glick of my imagination asks me why I want a cat.

Well, Pretend Dr. Glick, my orchids are not even in spike. The little African violets I buy in the Bronx Botanical Garden seem to have powdery mildew.

And then it comes to me—just the way it comes to me on Dr. Glick's couch: *I am lonely.*

And a beat later, I complete this thought.

A cat will not solve this problem any more effectively than does my windowsill garden. I need more than sunny green smells or a purring presence.

I need to figure out how I'm going to live this life and whether I'm going to do that alone or not. I need the kind of human contact that doesn't start and end with an oneg Shabbat.

Greeting Line Handshake

Every Shabbat I steel myself. And when, from the hidden rear door next to the ark, I step up onto the bima, I step into another self. I become taller and more dignified, older and wiser. I lose the bad posture and the ready willingness to say "fuck."

After the service, I steel myself again. When I step into my appointed place in the greeting line, after both rabbis, the rabbinic intern, and the congregational president, I inhabit yet another self. I become sincere and congenial. I pick up the tempo of my speech. I soften my gaze and harden my grip. I'm damn adorable as a greeting line caboose.

I have also perfected the greeting line handshake. Dad always said that a firm handshake is important. Of course he was talking to my brother, Simon—and not to little Sarah or to me. I'd never seen women shake hands. Not during my childhood, not on TV, not in the movies. I asked Dad to show me, and he gave my hand a proper shake. Then he demonstrated a cold-fish handshake.

At Beth-El of Great Neck, the greeting line is important and can last a long time, especially if there's a special service or a guest speaker. Events like that happen about once a month. But even after years of greeting lines, when men kiss me in the greeting line, I flinch. Well, except for two men. Ellis and Mike. They each have a twinkling presence and daughters my age, and they're so delight-fully proper and kind and carefully dressed. And there's something else. They have a trait so many men are missing, but one I see in my Bar Mitzvah boys. A sweetness. A vulnerability. An inability to pose.

So in the greeting line, I let my handshake tell all the men that I am friendly but not THAT friendly.

The not-THAT-friendly handshake technique I've developed works every time. So no longer does anyone succeed at the slip-pery stealth kiss. I smile broadly as I extend my arm, making defi-nite eye contact briefly but sincerely, and then turn my gaze, my full gaze, and rest it on whichever woman—wife, girlfriend, sister, mother, neighbor lady—is next. Behold, my pioneering-woman-cantor greeting line M.O.

I'm rehearsing this now because I've been asked to speak to the women students at HUC about things like clergy attire, clergy demeanor, the issues that confront women in our kind of work—things that haven't been specifically addressed before at HUC. Apparently these issues weren't relevant to men.

I'm pretty sure the reason I've been asked isn't that I'm the first woman cantor; it's that I work at Temple Beth-El of Great Neck, the congregation that, on the authority of its own board of trustees, is the "leading Reform congregation" in the New York area. (I joke about this with every assistant rabbi. Other temples are secondary, tertiary?)

I'm still honored to be asked. I prepare and present, worrying all the while—until the Q and A. I always begin to relax when I can rely on my immediate responses to questions. That feels like a conversation, and conversation is one thing I'm good at.

When a student asks about greeting lines, I'm ready. More than ready. I roll my eyes a bit, indicating how little I care for greeting lines, and the women snicker—even the newest student rabbi knows that greeting lines are gauntlets.

"Greeting lines give men excuses to kiss their women clergy," I say. "An excuse to grasp their hands and to display their plumage, which can range from pinky rings with diamonds to aggressive aftershave. Some men take forever to 'greet' women clergy, relating feats such as shooting an even par or finishing Pynchon's *Gravity's Rainbow*."

I laugh along with the students as I step out in front of the lectern to show off my patented greeting line handshake. I demonstrate the subtle adjustments to the angle and stiffness of my elbow and forearm. The Ostfeld Stiff-Armed Handshake—guaranteed to prevent all greeting line kissing.

My demonstration is hailed with delight, and the students actually rehearse the shake for my approval. We laugh some more.

We laugh because we know the truth. Women rabbis can't wear high heels or fashionable dresses. These are forbidden in the unwritten manual that instructs them to hide their attractiveness, their originality, their vitality in extra fabric and subdued colors. Women cantors can't pitch their melodies too high or wear bright lipstick. Our manual directs us to shake hands with femaleness, not to embrace it.

And I am here teaching these high-achieving women precisely what? How to avoid being handled.

Yes, we laugh. But not because it's funny.

Elmhurst High School Reunion

This is like a dream. I am some idealized version of myself. I weigh less than Sue Suconik and I did in ninth grade. My skin is clear. I have long hair, and I know how to care for it. I've learned how to dress up. I'm good at makeup, applying it like someone with OCD and low self-esteem would, which is to say with intense focus and relentlessly acquired skill. I'm divorced and without a boyfriend. I've attended so many Bar Mitzvah and Bat Mitzvah parties that I now know how to dance. I've engaged in so many oneg Shabbat conversations with so many kinds of people that I know how to chat. Also, I am far away from my congregation and on my own.

Unlike any dress I wore while we lived here in Elmhurst, this one is store-bought. It's pine green with white eyelet sleeves. It's no shorter than a dress I would wear on the bima, but it's more formfitting. I'm not used to being aware of a dress, feeling it on my body.

I wear my tenth-grade photo from 1968 with pride, pinned to my chest. I look much better now. And I have social skills.

Jeff hovers. Bob stakes me out. They dance with me. Closely. Jeff whispers in my ear, and I laugh. Bob moves his hand along my back. I squeeze his other hand.

Neither one had any time for me in high school. So THIS is what I missed.

Bob knows a place to get a glass of wine afterward. Jeff thinks a walk would be nice on such a perfect evening.

Jeff is far more articulate, funnier. He was in honors classes and went out with Sue Bodkin, who wore a skirt and not shorts to Beach Day and whose parents bought our house when we moved to Connecticut.

Bob is a twin. I always preferred the other one, Keith, who once shaved between his eyebrows in eighth grade. I thought of no one but Keith for several years. I thought I saw him in every car on the road. One time, at ballroom dance class on a Friday night, he told me that I almost looked human. I tried so hard to find a compliment in that.

Taking all of this in, I think of Simon and his friends, who used to play baseball after school. When a kid struck out, he would call, "Do-over!" The arguing that followed was endless. Every kid was sure he would get a hit if he just got another chance. But no kid ever got his do-over.

Now, though, I do. I get a high school do-over. It lasts one night, but for the whole night I'm pretty, slim, well dressed, and popular. I dance, and get asked out by two cute guys at once. They're pissed at one another. Over me.

I can almost hear the movie soundtrack.

Gramballs as Simon, Sarah, and I still call our paternal grandmother (the one everyone else calls "Chubbo") replies to my letter describing the reunion.

> You know, Barb, I think you enjoyed the reunion
> so much because it represented your childhood,
> your early youth, a time when you could be you and
> not worry about the impression you made on the
> members of your congregation. You ought to take
> a long sea voyage and try to be yourself without
> thinking about anything, except what you feel and
> what you wish to do—enjoy life and be young.
>
> Enough philosophizing.
>
> Love, Grandma

In her eighty-seventh year, my grandmother is telling me to enjoy life while I'm young. Maybe while on a cruise.

Gramballs, I won't be "enjoying life" anytime soon. I won't be reveling in my youth.

I do grin, though, on my way back to my accustomed rock pile.

Finding Dan

Some people have charisma, but Dan Gertz is magnetic, especially as a clergyman.

Dan graduated from the School of Sacred Music at HUC five years after me. He's a promising young cantor. His singing is nice, but his other talents are stellar. He is a gifted pianist, as Indiana U, Julliard, and Manhattan School of Music will attest. He actually has groupies in his congregation—usually women of a certain age who are at his beck and call. They cook for him, bring him treats, attend all his services, and make costumes and sets for his synagogue productions.

In turn, he pays them a certain kind of attention. He's like a puppy in that way. He listens attentively to their stories. He looks at them directly and with intent. He makes them laugh, which is easy for him because he knows just what they'll find funny. His attentions are never physical, so no lines are crossed, but sometimes crushes develop in his wake. Even these are within boundaries.

Dan is no threat to anyone. He speaks fluent woman. He speaks fluent child. He's a perfect cantor, happy in the music and the theater of it, successful as a teacher on all levels—and he has no equal in the schmoozing and name-remembering departments.

Well, there is one way he's a threat: The fact that he is very popular with the people who make things go in temples—the women—makes some rabbis jealous.

Women in temples. Without one of them in particular, I would starve. Literally. The one genuine meal I eat each week is a Cobb salad paid for by a doting elderly woman in my congregation. I bring my own zero-calorie dressing to the nice restaurant and listen to her for an hour. This works for both of us.

Dan. Dan loves my voice, its precision and clarity. He accompanies me on the piano for hours.

His playing is dazzling. Yes, Dan could have had a career in piano, but he hated the isolation of practice rooms.

He and I have been assigned to work together on planning this year's midwinter conclave of the American Conference of Cantors. We are the same age. We have advanced social skills. We are good at languages. We laugh a lot and understand the other's jokes. We're clicking.

Dan offers to drive me to and from the conclave. A talented and sweet cantorial student rides along. Ellis Gold is a wonderful tenor—handsome, open-faced, and funny. I wonder if he's gay. As we drive to the conclave, Ellis sits in the front passenger seat and I provide commentary from the back. I sit in the middle and lean forward so as not to miss a word. The long drive speeds by. Our conversation never lags and is punctuated by happy giggling.

On the way home, Dan asks me to take the passenger seat. Hours later, after Ellis is dropped off, Dan tells me that he would like to see me "not as a friend." I'm thrilled but taken aback. I pull a napkin from his glove compartment and tell him that I'm going to draw a dinosaur while I think. Yes, I say, completing the project.

By way of the apatosaur, who is green, we discover that we're both using green pens as our default writing utensils, and we take this to bode well for our relationship.

And so it goes. We begin to meet after services on Friday nights. He drives an incredibly long way to meet me, not caring about the time, the miles. We're old enough, but we know that we can't live together. Our congregations, so delighted with our relationship (How cute—two cantors in love!) would not tolerate our cohabitation. After all, we're teaching their adolescent children. We're leading worship. We're officiating at burials.

Consequently, we begin to plan our wedding. The planning stage is intoxicating. We both had early and unfortunate first marriages. This time is the charm, and we will celebrate! Our respective friends are happy for us and eager to see us married.

In the midst of the fun, though, I'm worrying about the forthcoming termination of my analysis. Although there's a new man in my life, I'm going to miss Dr. Glick. I see him five days a week. I'm not sure what it will be like to go day to day without seeing him. I'm aware that analysands are not supposed to make big changes in their lives while undergoing treatment, but I talk about this during my sessions. I feel good, clean, ready. And when Dr. Glick says, "You will always know you're on the right track if you are again Class Arguer," I think it really will be okay.

What matters is not so much that he says those words, but that I know exactly what he means.

So now, again into marriage while serving a congregation. I can do this. Work. Maintain a relationship. Be a symbolic exemplar.

Dan and I are good company as a unit, both of us amusing and verbal. We are becoming popular as a new couple. We socialize a lot, often both wearing green.

Wedding to Dan

I weigh 109 pounds at 5 feet 5 inches. I'm hungry. Yes, I've fasted, because it's traditional for brides and grooms, but my hunger goes back to my early twenties.

Thinking of appetite, I replay a Dr. Glick moment—a rare one in which he spoke aloud.

"Does Dan say anything about your eating habits?"

"Not a word. Even when I cry if there isn't any cantaloupe available for breakfast at our usual diner."

"Crying over cantaloupe?"

"No. Crying over the absence of cantaloupe. I eat melon for breakfast during the summer."

"You mean only melon."

"Yes."

"Cereal, juice, toast, coffee?"

"Only melon."

"Dan has not remarked on this."

"No. He likes me the way I am. Adorably compulsive about my eating habits."

Even though it's my wedding day, I have time to think. My bridal makeup is already perfect, and I've even passed an extra Q-tip under my bottom lashes to preclude raccoon eyes. I let myself think in the way that I think on the couch.

I know my eating is ritualized, and I am starting to know that it's nuts. Shouldn't an attentive fiancé express concern about the rigidity of the beloved's diet?

I will think more about this in a week or two. Today I'm getting married! Tomorrow we leave for our honeymoon.

Seven hundred people attend our wedding, some from my congregation and some from Dan's, which is two towns away. The sanctuary is as full as on a major Jewish holiday. Temple Beth-El provides a reception for all seven hundred.

Mom has made an aqua silk shift for Sarah. It has several layers in two shades. She is rosy-cheeked and lovely, although she's wearing her beat-up old Birkenstocks. I look at them and at her unpedicured feet. I love her and her footwear. For a moment I flash back to our shared joke about wearing Birkenstocks as a birth control method.

I'm wearing a vintage Edwardian day dress. My hair is tamed, partly French braided, and pinned here and there with baby's breath. I'd thought about getting a manicure, but I've never had one before, so I didn't.

Hands. I look at Dan's hands to remind myself of why it is that I'm marrying him. His fingers, ordinary looking, rest against his trousers, hiding their prowess. Dan and the other men in the bridal party are wearing silver-gray tuxedos. Dan's fair hair has been shellacked into place. We pose for photos on the bima of Temple Beth-El of Great Neck.

Co-officiating with Larry is Dan's best man, best friend, mentor, and sometime housemate—the petite, mustachioed, helmet-coiffed Rabbi Daniel Tannenbaum. Larry's wedding words to us are eloquent. Rabbi Tannenbaum's make me wince. The phrase "sharing and caring" features prominently.

Up on the bima, in the white sanctuary, it's Dan and me under the chuppa, which is supported at two corners by Ostfelds and at the other two by Rabbi Tannenbaum's children.

And now photographs. The Tannenbaum kids are in all the wedding pictures. One photo captures a happy moment between the two Dans, looking like cantor and rabbi salt and pepper shakers. I am the undernourished bride with punished hair, giddy and costumed. Adorned. In love. Ready for the ball.

chuppa: canopy—specifically, the wedding canopy

Canticle

Motherhood engages
Career thriving yet a blur
Years fly by in weeks

Wanting a Baby

I've always known that there was something wrong with my insides. Wasn't Mom always asking my pediatrician when I was going to develop?

I got my first period later than anyone I knew. There was never anything regular about its comings and goings. I bleed now only because a fancy regimen of hormones is injected at precise intervals into my ass.

Waiting for my examination, having passed through doors labeled "FERTILITY," I remember this *F* word from a different context—when Dean Metsch shamed cantorial students by pronouncing us fertile rather than cerebral.

I'm not superstitious. I'm not. I don't believe in the Evil Eye. But I remember my usher's vow and irrationally wonder if I've somehow sacrificed my ability to conceive by bearing a high standard instead.

Consequently, I'm going into this appointment with no optimism. It's just one more fertility procedure to check off my list.

I don't know why I keep taking fertility treatments anymore.

I enter Yale New Haven Hospital with Dan, who is expressionless. He's doing this for me and has no interest for himself. We walk down corridors, turn corners, take an elevator. Then I'm on an exam table in a gown.

The doctor says, "This process is called 'uterine sounding.' I will first insert a speculum and will then measure your uterus. It will be quick and painless, although you will feel some pressure. This is preliminary to all in vitro fertilization procedures."

Suddenly I feel pain like nothing I've ever experienced before, and then a welcome release.

Now I am being revived. I'm aware that Dan is angry, not exactly at me, for fainting, but at the situation. He doesn't want to be here doing this. We've already decided to adopt, and we both know that it will come to that.

The pain diminishes, and I ask what happened.

"Some patients react this way," the doctor replies casually. *And some doctors are inexperienced,* I retort in my head. In a way I'm gratified—as if the more I suffer, the more likely I am to get pregnant.

I'm used to shots. I'm at the end of the Pergonal phase. The human chorionic gonadotropin shot will be tomorrow, and then comes the harvesting of my eggs and their insemination in a petri dish. Poor Dan. He's made a lot of sperm donations. Little plastic cups with a ridiculously tiny bit of stuff in brown paper lunch bags.

The HCG shots hurt more than the others. The stuff is viscous and takes a long time to inject. It stings going in. Afterward my butt is sore.

Time for the laparoscopy. I've had one before. I'm shutting down the hope. I know from the ultrasound that there aren't many ripe follicles. We can afford only one cycle of in vitro fertilization. Dan doesn't wear boxers. How good can the odds be?

I wake up and am told that there were four follicles.

Dan has produced a sample during the procedure. I can't imagine the pressure. Again I think, *Poor Dan.*

We learn that only one egg is fertilized.

One day later, still sore from the laparoscopy, I'm back at the hospital. At least the cell division is looking normal and the embryo can be implanted. I can't assess my feelings. I am afraid to have any. I'm afraid that if I let myself be hopeful, I'll be crushed when I fail. Afraid that if I let myself be disappointed about not having more embryos to implant, I'll be a less commodious host. I don't want to talk to anyone, so I read.

Down more corridors, around more corners, into another elevator. I am gowned again and instructed to get onto a steel table.

I'm told to get onto my hands and knees and to lower my forehead onto my crossed arms, leaving my bottom in the air. A very long and thin plastic tube is inserted into my cervix.

The doctor says to someone, "Now take this and, yes, that's right. Yes. No, not like that. No. You don't want to . . . okay. Right. Slower. Yes. NO! With your left hand . . . now . . . well . . . all right . . . okay."

I AM AN IDIOT. I have the power of speech. I could say "Stop!" I could say, "I want the big boy doctor to do this, not the medical student." And yet I remain silent—tolerating, accepting—ever the compliant and therefore well-behaved girl. Even with all my hopes and dreams pinned on this. Even with my absolute devotion—all the money, the shots, the little brown bags of sperm, the anonymous corridors, the perfectly kept temperature charts, the full-bladder ultrasounds, the timed intercourse that isn't love-making.

Yes, I would like to have a positive pregnancy test. I would like to grow my own baby. I would like to nurse my baby. I would like to see if she or he has music or reads like a fiend.

But mostly I just want that baby. I want that baby.

Finally, Hana

We have been told to dress respectfully. This poses no challenge for a pulpit cantor.

I'm in my best navy suit, hoping that it will feel soft to the touch when I get my baby. I've never had to wonder about the softness of my clothing before today.

We're watching out the window of our hostel for the green-and-white-striped cab. Luis, the driver, pulls up right on time, so we arrive at the Foundation for the Assistance of Abandoned Children (FANA is the Spanish acronym) at 10:00 a.m.

We are whisked into a small, sunny room clearly intended for socializing. Its walls are covered with snapshots of some of FANA's children—the cute adopted ones, not the ones who have impairments or deformities. Niceties are observed. The director,

Mercedes—impeccably dressed and coiffed, even bejeweled—is somewhat withdrawn, though cordial.

We are asked to hand over the baby clothes we've brought for our baby. As I let go of the little pile of folded items, I feel my heart begin to pound. It doesn't stop hammering until nearly an hour later when Sister Laura hands me a swaddled baby, who smells sweet. Constanza. I am struck by her beauty. I wonder for a moment what one does with a beautiful child. But I already know. One sings.

I remember the lullabies my mother sang to me, and I learned some Jewish cradle songs in art song classes at HUC. Here in Bogotá, I start to sing a lullaby—for the first time to my own baby. I am someone new.

Like all new adoptive parents, we have numerous legal errands to run. Constanza needs a visa and a passport—all in her new name. An airline ticket. We have to buy gifts for all of the people we've encountered here. The gifts are to be of a certain kind and ranked by the importance of the recipient. Some want preserves and chocolate-covered tea biscuits. Others want American dollars. And still others want brand-name liquor. But I don't want to be out and about. I don't want the orphanage's housekeeper or her maid to feed Costanza for me while I am running errands. I want to stay with my baby and feed her myself.

Plus, the streets are scary. Luis locks the doors the second we enter his cab. Armed guards are stationed every two blocks. They stand in booths or pace the sidewalks. We drive through a sprawling city of homeless people, and a woman pounds on my window. Her breasts are flaccid and hanging low, half in and half out of her dress. She thrusts her baby toward me, screaming and red-faced. I sit up straighter and look with deliberate empathy into the woman's eyes. *Be professional,* I think. *Communicate concern.* But then Luis translates the woman's words. "She says, 'Take my baby—I can't feed him.'" Gone is my calm, professional clergy presence. My homeless sister cannot feed my tiny nephew. The world as I've known it has ended. With his arm, Luis prevents me from unlocking the door.

We arrive once again at FANA, this time for an official tour of the facilities. Sister Marion shows us classrooms, dormitories, the dining room, two play areas, the formula room, the kitchen, the laundry room, and children from the age of four months to eight years. We take some Polaroids, and the older children clamor for these, grabbing and showing them off to their friends. Many small hands find their way inside mine. My pulpit composure and teaching persona have deserted me. These little ones are neither my congregants nor my students. They are my unfertilized eggs, sloughed off monthly against my will. They are my potential babies. I feel as though I am rejecting each one. I leave them behind as we leave FANA behind, at the rate of one orphan per step.

Having left FANA and my would-be babies, Dan, Constanza, and I are now ready to depart our hostel for the airport, to fly home. As we are about to leave, the housekeeper, Petra, hands me the sweater she's been knitting. I didn't realize it was for Constanza until now. It's pale pink and lacy, with a matching pink bonnet. The work is delicate, and the yarn is fine and soft. A weepy new mother, I kiss Petra's cheek in gratitude.

My physical gesture surprises me. Up until now, I have never kissed a stranger. Maybe this new willingness to kiss has to do with the new mother in me.

Just as Constanza becomes Hana, I become affectionate.

How Naked?

Maternity leave ends, and I am ready. It's been hard work taking care of Hana. Hard, repetitious, and exhausting. I've read too many books about stimulating infants in their early months, so Hana's tiny head is chock-full of songs, rhymes, numbers, verbose descriptions of nature, and my own out-loud stream of consciousness. I can't keep up this pace at home. So it's time to return to synagogue life and its easier tasks. Yes, I'm ready to go back to work.

As soon as I do, Deborah presents me with her fantasy that New York's Leading Reform Congregation would embrace her, its first woman assistant rabbi, as a lesbian.

The Talmud says, "Kol b'isha erva"—that the open-air singing voice of a woman is as brazen as public nudity. Consequently all women are supposed to shut the fuck up. I didn't, and so here I am, in a position to be asked for advice.

It's 1984, but I just don't think so.

"No," I tell her. "The congregation just isn't ready for you, not as YOU. Larry isn't ready."

I play at being the voice of reason.

Deborah is such a dignified woman, so refined, so midwestern. I know she's a new rabbi, but I ask her if she is naïve enough to imagine that even the enlightened will be able to reconcile "esteemed rabbi" with "lesbian." I can almost predict that the eyes of any congregation will darken with suspicion if she comes out.

"It's one thing to be a woman CANTOR," I explain. "The buck will never stop with me. Today's synagogue pecking order starts with senior rabbi and ends with cantor, so it would be another thing altogether for a lesbian to be rabbi."

Does Deborah see the irony of my thought? It's there, the connection between Deborah's wish to claim her sexual identity with my own passion to pursue a career that had been male territory since the seventh century. But feeling confined in my hard-won, shiny-new seat of authority, I parrot the same old paternalistic crap. Given the chance to speak words of wisdom to Deborah, I default, lowering my voice out of fear.

Dr. Glick Dies

In the two years since Dr. Glick and I agreed that my psychoanalysis had ripened and the time had come for us to terminate it, I've continued to hear his voice. My mind regularly recreates his carefully modulated tones, asking me as he did, "What has become of Class Arguer?"

So when Dr. Glick telephones, I recognize his voice at hello, even after two years. He tells me that he has advanced cancer.

I react in stages. I get angry first—at him, thinking that he's been negligent about his check-ups; he's only in his forties. Before I fix on that, though, I'm struck by sorrow as a memory of his curly-headed son sitting cross-legged on the story rug at the temple comes to the surface in my mind. Reliably, anxiety follows. If he dies, where does my analysis go? Does it have a soul of its own?

I say some words, and I know Dr. Glick hears my sadness for him.

Imagine the bravery of a man who calls even his former patients to warn them of his death, to prepare them. Can these calls help him prepare too?

Then he says, "You would make a fine psychiatrist. If you need a recommendation in the very near future, you can have mine."

My gratitude for these words fills the world, and I stutter something back to him. Something about our work being an endless blessing and something about hearing even more from him now in my head than I heard in those five years on his couch.

And we agree that such was the point.

What Cantors Should and Should Not Kiss

When I have a day off, Hana likes to visit the temple with me. Although she's shy and won't talk to anyone except Dan and me, I see that she enjoys the praise she gets from the people there. She buries her head in my shoulder when congregants comment on her charm, but I can feel the pull of her smile against my blouse.

I point out a robin from the temple office window, and Hana lights up when she sees it. I plant little kisses on her head. No one is more affected by her appeal than her mother!

Saul Fogel, a newly retired board member, enters the office, folder in hand, to speak to the administrator.

"Hi, Saul!" I call from the window.

"Cantors should only kiss mezuzahs is what I think," replies Saul.

I am silent as this pronouncement penetrates.

Saul hands his folder to Rosie, the youngest and newest secretary, without a word. Then he leaves, making a show of closing the office door.

mezuzah: doorpost—a small encased parchment affixed to the exterior doorposts of Jewish homes

I take Hana home for lunch, which, as usual, she doesn't eat.

I think about Saul while Hana naps, briefly.

At first my thoughts center around what an asshole he is and always has been. Then I go beyond asshole to Neanderthal. I stop there and contemplate Neanderthal Man. He was on that famous chart, sporting his prominent ridged brow, but that's all I remember.

Is that it? I think. *Is it just that the world has moved beyond the willingness of primitives to adapt?*

And although I would like to spend more brain time on Saul, whose development never reached Cro-Magnon, I come to a full stop.

Every week I fend off kisses from men in the greeting line. But I shouldn't give one to my own daughter in the temple office? I've been a cantor for nearly ten years, and I've never heard from Saul's knuckle-dragging clan before today. Well, I vaguely remember some hate mail from somebody else that arrived in my in-box when I was a new graduate, but the words were misspelled and the grammar nonexistent. I paid it no mind at the time.

I think about it now and can't remember anything other than the words "shame" and "evul."

So wait. It's been ten years since my ordination, and I can count only Saul and some illiterate? They've been my only enemies in all this time?

I am the cantor of a "leading Reform congregation," a mother, an adjunct faculty member at the School of Sacred Music at Hebrew Union College, and an officer of the American Conference of Cantors. Professors from HUC come here once in a while to hear me chant from the Torah.

Hebrew Union College, the Union of American Hebrew Congregations, and Rabbi Larry Rappaport all call me Cantor.

Saul and Anonimouse Korispondent can go fuck themselves.

Finally, Tali

Hana is being surprisingly good on our very long journey back to FANA to adopt our second daughter. Her good behavior might be related to bottomless cups of soda and endless salty snacks, though. During the Miami layover on the way to Bogotá, she runs around and around the airport, making wide, mad circles. During the Panama layover, she runs in tighter circles, sensing the unfamiliarity of the place.

Worry is circling tightly inside my mind too. Hana is a skillful three-year-old, well socialized if shy, devoted to her friends and to anything that sparkles. Every inch of Hana is familiar to me, but her shyness, her confidence, and that attraction to sequins do not resonate. What will happen to my Hana once she has a baby sister? I worry that I won't be able to maintain the uncluttered neatness of our home, which we rent from the congregation. I live in fear that congregants will drop in and find fault with my housekeeping. With two children, will I be able to shelve all the toys just so every evening? Will the stickiness that threatens my countertops prevail over my regular assaults with ammonia? Maternity leave. Have I prepared the congregation adequately for my absence? Am I capable of getting two children into car seats, snowsuits, shopping carts?

Dan, Hana, and I report to the orphanage at 10:00 a.m. sharp. We wait endlessly. Hana is edgy and a bit flushed.

At 11:15 Mercedes walks in, regal as ever. She greets us with a brief wave of her left wrist, hand cupped, and leaves. Sisters Louise and Marion follow suit. They look no different than they did three years before.

Dan and I are getting increasingly anxious to see Leonor and to hold her. Hana begins to clamor for a snack. Sister Marion brings her three wafer cookies and a glass of soda.

Hana says, loudly, "I want to go back to the hotel."

I'm starting to sweat at my hairline. We're still waiting. I play rock-paper-scissors with Hana, forgetting the rules, and then we move on to pitching pennies into cups. We change her doll's diaper. I pretend it's a poopy diaper, playing for time. We put stickers on everything we own. I reach the far border of my mothering repertoire, even with Dan as backup.

Mercedes sweeps back into the room and says airily that there are no babies for anyone today after all.

I hate Mercedes with a terrible hatred. I have no sense of humor and no charity left. But of course, before I find my voice, she exits once again. At least I resisted the urge to drop into a deep curtsy, although it gives me a little satisfaction to imagine sustaining it until the door shuts behind her.

While she's gone, my mind circles to the evils of powdered formula. A normal mother would simply be tingling with anticipation. But me, I'm focused on my hatred for Nestogeno. It takes forever to mix and never really dissolves properly. And I'm never absolutely sure that the water boiled long enough.

A few minutes later, Mercedes returns with a baby swaddled in a white, lace-edged blanket. I realize, slowly, that the baby in white is ours. This baby with charcoal eyes is my baby.

Hana says, "Are we gonna keep her?"

As this question registers, my skin prickles.

Suddenly I feel like I'm cheating at motherhood. I've conducted many baby namings and participated in many circumcisions. I'm just an onlooker who officiates. Involuntarily, I begin to spin these thoughts out. *Who am I to have these two girl-children when I'm not an authentic woman myself? A real mother gets pregnant, throws up, can't sleep, and gives birth. A real mother has breasts that swell and leak and hurt as she feeds her babies. But here I am, playing with dolls, filling plastic bottles with chalky imitation breast milk, and calling these instant babies mine.*

But I stop myself. Is that Dr. Glick's voice in my head, trying to get my attention with his soft voice? It is. He asks me, *"Why do you always assume that a bad situation can never be redeemed? You solved the problem of not having children. Why do you refuse to see it that way?"*

He's right—exactly right. Okay, I know it's part of the psycho-analytic process to confer divinity upon one's psychiatrist. But he's still right! I get it, Dr. Glick!

Like lightning I feel little Leonor Paez become Tali Gertz and assume her place in this family. Dan and I named this baby in the same way that Adam and Eve named their fellow animals in Genesis. By assigning a word to a being.

Naming children is the same as blessing them. Tali means "dew." Leonor means "light." Only Tali-Leonor will figure out the true significance of her name. Only Tali-Leonor will figure out how light affects dew.

Nicknaming children is the same as blessing them too. Uncle Marvin used to call me Barbi Prim, or sometimes Zelda Prim, which he thought sounded tidy, Jewish, bookish. I understood it was teasing, but I liked the attention—and having my own nickname. Also, I AM tidy. I AM Jewish. I AM bookish. I'm prim. It was apt.

The Gertz-Ostfelds tour FANA once again. We see four rows of toddlers in high chairs precisely lined up along the four long walls of the dining room. They wait to be fed. Several are pointing to their open mouths and crying piteously. When we pass the nursery, I am struck by the incessant wailing. My stomach aches with guilt.

Here I am, parading through a South American orphanage again, this time with my velvet-clad three-year-old and my perfectly swaddled infant. I should take all these babies home.

Now I worry that my guilt will interfere with good mothering choices. Will I feel the need to overcompensate by spoiling my daughters? Will I constantly be seeing the other babies in their faces? Will I always hear the wailing from FANA's nursery or see the toddler fingers pointing to empty mouths? Will Tali and Hana be doomed by my persistent dark thoughts? Will they grow up in the orbit of my gloom?

On our last night in Colombia, I stop Hana from brushing her teeth in the bidet, conceding—because she's correct—that it's just the right height.

For some reason, firecrackers keep going off. Then, as soon as the dogs stop baying, the roosters begin crowing. I might not sleep, and I have bottles to prepare anyway. It's 1:15, and inevitably the powdered Nestogeno clumps in Tali's bottle. I wearily stir it.

"Barbi," I say, quietly but firmly, "you are about to fill your new baby's stomach!" I feel myself smile. I carry the warm bottle to my new baby on our last night in Bogotá. She makes quick work of it and falls asleep in my arms.

Leather Wedding Mentorship Opportunity

Larry is a parent too. Every summer, he, Carol, and their boys go to Martha's Vineyard to be a family. It makes sense. As Rabbi Rappaport, Larry doesn't take days off, and he's not home for dinner much during the year. His weekends are shot, what with the constant life-cycle events. So if he's going to be a dad or a husband, it's got to be during the summer. This means that every five years a new assistant rabbi comes on board at the beginning of July and finds the senior rabbi gone except for a few marathon wedding weekends. It's baptism by fire for the newbies. But the new rabbis have me. I save their cherubic, freshly powdered rabbinic asses.

Rob Krasner is about to conduct his first wedding. He's just been ordained, and he's in my care for the summer. I arrive and wait for him at one of the infamous cookie-cutter wedding hotels on Long Island. Five brides in five seemingly identical gowns pass each other on the way into and out of the one bathroom.

I sit in the lobby, marveling at the length and faux opulence of the chandelier and the obvious wear on all the trimmings, and wondering why anyone would think that post-guillotine Versailles is a suitable decorative theme for weddings.

Krasner will appreciate the glitz in exactly the same way. He arrives. I tell him to comb his hair and button his jacket. I straighten his tie myself. His glasses need polishing, but I rise above mentioning it. I ask a tuxedoed official where we might find the bride, and we are ushered into a cubicle where the overly made-up young woman is sitting in a voluminous white bathrobe. She doesn't want to see her groom before the wedding, so Krasner has her sign the license and the traditional marriage contract in front of the witnesses, who then follow us to another cubicle to find the groom, who is already three sheets to the wind.

The signing completed, Krasner and I find the chapel and get oriented. Behind a cheesy white trellis trimmed with flaking faux greenery, we don our robes and then, books in hand, take our places underneath the floral bridal canopy. A bad string quartet is playing a medley from *Fiddler on the Roof.* This sends Krasner into fits of stifled laughter, which I tell him to can completely.

"Could you LOOK like a rabbi?" I ask him.

Abruptly there is a squawk of strings, followed by what is meant to be a fanfare. It sets my teeth on edge.

Krasner whispers, "Ew," then, "Ten bucks says it's Pachelbel's Canon."

"No way," I whisper back. "It's gonna be 'Sunrise, Sunset.' You're on."

He wins. But it's a Pyrrhic victory.

The groomsmen stumble out and swagger down the aisle, barely suppressing their laughter. Krasner and I are no longer amused. This is a sham. The groom comes out with his parents. He looks sheepish, but a glance from his mother puts him to rights. I note that his suit is oddly supple looking, but my attention becomes fully occupied by the parade of bridesmaids, who are all in identical halter-topped black leather minidresses. Fishnets and strappy sandals complete the look. Their rose bouquets are blood red and dripping black ribbons. Krasner is not whispering now.

The music changes to Elvis's "Can't Help Falling in Love," and in comes our bride. Gone is the capacious cotton robe. Though also white, her skintight leather dress reveals more than it covers. Her legs are encased in white leather high-heeled boots. The tops of her nipples are showing. Furthermore, they've been dusted with glitter.

I decide not to look at Krasner.

I chant the opening blessings of welcome. I wait for the rabbi's translation. It does not come. The silence continues. I glance sideways at Krasner. He's in a leather-induced trance. I chant another verse, hoping that he'll snap out of it. Nothing.

I angle myself subtly to the side and whisper, "Krasner!"

He blinks.

This is a relief. I can rule out catatonia. I murmur, "The book, Krasner. Look only at your book!"

He blinks.

In desperation I knock the *Rabbi's Manual* from his hands. As it hits the floor, he startles. I chant something from Song of Songs while he picks up his book, finds his place, and reorders the pages of his address. Young Rabbi Krasner recovers, and we marry the leather-clad couple.

On our way out of the hotel after the ceremony, I point out the preposterous chandelier.

"What?" asks Krasner.

"Nothing," I reply.

The Real Rabbi Larry Rappaport

What I like most about Temple Beth-El of Great Neck is the eyes of the people who regularly come to services. During services I sit in my assigned high-backed chair on the bima—the last of the occupied chairs, the closest to my lectern. This is a good seat. It's high above the congregation and affords a stadium view of the people and their eyes.

I adjust my robe over my legs, which are crossed at the ankles, knees leaning left. I hope I'm looking back at these people with a like-minded expression, because I love these people—these smart, savvy, well-styled Great Neck Jews with New York accents and impeccable footwear. They are willing to hear the truth from Rabbi Larry Rappaport, no matter how finely he slices and dices it, and they nod their coiffed heads, reaching their manicured fingertips into their wallets for their hard-won shekels to support the causes we embrace together.

I don't see Larry's eyes from here. I see the back of his handsome head. His regularly trimmed, faintly graying hair and the backs of the ears that he can wiggle at will for the amusement of young children.

I think suddenly of Three-Piece. He used to tell us that when we were seated on the bima, our eyes should be focused on the back of the head of whichever rabbi was speaking. (He had three!) This would convey respect for the speaker and set an example for congregants.

I am a good listener and a careful observer of Larry.

Larry is like the newest model of the rabbinic Cuisinart food processor—or one that hasn't yet been invented. He does what other rabbis do, but better and faster, with fancier attachments, less fuss, and less cleanup. He even sounds better.

I watch the back of his head while he slices, dices, shreds, grates, purees, and kneads. As he preaches, teaches, counsels, exhorts, marches, marshals, marries, buries, and consoles.

If a congregant is sleeping while Larry speaks, that congregant is either very old or works a night shift. Or maybe has a new baby. Even adolescents listen to Larry's sermons.

Larry is a taskmaster. Everyone on the temple staff quakes upon hearing his distinctive buzz on the intercom. Krasner and I joke about this until tears stream down our faces. Other folks in the office will just buzz you if they need you. *Bzzz.* When it's Larry, we'll hear a frantic, percussive buzzing, like that of a rabid bee in heat. *Bzzzzzz-bzz-bzz-bZZZ-ZZZ.* (Bees don't actually get rabies or go into estrus, but that's the sound.) The staff member thus summoned will immediately experience a fight or flight reaction—or faint (thus far in my experience without an accompanying bowel movement).

But genius phrases just seem to come to him. He'll come up with passages like this:

> Houses of Congress, hostile to the true obligations of
> government, . . . look away from human misery, while
> cutting school lunches to fund military redundancies.

When I hear these words, goose bumps rise, tears threaten, and I have to swallow. Then I lose a bit of focus because I begin to hope that there's going to be some lag time between these mighty words and my sermon anthem—because I'll need to catch my breath.

It's not that his voice thunders. It's that his intensity flashes.

So heaven help the assistant rabbi who slackens his pace for a moment or flings his suit jacket on the robing room floor because he is late. Or the cantor who thinks she can squeak by with a less-than-stellar Sing for Fun Club presentation at the High Holiday children's service, regardless of the lack of rehearsal time between the beginning of religious school and Rosh Hashanah.

What I learn from Larry is that although you'd goddamn well better leave the corners of your field unharvested so the poor can glean, you'd also damn well better farm the shit out of every other available etzba that's left.

Ginsberg and the Garment Bag

The Shabbat morning service, one in which three kids are called to the Torah, is long. I get my usual second wind as we return the Torah to the ark. Just the speeches, presentations, a few more prayers, and the closing song, and then home. I sit, not allowing my back to touch the velvet back of the pulpit chair, knees together and feet crossed at my ankles.

I automatically check the knee status of the two Bat Mitzvah girls. I signal the smaller one by putting two fingers on my knees over my robe. She knows now to put her own knees together. The bima is much higher than the pews, so girls need to pay attention. Or, rather, I need to make sure that they're decent. Larry would not be happy if ever a kid were slouching or exposed. I myself have terrible posture, but not on the bima. Or at least I hope not.

Finally, I smile my way invitingly through the closing song, "Ein Keloheinu (Nothing can compare to God)," eyebrows raised, thus indicating (nearly always in vain) to the members of the congregation that it is not a solo. The service is over. Shabbat Shalom.

I congratulate the B'nei Mitzvah, as does Larry and young Krasner, and as usual we head out the back door from the bima into the rear hallway and then into the robing room. Donald Freedman, our building superintendent, is there, waiting for us, looking uneasy and a bit flushed. We look at him and wait for his news, knowing that it will not be good.

Larry starts grinding his teeth before a word is spoken. Krasner and I exchange an uneasy glance.

Donald tells us that Sue Ginsberg, a well-liked, middle-aged congregant, had slipped out of the sanctuary early in the service and had gone into the bridal room. He knows this only because he found her dress on the floor in there. Donald pauses to swallow. Larry clenches his fists and rocks forward on his feet.

"Come ON, Donald," Larry prompts.

"She went into the kitchen and started eating hors d'oeuvres. A LOT of hors d'oeuvres, and very quickly, one after another."

"Wearing what?" I ask.

"A garment bag," Donald answers and looks down at his shoes.

"WHAT?" This from Larry. "What do you mean?"

"You mean a clear garment bag like from the cleaners?" I ask.

Donald nods and looks toward the door.

Krasner says, "Gotta go," and is gone.

I stifle a smile at Krasner's maturity level. Larry asks where Mrs. Ginsberg is, and Donald shrugs. This infuriates Larry.

"YOU DON'T KNOW WHERE SHE IS?"

"No," says Donald.

Larry gives me a long warning look, which I take to indicate that pulling a Krasner is not an option for me. So Donald, Larry, and I go down the hallways and up the steps to the temple office, where Larry calls Dr. Ginsberg, Sue's husband, who responds resentfully and refuses to come to pick her up. His pique is audible through the phone.

Larry hesitates a moment and then pronounces his verdict.

"We've got to find her."

I'm thinking, *I'm the fucking cantor! Why do I have to find her?* And I imagine that Donald is thinking, *I'm the building guy! Why do I have to find her?* But Larry knows better than to launch a search by himself. Headline: "Great Neck Senior Rabbi Caught with Naked Congregant."

Off we go to the Hebrew school wing. No sign of Sue. Through the administrative offices. Nothing. The choir room, the organ loft, back to the robing room. Nothing. Everything appears to be in order, except a small disturbance gradually coming to my mind.

It could have been me gorging on hors d'oeuvres. Sue is a very skinny woman, even skinnier than me. And I am that hungry too, pacing myself between yogurts. It could just as easily have been me shedding a too-tight sheath, if I owned a sheath, and opting instead for a bag, so light and loose.

I don't remember the last time I allowed myself to eat an hors d'oeuvre. Or a cookie at an oneg. I avoid eating between meals as if it were sinful. I'm wary of even one small slip. A forbidden bite of cheese or chocolate might initiate the collapse of my entire persona. The self-denying, well-regulated woman cantor. Always at the ready, always hungry, always focused. I wonder, *What AM I focused on? Or is this all just denial of appetite? Denial of the flesh?*

Wait—I'm not a nun. I'm not, not, not a nun. I am not called upon to eschew the material world or a human appetite. I can fill my belly and be religious at the same time.

I want to bite into a slab of Jarlsberg right now.

Then, just outside the robing room, we hear a rustling sound. We follow it to a storage area in back of the sanctuary where extra chairs are kept. Here is Sue, curled up underneath two chairs, looking bewildered, swathed in a clear plastic bag that's sticking to parts of her body. Under the bag, she's wearing a high-couture bra, panties, pantyhose, and just one spectacular patent-leather pump. Larry and Donald turn to face elsewhere, and I get down on my knees.

"Sue? Everything's fine. Come on out now, and we'll get you home. Donald, would you grab a choir robe?"

Sue is quite biddable, and she comes out from under the chairs.

"What? . . . How?" she asks.

"We take this off," I say in a Mary Poppins voice, peeling the garment bag away from her skin and casting it aside. "And we put this robe on you."

I zip her into the white choir robe, and Larry regains his power of speech.

"Ah, um, Sue! Let's head up to my study."

Donald goes back to work. Larry shepherds Sue. He even takes her elbow.

I go home and think about her. She must have had some kind of episode. I imagine that her stomach contracted in pain, that the unforgiving fabric chafed, that after releasing and feeding herself, she looked for a protective cave. To rest in.

I hope she divorces Dr. Ginsberg, I think as I peel the lid off my evening yogurt. *And I hope she buys some muumuus, granny panties, and comfort flats to wear while joyfully eating toasted brioche with a Quebec chèvre and shaved truffles.*

B'nei Mitzvah Mill

OCD can be a blessing. My B'nei Mitzvah preparation regimen benefits tremendously.

During the very first lesson, I orient my students to the mechanics of our coming-of-age ritual. I do this by means of Krasner's cartoon handout. He's a great cartoonist and has created soulful biblical images to depict the three parts of the Bible: the Torah, the Prophets, and the Writings. He's great at caricatures—so Moses looks properly stern, Jeremiah wild-eyed, and Deborah sagacious. Ruth is actually kind of sexy. Opposite the cartoon side of this handout is some basic vocabulary. *Mitzvah, haftarah* (that's right, kids, not "half-Torah"), *Torah, maftir, tikkun olam, iyyun t'filah*—words and phrases that all B'nei Mitzvah need to understand now and forever. Amen.

I go over this material during each child's first lesson, regardless of her or his level of comprehension. Otherwise I'd be a fraud, a cog in the B'nei Mitzvah mill. Thank God for the cartoon. Each student gets a copy, and I refer to it from time to time. I put each Torah reading and haftarah in context, and damned if we don't go over the key Hebrew words in each student's readings, including their root meanings. I am no cog.

Thereafter, each lesson follows an immutable pattern. My students must ritually spit out their gum at the beginning of each tutorial session. No blessing accompanies the spitting. I just thrust my wastebasket at them and they comply.

maftir: the last part of the Torah reading, leading to the haftarah ~ tikkun olam: repair of the world ~ iyyun t'filah: concentrated prayer

mitzvah: commanded deed done from religious duty ~ haftarah: selected reading from Prophets

With their newly unimpeded jaws, they must proceed to master
all of their Hebrew blessings, prayers, and texts. They must do this
one phrase at a time, all the while employing clear diction. And then
they must proceed to grasp them.

They must practice their speeches, counting one beat for each
comma and two beats for each period as they recite.

My OCD is necessary.

The pace is hellish. There are so many students—a hundred
in some years. Triple B'nei Mitzvah some Shabbat mornings. It
is my job to orient the families and to rehearse the Torah blessings with everyone in sequence during the hour before the service
begins. Ours is no casual shul. We've got ushers with carnations
and an electronic signal system. There can be no screwing up.
Over and over the routine I go, emphasizing the correct pronunci-
ation. Reminding the family members when to ascend and descend
the bima. Asking them to refrain from strangling the B'nei Mitzvah in sloppy embraces. Displays of extreme emotion are just not
appropriate here, I've been told. And when there are three students
per morning, time will not allow for all the smooching and cheek
pinching.

For everything there is a season. The whole B'nei Mitzvah cycle
at Temple Beth-El has benefited from my compulsions. I just can't
leave anything out—I have to go over every step in every rehearsal.
Very few family members come up to the bima at the wrong time
or spend prolonged periods weeping into the necks of their featured
progeny. My students' tallitot are carefully aligned and perfectly
folded, even if they need periodic tweaking (by me) during the service. My students make very few mistakes, and if they are about to,
I catch them and correct them in an undertone, as all cantors do.

I love many of them, though not all. But I'm fierce about each
one who stands on the bima. They are mine on that day. Sometimes
tears come to my eyes, too. I know their struggles and their secrets.
I've listened to the hesitating girl and heard hints of the woman
emerging behind her floppy bangs. I've listened to the clammed-up
boy and heard a word or two from the man he'll become.

tallitot: the plural of tallit (the fringed Jewish prayer shawl)

I am no cog in the B'nei Mitzvah mill. I am a cartoon-wielding obsessive companion for the grinding of the grain.

Behold Me

Hin'ni (Behold Me)—

Yes, I am here, on the bima, standing at my lectern on Rosh Hasha-nah evening. My prayer book is open to page 18 in Gates of Repentance. *I am worrying. My kids are miserable. Rosh Hashanah dinner holds no joy in our household—I'm too tense to pull either girl onto my lap or to linger over blessings. Am I failing them as a mother? Specifically, as a Jewish mother? They'll be asleep when I get home, having missed my lul-laby. Here I am—mother, daughter, cantor, and failure.*

Empty of Good Deeds—

Have I told my mother that the smells of the soup and challah she makes, burned or not, are the only holiday smells that my daughters will remember from childhood, and how much I love her for that? Have my hugs been long enough? Have I shortened them in my haste and tension and worry about my makeup?

Trembling and Frightened to Death—

Oh yes, I'm afraid. There was the Rosh Hashanah when my gray stack heels were criticized for being too casual for the bima, and the year that my skirt hung lower than my robe and was brought up for a brief discussion in the Ritual Committee meeting. Some, I know, still compare my voice to that of my predecessor, Neil Gluck, who sings like an angel and whose high notes open heaven's gates. And of course, I might cough. But mostly I agonize about whether or not I am fit for this task. At night dur-ing Elul I read S. Y. Agnon's Days of Awe. *I confess that only the folksy material sinks in and remains with me. So, oh yes, I am afraid. Also, it's true that I'd rather be reading fiction.*

Praise before the One Whose Throne Is Israel—

When I look out on the congregation, my eye skips over the people I don't know or don't like. It lingers each year on the people I love, and I love them even more on this night than I do on all the others. I see all

Elul: Harvest—the twelfth Hebrew month, a time of preparation for repentance

shofar: a ram's born, ritually sounded during on designated holidays ~ Zohar: Shining—the primary work of Jewish mysticism

Levi-Yitzchok . . . : a Chassidic rabbi of the eighteenth century who bargained with God

the gestures of affection and all the reaching for hands. Yes, I see the self-admired new shoes and hear the tinkling of bracelets. I imagine no reproach from on high. Even the Eternal One likes things that shine.

These are good and generous people, for the most part. The best part, the very best part, is the sound of the voices all together. I wait with antici-pation to hear "to bring the captives out of prison and those who sit in darkness from their dungeons." This is the Israel I love—the Israel that speaks of liberation and of light.

I Have Come to Stand before You and to Pray on Behalf of *Your* People, Israel—

It's just the beginning of the service, of these holy days. Here, from my lectern, I will give You all that I have. I've rehearsed all the music—the solo music, the instrumental music, and the choral music. I've drilled the junior choir. I've practiced many times over with the blower of the shofar, Larry's brilliant son. I've exercised my voice. I've gone over my Torah readings. Over and over. Yet I stand here remembering only the folksy tales from Agnon and not the passages from the Zohar or the Talmud. I am like Agnon's flute-playing boy in Days of Awe. *I know only my melody. Let it be good enough for this good community.*

Please Do Not Hold Them Accountable for My Sins—

I don't want to start thinking of my sins now. I'll start to cry. Even now my eyes are tearing. It says right here in the liturgy that I'm not deserving of this task. As hard as I work to become worthy, I will always beg You in this moment for forgiveness. I am like a child begging You, even as I try to shake off that imagery. Let me not fuck this up, and I will work to become a better person in this New Year. Ha! I am no Levi-Yitzchok Son of Sara of Berditchev to haggle with You! Go away, primitive reptilian bargaining voice! A cantor shouldn't sing as if she were a reptile!

I Am a Willful and Careless Sinner—

For the first time this year, I say I have sinned. I know I said it last year and that I will say it again every year. Still, let me do justice to this work! Let me feel Your presence. Then I will weave all that I feel and know and sense into the cloth of my prayer. Even my particular sins will color it. It will be an honest prayer, with uneven filaments, because its source is just one more Jew with a broken heart. I just happen to be stand-ing in the cantor's spot. Uphold me.

Bomb-Sniffing Dogs

The sanctuary is mostly clear of people. Donald Freedman, the ever-vigilant superintendent, is looking pretty pale. He's pointing at something. A bag lunch under a front row? On Yom Kippur? The Day of Atonement, a fast day? No, it's empty.

One of the maintenance men opens the door to the roof gar-den. I wish I could feel the breeze, but the door is too high above the bima. I am checking and double-checking my cue sheet and my music and my holiday prayer book. Of course it's all in order and has been for years now.

We're between services on Yom Kippur, and we're in the middle of a bomb scare. Larry announced it during the previous service. It happened while the choir and I were singing the words "The ways of the Torah are pleasantness and all its paths are peace." A note was passed from Donald to an usher to the president to Larry. The note passing generated considerable hushed discussion in the pews. Larry waited until the last chord evaporated. He got up from his seat and said into the microphone, "An anonymous tip was received by the Great Neck police that a bomb has been planted here in our sanctuary. If any among you wants to leave, please feel free to do so now—in a quiet and orderly manner. Rest assured that the police will be thoroughly checking the building during the break between morning and afternoon services. We continue on page 347."

What sangfroid! Perhaps fifty of the five hundred congregants left. Maybe some were bored or looking to escape the one inevi-table disaster of the day, the holiday parking lot scene. Maybe some were actually scared. Hard to say. I'm so used to steeling myself during worship that I don't know how I feel. Wait—here come the uniformed police officers and their dogs. The dogs are wearing har-nesses and straining forward, their tongues hanging out.

Do I feel something? I might. This might be nervousness. Or fear. Am I afraid? Why would someone call in a bomb threat? Why would someone place a bomb in a crowded synagogue on a holy day? People do these things, I know, but not to me or to my temple. Not to my Jews.

I'm too young to be obliterated in a matter of moments.

Wait—am I actually thinking that instant obliteration is the fate only of older people? Of only, say—older cantors? Of noncantors? Of non-Reform cantors? Of non-Jews? Of men? Older men? Male cantors who are Orthodox or maybe only Sephardic male cantors? Wait—are there any women Sephardic cantors? I don't think so.

So, what are my chances of being blasted to smithereens today? If it were today, the gates of heaven would be open, and my sins would be lighter than a feather and whiter than snow. Still, this is improbable at worst, right? A crank call from an anti-Semite to shake up a load of Jews on their holiest of days, right? What are the chances? Nil. Of course nil. Ridiculous. And in any event, I am a Jewish leader and a woman. I must stand firm, showing no fear. Imagine a cantor quaking in his boots. Preposterous! Imagine the first woman cantor running for cover as her people are blitzed to kingdom come. Some heroine! Whatever comes, I will chant penitential texts with all due focus, knowing that as my flesh is consumed, my people will ascend heavenward with my song between their souls and all pain. Yes! This is what I was born to do.

Am I listening to what I'm thinking here? A bomb-sniffing dog is probably pooping under the Eternal Light while I'm beatifying myself.

Now I'm worried that my heavenly armpits might smell. This black robe is a curse. Lightweight as it is, it's another layer. Other congregations don't require their clergy members to wear these relics!

Should I check my makeup? If I do, I'll never stop fixing it. Better not.

Maybe I should hit the robing room, take off my robe and atarah, and retie my bow-neck collar. Then I could tuck my blouse farther into my skirt too. No, I should leave well enough alone.

Should I sit down in my office for a few minutes? No, can't relax too much. It'll be too hard to relaunch. Maybe I'll find Krasner and we can chat. Swap some bomb-sniffing dog jokes. Make fun of something. Imitate a congregant's Brooklyn accent. Do something we'll still have an hour or two to repent for. I'll ask him for the hundredth time if my butt looks big in this robe.

atarah: crown—a prayer shawl with a special neck band worn by officiants on the bima

Blessings, Ad Nauseam

Somewhere I read that a baby who doesn't have a toy to play with will compulsively twiddle her hands instead. This begins to make sense to me as I teach the Torah and haftarah blessings to scores of kids every weekday afternoon at twenty-minute intervals between 3:50 and 7:10. The blessings share twenty-two words in common, and it is mind-numbing to hear the same words over and over, recited at the same pitch. So I put my mind elsewhere, set my voice to patient, congenial mode, and have child after child repeat phrase after phrase time after time. Between students, I ritually imagine punching a hole in the leaded glass window of my study. This is how the days go by between Sabbaths.

During the inaugural lesson, I obsessively explain the structure of the Bible and the greatest hits in that kid's portion. Like why Miriam sang an encore after Moses's long aria. The hits ensure ringing Bar Mitzvah Speech Sound Bites when the kids fill in the Mad-Libs Bar Mitzvah Speech puzzles that are handed to them by the assistant rabbi.

I do the text talks well, but most kids don't care much, and my energy wanes. And there is much more drilling of text than time spent in discussion of text. Every single child must be letter-perfect on the bima. Or the family will feel cheated. And will quit. And membership numbers will go down. And the cantor's reputation will be shot to Gehinnom. And there will be BUDGET PROBLEMS. And the cantor will be fired. And I will be known to one and all as a ne'er-do-well. The first shall be last.

I think of my weekly three B'nei Mitzvah students, whom I have been instructed to align according to their abilities—so the weak one reads his portion in the middle, between the average pupil, who goes first, and the inevitably gifted kid, who goes last. I imagine the consequences of putting the weakest first, and the travesty of placing the strongest in the middle. I smile. To remain conscious between lessons, I fill in assignment sheets with colored markers—nine of them. I clean my desk with Windex between twenty-minute tutorials. I apportion one dietetic chocolate mint candy per three students.

Gehinnom: essentially Hell, or a place of spiritual purification where a soul lives for a while after death

I am playing with my hands. Like an understimulated baby.

My baby, Tali, gets plenty of stimulation from her parents and her other dedicated caregivers.

Her older sister, too, gets a good amount of encouragement and challenge, at home and at Temple Beth-El's nursery school every day. Hana's in good hands there, but I see that her wardrobe marks her as poor. Her cheap cable-knit tights pill all over and sag at the crotch. Her budget hair ribbons go limp at the tips. The polyester lace on her socks is fraying. Fortunately, from time to time she is generously offered Erica Troyan's hand-me-downs.

I look down at the long, plain wool skirt that Mom made me and the lace trimmed, high neck white blouse from Sears. I think of their identical sisters in my closet, and I sigh. I can't afford designer outfits. Occasionally, if I find a sale, I'll buy a Laura Ashley dress to wear on Shabbat. But the dresses aren't actually any more fun, just more floral.

I'm not the only one who notes the slight shabbiness of my wardrobe. Generous Susan Troyan starts giving me her hand-me-downs too. These are spectacular—bright and well cut, made of beautiful fabrics. But the red-and-black fit-and-flare dress that looks smashing on Susan washes me out.

I am not destined to fit in with the Great Neck crowd. I will always feel either scruffy or costumed.

I start fantasizing about a smaller Midwestern synagogue— where life is less frenetic, where the dress is more casual, where there is more parking. I imagine the relief of parking my car any-where within inches of my destination and reducing my worry about the long-term presentability of my winter coat and boots. How badly does the salt show? How is it that Great Neck women don't get salt on their boots?

It's 3:30 on a weekday, and the B'nei Mitzvah Mill machinery is revving up. I so hate that phrase, and yet I am the master miller of Beth-El. I oversee the breaking, winnowing, and rolling of the grist. I don't know how much longer I can add gluten to artificially enrich my so-called deficient middle students. Sometimes that middle boy—and it's usually a boy, still playing obsessively with Transformers—is proficient at some one thing that is not displayed on the bima during a Shabbat morning service.

If we were less of an assembly line, middle boys could be helped to draw some analogy in their speeches between whatever that proficiency is and whatever happens to be the assigned Torah reading on his particular date.

How many hours I spend standing, rehearsing with these boys in the sanctuary, calling, "Louder, Sammy! Pause for two counts after each period! Wait! I can't understand you; you're going too fast! The word is 'Eye-ZAY-uh' or 'Nee-ha-MY-uh.' One syllable at a time, Sammy!"

Between the stress of maintaining Bar Mitzvah Performance Standards and the lack of parking, I don't know how much longer I can be grateful for hand-me-downs or worry about the suitability and breadth of my shoe collection.

I fish out the clear nail polish from my purse. I have a run in my drugstore pantyhose. I need to end this chapter of my career. I need more stimulation. My fingers are all twiddled out. As the polish dries, I call Cantor Richard Abravanel, placement director of the American Conference of Cantors. It's time for these fingers to reach farther, to perform other tasks, tasks that feel like building something.

Interview Gauntlet

The job interview is going well. Still, it's so bright in Santa Clara that I'm not sure I would easily adjust to it after Great Neck. Everything here is yellow and blue. Great Neck is pretty gray, now that I think of it.

I've kept up the obligatory banter with the search committee chair. I've used every ounce of my strength. I do this well, but it's been a strain. I left Dan, Hana, and Tali to finish up our family vacation without me—so I could fly here—and I am worrying about them. Not that Dan can't take care of everything. But it seems unfair that he has to travel back from Maine without me. That's a long car trip with two little girls—two crabby little girls on the way home from a fun but exhausting vacation.

My spirits are flagging. There were many connecting flights between Maine and here, and I arrived in the San Jose airport with a mighty migraine that shows no signs of dissipating.

I am on my way to meet with the senior rabbi. My audition suit has traveled from Great Neck to Bar Harbor to Santa Clara, and I've ironed or steamed every inch of it. Of course it's wrong for California, but it's what I have. Wool, charcoal wool—dark and heavy. All of my blouses are white, but of course I deliberately choose the right one for each occasion. I've brought the one with the wide-winged collar. I hope I radiate seriousness and dignity because this meeting is, well—it's pivotal.

I am invited into the senior rabbi's study, and I sit in the chair opposite his desk. We begin to talk. We talk about trust and confidentiality. We talk about how to disagree. Suddenly, somehow, the rabbi is talking about "sharing special moments." His eyes are boring into mine, and the intensity of his stare sets me a bit on edge. I am not sure what to make of concentrated eye contact. A brief knock at the door, and the assistant rabbi comes bounding in.

Abruptly he dismisses her. "This is a private interview—you're not needed," he tells her.

She withdraws, deflated, without a word, but the atmosphere is charged. Then he says, "Odd that she would insert herself between us at this moment, no?"

I think, *Um, no it's not—she's your assistant rabbi,* but I don't say a word.

He asks me to "go into *D*epth about my *P*ersonal *P*assions." He stresses the *d* and the *p*'s.

Thinking, *Uh-oh,* I launch quickly and a little loudly into something about literary fiction.

He quotes *Anna Karenina*: "He stepped down, trying not to look long at her, as if she were the sun, yet he saw her, like the sun, even without looking."

Then his intercom buzzes, sparing me from having to think up another way to seem oblivious. It's time to meet the rest of the staff.

And then it's time for lunch. My headache has blossomed and is pressing against my right eyebrow. I will not be able to eat. We are in a lovely, open greenhouse of a restaurant. The light is attacking my eyes. When I move my head, my stomach seizes. Black dots appear at the edges of my field of vision.

The maître d' seats me between the senior rabbi and the president of the congregation. Although I have a menu, the rabbi spreads his in front of me and puts his hand around my waist to pull me closer. His thumb extends upward, under my jacket and blouse. It brushes against the lower edge of my bra. As subtly as possible, I shift away in my seat, retuck my blouse, and take a sip of water. After lunch I confess my headache and ask to be taken to the hotel. I throw up before I close the door to the room.

By the next day, I am rejected by the search committee.

My audition at Temple B'rith Kodesh in Rochester, New York, is as smooth and straightforward as my Santa Clara interview was bizarre and disconcerting. The senior rabbi's politics are right up my alley. The leadership is strongly aligned with the Union of American Hebrew Congregations. The executive director is a Soldan High School contemporary of my father. A well-known Jewish composer, Professor Samuel Adler, who is chair of the Composition Department at Eastman School of Music, is a member of the congregation. His late father, Hugo Chaim, was a famous Belgian cantor-composer!

The stars seem to align. The salary is an improvement, and housing costs are low. It feels so right that I am not even surprised to be offered the position.

I take it without hesitation.

Day Sledding

Nina—a congregant, neighbor, and friend—suggests a winter outing, and I'm overjoyed. Or at least I *want* to be overjoyed. I have no ideas for my girls beyond museums, greenhouses, and zoos. We set out in her station wagon for Greece Canal Park. She has daughters who are six and three, a little older than mine. Nina and her daughters are many inches taller than my girls and me.

We arrive to find that the snow in the park is deeper than we expected. The girls are delighted. Nina is undaunted—the snow is hardly over her ankles. It's up to my calves. I wish I were at the Lamberton Conservatory in Highland Park. Preferably the desert section.

It's so quiet that the girls attempt to tiptoe with their boots. So immediately, and with a great flourish, Tali falls down and everyone laughs. Nina tries to restore the mood and whispers that we might see chickadees. She reaches around for her pack, taking out the sunflower seeds she's thought ahead to bring. She shows the girls how to hold out and flatten their mittened palms, and then she stands stock-still, hand out herself. We all try to imitate her perfect posture. *Please*, I think, *please let a chickadee land on Hana's hand.* And after a few moments, one does. Hana freezes, perhaps with fear or perhaps with wonder. The tiny bird stays long enough to grab a seed. A second lands on her mitten one heartbeat later. Soon all but Tali have fed the little birds. I undergird Tali's hand with mine and still it, even as she shifts in her boots, getting bored.

I whisper, "This is it. Here it comes, Tali!"

And yes, one brave chickadee lands long enough to be catapulted off as Tali squeals with delight, scattering her seeds in the snow.

We continue on our walk. Nina has also brought trail mix in little hand-sewn cloth bags. (I left some goldfish cracker packets in the car. I must look wasteful and unimaginative.) Tali picks out and eats all the carob chips and leaves the rest untouched. Hana picks out all the pretzel pieces.

We come to a downward slope, slick with ice. Nina declares that there is only one way to conquer it and promptly slides down on her slender butt. Have I mentioned how much I envy my willowy, cello-playing neighbor?

The girls follow suit, on their butts, screaming with pleasure.

That means it's my turn. An attempt at judiciously lowering myself to the ground is unavoidable. I plop instead. I force a smile. But then, whooshing down the hill, I surprise myself and succumb to winter's magic, realizing that it's been too long since I've let myself whoosh—maybe even since that furtive midnight sledding trip on Homewood Avenue. Whoosh, indeed! How primal!

I still prefer prim to primal.

Peace with Christmas Carols

NPR sings them to me. Elevators sing them to me. Shops sing them to me. I have a new relationship to Christmas carols, and I love them anew each winter. It's been many years since I've been compelled to sing them in school or in chorus. I no longer resent them or feel guilty about singing them softly in the mall. I love the ones with many verses, all of which I remember. "Good King Wenceslas." "The Twelve Days of Christmas." I picture five golden rings on those sustained notes. Those old carols, despite their focus on a holy baby, soothe my soul. Every year I hum my way through Christmas.

A Short Stay in Sacred Covenant

Temple B'rith Kodesh is located conveniently between the Brighton Public Library (about which the temple's cantorial search chair had remarked, "They got a lotta books in there, my wife tells me") and the Princess Diner. My shiny-haired, baby-cheeked organist, James Cochran, calls that eatery "La Principessa." After services on Friday nights, organist James, assistant rabbi Judy Levi-Green, and I can often be found laughing over a glass of wine or cup of coffee at La Principessa.

That is because no one at B'rith Kodesh stays for long at the oneg Shabbat. I barely shed my robe before the cookie trays have been ravaged and all but the infirm elderly have vanished. Eliezer Behrmann, our senior rabbi, does not tolerate receiving lines, which he calls "goyish." I wince at the word. I know what he means, but still.

Rabbi Behrmann confounds me. Some days I am welcome in his presence, and some days he is curt, even sullen when I enter his study. Then he'll apologize, but without looking me in the eye. I love his politics and respect his views. He's my kind of prophetic Jew and my kind of injured man. His sermons are not always written with three points in mind, but they ring out, especially if the daily news is bad or a particular theme has struck home with him. But his behavior veers between sublime and ridiculous. Once during a staff meeting, Rabbi Behrmann trimmed his fingernails with the office paper cutter.

Judy and I often try to decipher or articulate the nature of his rabbinate and just as often fail.

Judy, for all her radical ways and advanced feminism, loves to shop. I accompany her. This involves shoe boutiques, regardless of snow or cold.

In the summer months, when James and I meet for lunch, he'll ask me to drive him around the temple grounds beforehand, on the lookout for lawn workers. He'll tell me to slow down or even to stop if he catches sight of shirtless, fine-looking lads.

James and Judy are my Rochester siblings.

I like Rochester, its music, its quaint downtown, its lilacs. The temple folk are smart and talkative. It's a given here that each bar mitzvah, each bat mitzvah, is taught as an individual. There is no single Standard of Bima Perfection. I do less rote teaching and enjoy figuring out a solid Mitzvah curriculum with Judy. Services are informal, and Rabbi Behrmann laughs unabashedly from the bima. The junior choir rejects the idea of choir regalia. For services, most of the kids wear whatever they wore to school that day. Others dress up. (One of these is conscripted junior choirgirl Hana Gertz.) My work is less onerous, and I can park anywhere I want, moments after arriving.

But there are underground synagogue politics and machinations afoot here. I can't even play chess or Stratego, so I can't figure out how to maneuver in life or in temple politics. I can recognize when others do it well, but I don't know how to do it myself.

I am asked to attend a private executive committee meeting, and so of course I do. Insinuations about Rabbi Behrmann are being made as I enter the room. His car has been spotted in a seamy part of town, and that can only mean one thing, they say. I am left to wonder what one thing that is. Might it not be a social action project?

I now remember him saying to me, "Mouthwash. Listerine. That's all it was."

Another thing Eliezer always says: "Remember that what they tell us in AA is true. When you point an accusatory finger, three other fingers are pointing back toward you."

I have no time to work this out in full, but some pieces fall into place.

"Cantor, we're glad you came. We've got a few questions about the workplace environment. Gerry, would you proceed?" (Gerry is the St. Louisan who long ago attended high school with my dad and aunt. Now he is the temple's executive director.)

"Barb," he says in his Missouri accent, "how is it for you working with Eliezer?"

"Well, we're just getting to know each other, but I really respect his values and his goals for the congregation."

"Okay, but how is he to work with?"

"Fine. What do you mean?"

"Well, would you say he is even-tempered?"

The president interrupts. "Cantor, we know it's not easy working with Eliezer. He's volatile in the workplace. Everyone says so. We want you to know that we're on your side. We have great hopes for B'rith Kodesh with you on board. When Judy finishes her time here, we'll find a new assistant, and we'll be moving forward. With or without Eliezer. You're a part of our new vision. We want you to know that you have our support going forward. Here's the bottom line. Eliezer has problems. Hell, we ALL have problems, but we're not ALL rabbis. Last week I had three complaints about the rabbi. He didn't wash his hair. He wore jeans to work. He smelled like whiskey. YESTERDAY I got a call that he didn't get out of his chair to see a lady out of his study! What have YOU noticed, cantor?"

"Um. Nothing."

"Well," Gerry says, "we know you've seen something. The ladies in the office have. I'm guessing Judy has. I have."

"Um, I, uh, I've just been trying to plan out services with him and do my teaching. I haven't been spending time looking at the rabbis. We plan which one of us goes to which hospital on which days and, um, we had to cancel this week's staff meeting—"

"Yes, the Schulman funeral."

"I heard they didn't want HIM there," says Gerry.

"Really, the family didn't want the rabbi?" the president asks.

I remember that we were told in our human relations class: Never defend your rabbi. At the time, I assumed the point was that the lowly cantor should not even presume to weigh in on a subject other than liturgical music.

But this is a new time. Cantors are beginning not to PRE-SUME, but to ASSUME expertise. I know what I know, and I am qualified to speak. I am also able to refuse to rat out my rabbi and align myself with a false cause.

And I identify with Eliezer. And I feel bad. I've also made no friends in Rochester other than the assistant rabbi, a few officers of the congregation, the organist, and Nina. Dan's been working in Buffalo and has to commute daily on the Thruway, so it's been hard to socialize. It's been lonely. And now this.

I start to think about leaving B'rith Kodesh.

Exposed by My Teeth

At first I assume my teeth are yellowing. Then I notice that I can't bear cold liquids—particularly on my back teeth. When I look closely, I see that it's not that my teeth are yellowing; it's that the enamel is worn away in spots. And my gums are receding here and there.

It must be from the tons of tea I used to drink. Enough, appar-ently, for it to darken and erode my teeth. It could also be from the packets and packets of Sweet'N Low I used to put in the tea and on my grapefruit and cantaloupe and apples and then on my oatmeal. That might have had some effect.

I'm too embarrassed to see the dentist. I mention my bad teeth to Trudy Lewis, a rabbi friend, whose father is a retired local dentist. She suggests that I see him to get his opinion. He is kind enough to see me in my office at B'rith Kodesh. I position my desk chair under the high windows. Dr. Lewis is soft-spoken, serious, and bearded. I sit in my chair and tilt my head back, opening my mouth. He turns my head this way and that, angling it in relation to the light.

"You'll need crowns," he says.

He tells me to go to the Strong University Dental Clinic, which is mere blocks from the temple and from my house.

His matter-of-fact statement and lack of surprise at my evil-looking mouth give me the courage to phone for an appointment.

I consult with a Dr. Samuel Kahan. After he gently examines me, without comment he reaches up to snap off the overhead light. On the chair he pushes an invisible button, and I find myself upright. I turn to look at him.

"Are you still making yourself throw up after meals?" he asks.

I swallow hard. "No, I haven't done that for nearly ten years."

"Well, you have bulimia teeth."

"Oh."

Dr. Kahan fixes my teeth in eight sessions, each lasting about four hours. My mouth is filled with porcelain. Although I am thirty-six years old, I ask my parents to pay. This is bold. I think the total cost is twelve thousand dollars. I don't tell them precisely how I damaged my teeth.

I'm not sure that I will ever earn Rabbi Simon's proverbial crown of a good name, but Mom and Dad buy me many tiny crowns that hide, if not adorn, my shame.

Oma and Opa Come to Visit

Mom and Dad (Oma and Opa to the girls) are visiting us at our house in Rochester. They won't stay long. When Dad is with

In Pirkei Avot (Ethics of the Ancestors), Rabbi Simon said, "There are three crowns: the crown of Torah, the crown of priesthood, and the crown of royalty. However, the crown of a good name is greater than all of them."

the girls, he's always detached, anxious to escape, or somewhere in between.

Predictably, dinner with the Oparents (a nickname coined by Uncle Simon) is a disaster. Dad finishes his generous servings of food immediately and begins fixing to go upstairs to the guest room, not to reappear until breakfast, after which the Oparents will depart posthaste. Mom uses practiced, gentle words to suggest that he remain at the table so we can have an intergenerational dinner conversation together. Dan tries valiantly to find a topic. I worry about our white dining room carpet and the possible consequences of a dinner with the girls over it.

Hana and Tali have wanted to be excused since minutes after the meal began. Dan and I insist that they stay in their chairs.

I suggest that Hana tell all of us about the Native American diorama she's making in school.

Opa actually expresses interest. "Yes, tell me about your diorama. You know, I've been collecting Indian artifacts since I was your age, Hana. Which nation's culture are you depicting?"

Hana looks down and whispers, "Indians."

Opa tries again. "Which tribe? Although it's preferable to say 'nation.'"

"I dunno."

Then, inevitably, Dad moves on. "Well, Ruth, I'm going up to bed. It's been a long day." He addresses none of the rest of us. While he heads for the stairs, Dan and I exchange a knowing glance.

Oma makes an attempt at starting a conversation. "How is your work at the temple going, Dan?"

As Dan begins to answer, Hana throws her spoon at Tali's head—hard and probably for a good reason.

I get up and go find the *101 Dalmatians* video, since dinner is clearly over. I park Hana and Tali in front of the family room TV.

With the girls thus diverted, Mom starts to steer me back into the kitchen. Dan goes to the study to work.

"I just need to fill you in on Dad's depression," she whispers.

I tell her that I'll be all ears in a minute or two, but I'm lying. I don't want to know how much he's sleeping during the day. I don't want to know that he regularly wonders if his life is worth living.

Dad, Dad, Dad, and Dad! He's been circling his drain, and Sarah, Simon, and I have been trapped in his vortex for as long as I can remember!

I don't ever want to be sucked toward that drain again.

I turn toward Mom, dutifully, eyebrows raised, but my brain is screaming, *So let him kill himself already and leave us in peace!*

But Tali comes in, grabs Mom's hand, and begs her to come see the dramatic entrance of Cruella de Vil. My relief comes in a gust.

Mom proceeds to the family room couch to snuggle with Hana, taking Tali onto her lap. The sinister music coming out of the TV is like a balm to my irritated mind. I won't hear about Dad's depression tonight.

Before Cruella can reveal her diabolical plans vis-à-vis the adorable coats of many Dalmatian puppies, we begin to hear deep snoring coming from the guest room above us. Its resonance and cadence make it impossible to ignore.

Dan returns and begins to clean up the dishes. I rub club soda into four stains on the carpet and then begin working over the kitchen counters with Windex.

Another visit from the Oparents nears its conclusion.

A Better Place

After two fraught years, I do leave B'rith Kodesh. We move to suburban Buffalo, near Dan's congregation, Temple Beth Am, which was ready to give me a part-time cantorial position. I also take a thirty-hour-per-week job as director of adult services at the Buffalo Jewish Community Center. I am lucky to have landed here with work, meaningful work.

The JCC has assumed the responsibility of introducing newly arrived Soviet Jews to Buffalo. I sit at my JCC desk, trying to come up with programs that will appeal to "New Americans." No single program will work for all new Americans though, of course. I puzzle over the challenge. What will be helpful? What will be popular?

Beth Am: House of the People

What will bring groups of families together? I know what it takes to be a cantor, but I don't know how to be a program director.

So as my first workweek ends, I'm eager to stand on my new Buffalo bima.

We're in the early days, but things at Beth Am look like they'll be uncomplicated. Robert Nussbaum, the rabbi, was at HUC with me, as was his wife, Lois, who was a fiery religious education major. These are people I know, working in a synagogue that will soon feel like home.

Erev Shabbat arrives, and I stand at my new lectern smiling. This is going to be fun! Robert reveals himself as a stellar guitarist who happens to sing like Bob Dylan. His fingers grind out a bass line that struts rather than walks. His twelve steel strings sing along with Dan and me.

My mind wanders happily. Robert, Lois, Dan, and I are going to be friends. Nancy Nathan, the temple administrator, is a hard worker, friendly, and funny. Congregational life is going to be good.

We rock the closing song and head for the social hall. At the oneg Shabbat, I am introduced to Greta Rachilson, the religious school secretary. Five minutes into conversation with her, I realize that she has the IQ of a rocket scientist. She looks like another friend in the making.

Okay, so I hate the ark. It's ovoid, with horizontal bars that bisect it in freakish ways. The stained glass on its outer edges is fluorescent yellow with blood-red tentacles woven through.

If the only drawback to life in Buffalo is an ugly ark, I am definitely in a better place.

The Viper in the F

I've been taking voice lessons continuously—singing scales, performing vocal exercises—since the age of eleven. And every time I've ever gone for the high F, I've felt the crackle. It doesn't hurt; I just hate the sound. So I've learned to stop short when the crackle threatens. (I can feel it coming, always.) I can't allow ugly to come out of my throat as did toads and vipers from the mouth of

erev Shabbat: the evening on which Shabbat begins

the unkind daughter in the French fairy tale *Diamonds and Toads*. I'd rather sing within a limited range than risk the emergence of a snake—than expose the truth that I'm not a real singer.

And there's another truth I'm avoiding too: I'm feeling invisible to Dan.

If you are ugly, you work very hard. You are a dazzling conversationalist. You remember particulars about people and trot them out to your advantage. You stay thin, or at least keep the fatness at bay. Always you are polite. You make a life's work of ferreting out the most flattering and long-wearing cosmetic brands. You travel great distances for good haircuts. You maintain a long, complex beauty routine that must not be attenuated or interrupted. When you speak to beautiful people, you are distracted by your envy and you think, *But I can sing*, knowing very well that one doesn't say such things out loud. Certainly a dazzling conversationalist doesn't.

Once Tali was toilet trained—an event that, in her case, was a small miracle from the Eternal One—I had time to talk to friends in my book club about marital love. We would talk in fits and starts about husbands and their ever-declining libidos. Mostly we laughed, making sure that we all understood the lightness of the subject.

But for me it isn't really light. I'm still trying to be a dazzling conversationalist, still tending assiduously to my makeup and to my weight, but my husband no longer seems to notice. My verbal flirtations now seem to fall on deaf ears.

Dan and I talk about our girls, about work, about people we know in common, but these conversations are no longer lively and bright, like they were earlier in our marriage. Am I making enough effort?

It must be me. Me and my impossibly high standards. Or maybe it's just that I've reached a new, nonsparkly stage of life. Nothing shines forever, right? These changes are common in marriages that are as old as Dan's and mine, right? Dwelling on the ordinary and inevitable process of fading is just a manifestation of my vanity. Everything fades. Besides, what would I do to stop something as unavoidable as the passage of time?

I would be a better singer if I took risks and vocalized beyond the crackling notes at the upper end of my range. This is what a true singer would do. Am I a pretend singer?

Am I also a pretend wife? I would be a better wife if I called the question.

So I am dealing with this truth the same way I deal with my high F. I hazard nothing in my marriage and I hazard nothing vocally.

There is only so much truth, only so much ugliness, I will allow to be exposed.

"We Are the World," Buffalo-Style

Reverend Bennett Walker Smith and I have been working on our interfaith children's choir concert for months now. It's a fund-raiser for African famine relief. The performance itself will start in twenty minutes.

St. John Baptist Church here in Buffalo is packed. My choir kids have been behaving nicely until now, but watching them, I feel the first buzz of a migraine. Is there time for me to inject my medicine? I dig into my purse and find the vial. Where's the needle? Got it. Clutching both, I duck into the washroom and pop off the bottle's yellow cap. I draw up .5 mg of sumatriptan and plunge the needle through my pantyhose and into my thigh. Heading back to the sanctuary, I breathe slowly in and out.

Each of the two children's choirs will perform a set of songs, and then we'll conclude (no intermission) with a final song all together. One hour, tops. Then cookies.

The Beth Am kids will sing first, in a few minutes. They're getting even more restless. We need to assemble them right now.

I'm worried. During rehearsal, we gave the kids instructions about logistics. We told them the order of the songs they would sing with their groups. All the kids have assigned spots for performances. I'm not too worried about that. What I'm worried about is the mechanics of the combined choir piece. Reverend Smith told his kids and I told mine that before our final piece, each child should find a spot next to a singer from the other group.

Now that we're here, I'm thinking, *This isn't going to work. We already have chaos, and the concert hasn't even started.*

I try to track Tali's whereabouts but can't. She is everywhere and nowhere. Tali is at the youngest age for junior choir—seven. What was I thinking?

Wait. Dan must have sprung into action! The small soloists are coming together right in front of me, eager to grab the microphone, ready to sing. Do we have a shot at success?

I tell myself to relax and switch off the radar. I realize that my headache is gone.

I signal to Dan that we're as ready as we're ever going to be. He begins to play the piano introduction, and the room becomes quiet. Miraculously all forty of my kids are in place. The sixty-odd St. John kids are seated and waiting their turn. Maybe God exists after all.

My students sing "Miriam's Song."

> Miriam was a prophet
> > and she played a tambourine.
> The women, they all followed her
> > and danced in a line.
> Miriam and the little girls
> > they sang out loud:
> This song is high
> > and belongs to God!"

What follows is the sound of thunderous applause.
Then Reverend Smith's kids are up. They sing:

> Wade in the water
> Wade in the water, children,
> Wade in the water
> God's gonna trouble the water.

See that band all dressed in red
God's going to trouble the water
Looks like the band that Moses led
God's gonna trouble the water.

Wade in the water
Wade in the water, children,
Wade in the water
God's gonna trouble the water.

Now the applause is endless, fervent.

The armpits of my blouse are wet.

It's quiet again while everyone waits for the finale that these hundred-plus children have learned. They have memorized every word of Michael Jackson and Lionel Ritchie's "We Are the World."

Rusty, whose light brown hair is gelled into little spikes, begins the song with the first line—his voice high and clear.

He is our muezzin, calling out that it is time to do God's work.

Shameeka, her hair in two exploding shiny ponytails, joins him—her voice a sweet tremolo.

She is our Deborah, chanting the magic pitches that transform prayer into action.

When the other singers join them, the precision is gone, but not the message.

In the very front row, Rachel's pink butterfly clip catches on the tip of Jayani's braid. They look at each other warily for a second. Then they giggle as Jayani expertly releases her hair without missing a note.

The audience holds its breath, listening as their kids sing the same notes and the same lyrics at the same time. Together, if not quite synchronously.

I blink hard to prevent actual tears and look for Tali.

Things That Shatter

There is a famous omission in the fourth chapter of Genesis, a gap in the story.

The Torah text says, "Cain said to his brother Abel . . . and when they were out in the field, Cain went up against his brother Abel and he killed him."

To acknowledge this gap, we use an ellipsis, three small dots in a row.

Those three dots appear in this story because the details omitted are not what's important.

~ ~ ~ ~ ~

If I just glue the two pieces together and put a rubber band around them, that'll fix it. No, a big clasp will do a better job.

I'm at the kitchen table mending the Israeli-made ceramic matchbox I use to store Shabbat matches. I am anxious and assigning myself little tasks because Dan is late. He's never late. His mother, Martha, has just called for the second time, wondering where he is. He always picks her up to bring her to our house for Shabbat dinner. Where is he?

I'm happy for the moment that Hana is away at an out-of-town synchronized swim event. She would be irate about the delayed dinner, wanting to get on with her evening. Tali doesn't keep track of time yet, fortunately.

It's now been a half hour. I have to be on the bima, welcoming Shabbat, in an hour.

Okay, that's it. I call Robert, our rabbi, and ask him if he knows anything. I know this is futile, but I expect to be reassured—Robert is so laid back. I prepare to relax. Instead he says nothing consoling at all and tells me to call Nancy, the temple administrator. I call her, and she asks me in a soft voice if I've called the hospitals.

"No," I say, "but they would have called me, wouldn't they?"

"Yes," she sighs.

My heart is noisy in my chest, and I ask if I should call the police, and without hesitation she says yes in that soft voice. I do.

I register the sardonic tone of voice before I understand the words. The officer tells me that my husband is being held. . . .

I hang up the phone. I take out my car keys. I take Tali to her friend Adam's house and tell Adam's mom, Jeanette, that I need to pick Dan up. . . . She gives me a quick hug and assures me that she will keep Tali as long as necessary. She shows no surprise and doesn't ask a single question. In that moment, she is heaven-sent.

I arrive at the police station and meet the arresting officer. Hardly a "plainclothes" cop, he's wearing tight, artlessly frayed denim hot pants, rainbow suspenders, a muscle shirt. Tan and sleek, he is Steamboat Park's God of Entrapment. . . .

I post bail. I drive Dan home.

The next morning when I get up onto the bima, I do not know if any sound will come out of my mouth. It does, and I sing, and then I sing again. I pay attention to my student and guide him. The Bar Mitzvah boy asks where Cantor Dan is, and I say that he's not feeling well. I wonder for a moment if this boy will have good memories of his Bar Mitzvah day. By the end of the service, the news has gotten out.

I've made an emergency appointment with Eva Fried, my friend and an experienced psychiatrist, and I head to Erie County Medical Center to see her in her office. I feel like my next steps are in her hands, and I drive with a sense of purpose.

When I return, I find that Tali is home and Hana is too, watched by their downcast but determined grandmother. I don't see Dan, and I don't look for him.

The news of Dan's arrest is on all the local TV and radio stations and in the paper. There are news cameras shooting through our windows. On the screen there is footage of our backyard swing gently swaying back and forth behind a reporter describing Dan's position as educational director at the temple and his work with nursery school children.

I can hardly contain my anger at the almost gleeful sensationalism. My hatred expands to the furthest edges of my mind. With this anger that pushes all other thoughts out of its way, how will I find the words I need to explain this to my eleven- and eight-year-old children?

Hana cries, and Tali copies her out of confusion and anxiety.

That night, I don't sleep. I just go over angry things. Over and over. This is just the first of many nights like this, I'm sure, and I am angry about that too.

Meanwhile there is tomorrow's junior choir performance of *Brundibár*, an opera originally performed by the children imprisoned in the Theresienstadt concentration camp. We've been planning and working on this nonstop for over a year. The choir children, Dan, and I have been rehearsing intensively.

Junior choir parents have designed and painted sets, sewn elaborate costumes, created backdrops, developed publicity. I've drilled voice parts and coached diction, taught about the folktale itself and judiciously, cautiously, about the tragic setting. The children have even met a survivor of the camp who sang in the *Brundibár* chorus as a boy. Throughout, Dan has sat at the piano, patiently rehearsing every voice line, every soloist, hour after hour.

In light of what's happened, the temple officers have asked the entire temple board to attend the performance, which is at the local high school. This is kind, I know, as well as politic. We all worry about the press. If reporters and cameras were to invade and taint this project, it would be unbearable.

Hana and Tali are both in the chorus. Dan will be at the piano, as always. My parents are driving in for the performance. My parents! I have to call them. I tell them about Dan's arrest in a few words and ask them not to visit, not to ask questions, just to support me. I tell them that I will be okay.

The opera begins. The opera ends. The audience is huge and claps wildly. The children have outdone themselves. I signal for the junior choir to bow. I sweep my hand across them and gesture toward Dan. Expressionless, he nods and exits.

I ask Dan to take the girls home. Other groups will be performing in the auditorium afterward, and I stay through them, sitting in an unobtrusive spot on a squeaky, sticky seat. One performance after another. Various people sit next to me. I know some of them. They don't talk to me.

After the last performance concludes and the lights go up, I get up and go to my car. I sit in it for a while. I think of tomorrow night, when I have to sing "The Star-Spangled Banner" and "Hatikvah" for the Israel bonds dinner. I drive home and reason that sound will come out no matter what.

I am late getting home. The girls are asleep, and Dan is quiet in the guest room. Jasper the cat follows me to bed.

When I come home the next evening, Dan and the girls are watching TV under a blanket. I wish that the girls were reading instead, and I'm angry.

I don't want to explode, so I sweep past them into the kitchen.

I see the matchbox cover on the counter and pick it up. It's dry. I take off the clamp. One of the two pieces comes with it and shatters on the counter.

Fraying, but Finding Arlene

Scott Balaban, a temple vice president, reassures me that my job is secure. He has more responsibilities now than when he was the temple treasurer, and among them, apparently, is trying to shore me up. This infuriates me. When people start dropping off baskets of home-baked cookies for Dan, Scott brings me a punching bag, thinking that it will help me relieve my angry feelings. I nearly punch Scott. Who does this skinny guy think he is? A Republican evidently, considering the way he dresses.

I need Eva again, so I schedule a second session. Soon I learn that I have said a wrong thing to Tali already. I try to say the right things. I'm trying not to boil over with fury from holding back what I want to say—to keep from poisoning them against their daddy.

Please, please let me say only the right things.

Dan and I begin marriage counseling before he takes up residence at the St. Luke Institute in Maryland to do a twelve-step program for clergy. With the girls, we are also pursuing family counseling.

I am losing weight. Eating seems frivolous. When I poke my fork into something, I think, *How ridiculous. My life is over, and I am sticking this implement into a food substance.*

My friend Aviva comes over to talk to me and to get me to take walks with her. I wear sandals and get blisters on these walks. I know I'm not using good judgment.

Eva has given me a prescription for sleeping meds.

I take my first pill, fold my pillow, position my head for sleep, and wait. While I wait, I shift my hips, rearrange my legs, pull down my nightgown, and fold the top sheet precisely over the comforter. And then I wait some more. The waiting alone is bearable. But my brain kicks in and starts spinning evil threads. The longer the threads, the more likely they are to tangle. And loop and twist and snag and knot. If sleep actually happens, I don't recognize it.

I don't like to move from any one thing to any other. Not from waking to sleeping. Not from sitting to standing. When I arrive anywhere, I can't get out of my car. I can unfasten my seat belt, but I'm stuck after that.

What I need is a therapist, without delay. Our family has been traveling to Rochester to see a family and couple's therapist, but I've been coasting along without my own for several years. As I wait for a referral, I vow that I will never again go without a therapist.

Eva calls to give me a name: Arlene Warren.

I go to my first appointment with her. But now, maybe because I can only spend so much time fixated on myself, I examine her. I wonder: *Why is this therapist so dressed up and wearing so much makeup? Why so many accessories? Why is her hair so red? Why isn't she more soberly attired and more subtly made up?*

In my primness, all of these things bother me. Yet I fall for her. How I fall for her.

I should color my hair too.

I make a salon appointment and emerge as a redhead. I want to show my hair to Hana and Tali.

Where are they exactly right now? I take my pungent newly red hair from room to room, looking. And here they are on the back deck, fighting.

So I slide open the glass door and look from Hana to Tali and back again. They stare, but are silent.

I leave them alone and drive to the bead store.

These days I spend hours stringing beads. I want to make brace-lets for the girls—a gesture. I want to make necklaces for my friends and for my sister, Sarah, for Eva, for my dentist friend Patti, for Aviva, for my mother. I love them all, but I have no words for them.

Long necklaces. I begin to twist gold wire around large beads and to use more elaborate techniques and more semiprecious stones.

Bead after bead and my brain kicks in, but nicely. It only chants words like *pretty* and *perfect*.

Hana gets her period for the first time while Dan is at St. Luke and I complete my hundredth necklace. I try to think of what a good mother would do.

No longer reliable, my mind kicks in and out of focus. Still I manage to get excited for her. I ask her if she wants a Jewish ritual. Of course she wants nothing of the sort. I am prepared with prod-ucts, and I do some explaining. I'm good at explaining; that is, when I resist the urge to go overboard. I tell Hana that I think we should call her dad with her news. My brain says, *"You are a good mother and a diligent wife."* But I know better.

Hana is embarrassed. Dan is embarrassed.

I think about cake, ice cream. Red candles? No. Too explicit.

I'm aware for just a second that Hana's memories of this event will be forever tainted.

Desiccated in July

The girls are upstairs getting ready for bed and screaming at each other. I used to monitor each and every step of the bedtime ritual. I lived in fear that they might go to bed dirty. I still live in fear that they'll go to bed dirty—or that they won't have read enough. I just don't have the energy to go upstairs and get angry at them.

We had to buy a new car today. The old car finally bit the dust. It was my car, but I felt completely detached from the whole process. I suppose I don't care. Except I was angry that Dan wasn't dealing with the details of the transaction. I had to do it all. It may be that I'm more capable; I just don't want the responsibility. Actually, I don't want any responsibility. I just want to lie down and read and be engulfed by perfect, excellent books.

Everything I look at always needs fixing, adjusting, or cleaning. I can't abide not tending to things, but now I think that if I get started, the process will suck me in and I will disappear.

Tali is complaining because I don't know where her book is and because I won't help her find it.

I can't stand it that Hana didn't wash her face properly—again. I know I scrub mine too hard. I've been doing it that way since my freshman year of high school. Maybe if she scrubbed her face, we would understand each other better.

Up until now the biggest problems Dan and I had were paying the bills on time and finding the energy to make nutritious dinners. Oh, and me feeling like he didn't see me. Now I see myself as an ugly, pasty, sour drudge who is way beyond whatever passed for her prime. I can barely scrape together a smile for my wounded daughters, much less sit up straight. There she is: the woman whose husband . . .

How could Dan—the man who I thought had rescued me from feeling so woefully drab and unattractive—become the instrument that saps me of all my substance? Maybe I've lost all this weight to show everyone that my essence has been bled away. Maybe I want my body to be an object lesson for Dan: See what you've done to me?

My periods are heavier than ever these days. And just when Hana is becoming ripe and beautiful, my skin and hair are drying up. Does the whole world see just how drained I am?

I've lost almost twenty pounds, and I'm still losing weight.

In our family therapy sessions, Tali has trouble putting together a coherent sentence, but she keeps trying, so it seems as if she is monopolizing the gathering. Dr. McWilliams shushes her, which leaves her in tears. Hana is too embarrassed or too shy to say much. Dan is trying, but he has trouble finding words too. Maybe because he doesn't understand his own thoughts.

I'm trying to be a good patient and a nurturing mother, but

I succeed only when I'm at a therapy session and when I'm not in some obsessive mode—so, rarely.

In this state, my infrequent and mild migraines mutate. Twice or three times a week, I am laid low by pain behind and just above my right eye. I don't want to move my head even slightly, and I need to be in the dark.

Nights like tonight, when I start to think about dirty faces, car payments, or missing schoolbooks, I feel the first pulses in my forehead, at my brow line. I head for the bathroom, unwrap a needle, and grab a waiting glass vial.

Tomorrow I will teach and lead prayer and perform whatever custodial tasks are in front of me, but I am no good for the girls— it's as if I no longer recognize them.

Nonetheless, I'm sticking with all of the therapy and taking my meds.

Repentance, Charity, Righteousness

Tomorrow is Labor Day, and I think we have plans. Do we? The day after that, school will start for the girls, and then it'll be Rosh Hashanah. Unending services and hundreds of people to greet.

I'm tired, and I don't want to do anything. I have no interest in today, tomorrow, the school bus routine, or the holidays.

Hana is loudly sulking in her room. I can hear drawers slamming shut. Tali is thinking out loud about what to wear on the first day of school. She describes every combination of top-and-skirt, top-and-overalls, and top-and-jeans. How do the colors look together, Mom? The periwinkle with the denim? Yes or no, Mom? Mom!

And I wish I could just take a nap. Actually, I wish I could nap like I did when I was a teenager. I loved those dead-to-the-world afternoons.

My dad got away with ignoring us kids. Shit. I'm doing a pretty good Dad imitation right now.

If only my brain would stop digging around for dirt and probing every wound. Always the relentless digging, the rubbish results. The whirring and hissing last longer than holiday services.

Dan suspects that Robert won't allow him to sing certain texts during the High Holidays. I agree and think that Robert may well be unhappy at the prospect of Dan chanting Kol Nidre. Does he want Dan to be publicly branded? Does he think that Dan is not worthy to lead the congregation in prayer? Does he think that congregants will be distracted by feelings of sympathy for Dan or for me? Is he simply trying to avoid controversy by allowing time to pass before having Dan in front of the congregation again? Have congregants expressed anger at the thought of seeing Dan on the bima?

A sinner needs to repent. He needs to ask for forgiveness from all whom he has wronged. He needs to pray with his community for pardon. His contrition should be recognized by all who see him. Dan's sincerity and efforts toward health and wholeness need airtime now. Only those things can begin to restore his dignity—and mine.

Repentance, charity, and righteousness avert the severe decree. That's a central Yom Kippur declaration. We are also taught that the gates of repentance are never barred. Dan's right to work toward conciliation, pray in his community, and do acts of justice take precedence over any person's reluctance to see him on the bima.

May Dan's voice ring true during this Kol Nidre service.

And let the girls' first day of school be a good one. Let the other kids be forgetful about Dan's arrest and the TV descriptions of what happened. Let a few of their teachers be somewhat inspired.

Wrathful in September

When will I stop being angry?

People in the greeting line after Shabbat services say to Dan, "It's so wonderful to have you back." "We love you."

I react like a jealous sibling. *Hey! He's a sinner, and I am a saint!*

I guess I'm also thinking, *What about me, the martyred, long-suffering, betrayed wife?*

The congregation's sweetness and generosity conspire to rob me of my righteous indignation, but I am not willing to let it go just yet. I need to nurse and savor it for a while. So it's odd to me that I am especially furious at people who don't want to see Dan on the bima. Who are THEY to bristle? Especially when I'm not ALLOWED to?

I am also disdainful of the political beliefs I automatically ascribe to people who don't want to see Dan officiate. Certainly they must all be right-wing, reactionary Republicans.

What do I do with all these conflicting thoughts?

I'll focus instead on devising new combinations of beads in rigid, endless patterns. Three ceramic beads, a crystal bead, two contrasting agates, one vintage Czech glass bead, now a Bakelite bead, five seed beads . . .

Dan is losing weight too. He now weighs 147 or 148. Losing weight is MY territory. It's my way of saying that I am less than my former self. I'M the one who's been diminished by Dan's arrest. Who is HE to be shrinking? He brought this all about. And he's won. He's become the innocent, much persecuted victim. He's elbowed me right out of my role.

Hana Is Called to the Torah

I can hear the people in the congregation shifting their weight to lean forward in the pews. Will they be able to see such a small girl? Yes, she's standing on a box at the reading table.

Hana conducts herself with poise and dignity. She sings sweetly, and her Hebrew is dazzling. Her speech is delivered with grace. Where is my shy, embarrassed, easily provoked girl? Because of her shyness, no one has expected the clarity of her voice, the sternness of her posture, the freshness of her singing.

In the front row I see my father's eyebrows go way up—an unmistakable sign of approval.

I feel the sweat prickle under my arms.

Before I can memorize the moment, Hana steps off the box, and again she is tiny.

The congregation throws soft candies in plastic wrap.

Miriam and Janet, my cantor friends, join me at my lectern. We sing.

Seek the shade of the house you build.
Eat the fruit of the trees you grow.

It's a canon, and our voices play games with each other as if they were children in a yard. Sugared disks rain down, and we duck as we sing.

Sweets, yes. But today Hana begins to make her way out of childhood.

I stare at her and think of chalk art on a new sidewalk. I blink and see her in an ivory suit, shielded in a pastel tallit, sticking a red candy into her mouth. I blink again more deliberately to see if the image remains. And it's gone. She's disappeared, off the bima and into her own garden. I am too late to kiss her round, perfect cheek.

Fire-Breathing Barbie

Dr. McWilliams, our marriage counselor and family therapist, has advised Dan and me to have a daily controlled anger moment. We decided that 3:00 p.m. is best for us because religious school doesn't convene until 4:30 and I don't begin tutoring until 3:30 at the earliest.

I like the idea of forcing myself to be angry out loud. And I understand that it's therapeutic to express anger in a timely way and on a regular basis.

Just inside my office door, Dan stands ready for the invective I will let loose when the clock strikes three. He's bracing himself.

I open my mouth to expel my wrath, aware that we only have a few minutes before Greta buzzes Dan to ask if his religious school ducks are in a row. As I turn to face him, I inhale and rear back.

But . . . pfft.

I suddenly can't manage to light my own fuse. I have no fire to breathe. There is only air. I exhale raggedly.

Dan makes use of the void and remembers that he has to leave right away for a twelve-step meeting. He tells me that Greta will be handling religious school today.

He leaves. The door shuts behind him.

Fuck this. I will inform Dr. McWilliams that moments of controlled anger are bullshit.

But after a moment, I think, *THIS, this failure to strike, is the problem. THIS. My inability to spew. My refusal to let the burning vipers and red-hot toads leave my mouth.*

I need to remember how to breathe fire like Class Arguer did.

And I'm going to need to tell Dr. McWilliams that I require props of some kind—props that will help me eject some serious heat. Or some magicked costume that will reveal my powers. A dragon suit. Yes. One that comes with wings, claws, and fiery plumes.

I should suggest this to the designers at Mattel—Barbie should have one of these too. She has to wear a smile every second of every day, but when the moment calls for it, she should be able to put on a dragon suit that screams FUCK THIS.

Tali in the Wilderness

Nat Kirchenbaum, an environmentalist and friend, offers to take Tali and me on a nature walk. It's a lovely day, and I say yes. This will be good for us, mother and daughter alike.

Nat names trees and herbs, and points out habitats, nests, and burrows as we stroll through the Reinstein Woods Nature Preserve. I keep exclaiming with delight, but Tali drags her feet, saying nothing, widening her eyes with false interest. Looking at her face, I realize that, at nine, she is old enough to resent being figuratively frog-marched "for her own good" in the great outdoors. She is also sophisticated enough to let me know that she's enduring the indignity to mollify me. Tali is my sacrificial captive, as well as her father's.

Although my parental skills have receded, I manage to register Tali's sadness, and so I take her to Steve's Pet World. I buy her a baby ferret, and it falls asleep in her lap.

But now there is a ferret living in my house. A ferret whose fragrance, I might add, belies Steve's claim that her anal scent sacs have been removed.

Descending and Ascending

Communication between Dan and me deteriorates. We've been sleeping separately for a long time. I think he has stopped going to twelve-step meetings. Although the family therapy continues, there are fewer family sessions and more couples' sessions. There are no disclosures about Dan's sexuality. This leaves me stuck in a continuum of betrayal. I will not be fooled any longer. I don't want a sexless marriage. I am angry to some degree all the time.

We go out to dinner with our dentist friends, Patti and Lou, and with Scott Balaban and his wife, Mary. The conversation is desultory. I talk about the advent of email, which I have just gotten on my computer. I almost get into a fistfight with someone at an adjacent table who is bad-mouthing gay people.

Scott starts emailing me—or perhaps I start emailing him. It's not long before I find myself waiting the whole day for the time when I can check my email for a message. Nightly it is there. Nightly I compose a perfect response. The content is trivial; the ease of conversation is earth-shattering to me.

Dan is sullen. He knows that something draws me to the computer and knows, too, that it is a threat to him.

I discuss this with Arlene, knowing what she will say and hoping for mercy. She tells me that I must stop distracting myself this way and concentrate on my primary relationship. I agree.

I stop emailing Scott, but my days turn dark.

At the end of the next board meeting, he offers to walk me to my car. We go to my office, and I put on my coat, but I don't change into my boots; I don't want him to see my feet.

In the parking lot, I slip on the ice.

In a staff meeting the next day, Robert announces that he and his wife plan to head up a congregational trip to Israel over the summer. He tells me that, should enough people sign up, there will be a spot for me. I can lead songs on the bus.

I smile. Something to look forward to. The girls will be away at camp, so I hope that the registration numbers go my way.

Scott and Mary and their two boys sign up for the Israel trip.

I learn this and say nothing to Arlene. I know this is wrong. This is my secret.

The trip is fully subscribed, and I will be going. I start thinking about a bathing suit. I don't own a bathing suit or shorts. I haven't in years.

I am very excited about the trip.

I write to the girls at camp, winding up, as always, with exaggerations about the cat's antics. Jasper has no real antics. He just attacks everything at random because he's feral. I have nothing authentic to report.

In Israel I am happy. I room with Patti, and at night we laugh, talking until one of us doesn't respond. I tease the kids in the group and feel like myself. I remember that I like teenagers. Patti and I sit together on the bus, eat together, and are a pair. The kids on the trip joke that they can't tell us apart.

Scott seems to be behaving strangely. Often, when Aryeh, the guide, gives a lecture or when I stop to look at something, he finds a spot next to me. I glide away, seeking Patti. I mention this to her, and she tells me that Scott had suggested that the two of them make it a goal to see that I have a good time in light of my year from hell. Yet again he infuriates me.

In the market, Mary models a pair of harem pants for Scott and asks what he thinks. He's critical, dashing her hopes for a purchase. I resent him on her behalf.

He holds Mary's hand on the plane ride home.

Scott's kindly dad picks up the Balabans at the airport. Patti and I wait for Dan.

I am bereft.

Angels Are Bullshit

Another Rosh Hashanah. The sanctuary has been opened at the back to allow for the huge High Holiday crowd. I do not experience this year's holidays as high. They are low because I am low. Very low.

Late in the morning service, Robert begins reading from the Torah, and I experience my usual jealousy. I covet the reading of the Binding of Isaac. I not only want to hear it chanted according to High Holiday cantillation, I want to chant it myself as I did in Great Neck and later in Rochester. I love the way it feels to chant it, to have the story go from the parchment to my eyes to my throat to the air.

In the middle of the second section of the Binding story, Robert stops abruptly and comes over to my bima chair. I think he must have some emergency to report. I prepare myself to slip off the bima and deliver a message.

But instead he says in a high-pitched voice, "I'm not sure where I'm supposed to be right now."

"Okay. That's fine, Robert," I tell him.

In the Binding story, as Abraham is about to plunge the knife into his son's neck, an angel calls out his name, stopping the action.

And suddenly a real-time freeze-frame is in progress, a caesura right here on the bima. The Binding narrative is paused, and the congregation must be wondering why.

Between one moment and the next, I consider. I know I need to rouse myself to act, that this is an important moment. But I'm also nervous. I've never chanted this or any Torah portion without having practiced.

I ask the temple's past president, who is seated next to me, to take Robert quickly to his office and to have one of the many doctors in the congregation look him over. The former president, himself a clinical psychologist, stands up and takes Robert's arm with a reassuring smile.

I walk over to the reading table and begin chanting in Hebrew the Torah text where Robert left off. "And Abraham took the wood for the offering up . . ."

I feel the drama of the story infuse my voice now. The congregation is listening. As I finish, I feel the echo of my cantorial powers and wonder if they will be here tomorrow or back in the tank.

Nancy passes me a note as the scroll is being closed. Letting Dan take over, I read it and walk down to where Robert's parents are sitting. I whisper slowly and calmly that Robert is being taken to the nearby hospital for observation. They leave, and I return to the bima.

A lay reader begins to recite the haftarah, and I register with a jolt the presence of a manila folder marked "Rosh Hashanah Sermon."

But there is no time for me to worry about sight-reading someone else's words. Or about whether I will read them well in this overflowing sanctuary.

I deliver Robert's sermon on his behalf with an explanation that he is feeling unwell. I go for a laugh when I address my empty bima chair with a scripted remark to "Cantor Ostfeld."

A little later, during the announcements, the president is able to inform the congregation that Rabbi Nussbaum is fine.

I am greatly relieved to hear it, stifling an emotional cough. I hear other such coughs from the pews.

He's okay.

How would I go forward without the equanimity of Robert Nussbaum? My impulse is to thank God, but I stifle it.

God sent an angel to save Isaac. Yeah, right. Angels are bullshit, and anyway, on this Rosh Hashanah, I was able to do without one.

Beads, Beads, and More Beads

I position the white plastic tray on my kitchen table and begin. It's late fall in Buffalo, and a weak early morning sunlight shines on what I've spread over the table. First I line up five moss-colored seed beads and then three malachite rondelles. I end the pattern with a single vintage lampwork bead that reflects all the greens.

This, arranging beads, is the only thing I want to do. It's even better if Jasper sits in my lap.

I take off my glasses for the actual stringing. Nearsighted as I am, there is a sweet spot, up close to my nose, where even tiny things come into sharp focus. I need this clarity in order to string the smallest seed beads onto the clear, stretchy plastic thread. Today I am making a necklace, and it will be beautiful.

Midmorning I get into my car, but I don't head for work. Instead

I find myself en route to Beadnik—Where Beaders Bead. I'm supposed to be at my desk.

On my route to Beadnik, there's a tree that must be hundreds of years old. Each time I drive past it, stolid and beckoning, just yards from the road, I think, *No one else would be hurt. It will just take a fraction of a second. Who cares about the car?* But I drive on.

Back home, I have an hour of beading ahead of me before I have to go teach. So I'm angry when the phone rings—and angrier when Tali's principal identifies herself.

"Tali has been fighting in the school bathrooms," she tells me without preamble. "She slapped another student across the face."

This registers, and instantly I'm full of anger. Angry at Tali. At the principal. But mostly with myself, for fucking everything up.

"I'm sorry to hear that, Mrs. Mayer. What precipitated this fight?"

"It's unclear at this time, Mrs. Gertz."

Though bristling, I do not say, "That's CANTOR OSTFELD," as I want to.

The conversation ends, and I know that I have to focus on Tali. I put my glasses back on and put the beads away, each color back in its own cylindrical container.

I'm overwhelmed. What should I do? How many times have I talked to the girls about the virtues of nonviolent solutions?

I seize upon the first answer that comes to mind. Aren't we taught that when taking exams, we should go with our first answers?

I call my mother and ask her to take Tali for a dull weekend alone with the Oparents in Connecticut. There will be no phone, no friends. She will be in purgatory, if not in hell.

Perfect. Tali will be out of my hands. I imagine how many beads I will be able to string in her absence.

Tali returns from her Connecticut exile subdued.

The week passes, and I fly by myself to attend my brother's wedding in California.

When I return, Dan tells me he's found an apartment and announces that he's moving out over Thanksgiving. I take a deep, relieved breath, but by the time I finish releasing it, I'm already worrying about Tali and Hana.

Bottom Notes

I rush into the temple just in time for the Monday morning staff meeting. I've been downtown, meeting with the lawyer who is representing me in the divorce. Dan's engaged a lawyer too, and they argue over terms.

I don't miss Dan at home, and even though there's tension between us at the temple, services take place, lessons are conducted, and classes taught. Meetings are shorter than they used to be, but still efficient. There's no longer any chitchat or laughter, but Jewish things get done.

Robert opens the meeting with dramatic news: He's leaving the temple for a new rabbinic position in Chicago.

I understand his reasoning. It's a good career move for him. But it's a loss for us, and for me. Robert can only grow in a new community, one in which he isn't consumed by the daily demands of damage control.

I am sad. Robert and Lois have been my friends since our days at HUC. Our big temple family was lively and boisterous. I wonder if these rare qualities will be lost to the temple for good.

The temple president appoints Scott to chair the rabbinic search committee, and he in turn asks me for advice on how searches should be conducted.

I appreciate being consulted—being respected for my experience in the synagogue world and in the Reform movement. It's reassuring to be included in plans for the temple's future.

The conversations with lay leaders and staff seem to rely at least to some extent on my opinions. As others begin to cite my thinking, I can't help feeling a touch more confident.

Mother Abbess Goes on a Date

I've just been talking with Gershon Fishman, who will be starting as our new rabbi in July. He seems smart, funny, and scholarly, and he treats me with respect. I'm pretty sure I'm going to like him.

As soon as I hang up, Dan knocks on my office door.

"I just wanted to tell you that I'm leaving the temple in June to become the director of the Bureau of Jewish Education."

Another surprise. But just the latest in a series.

What will the temple feel like without Robert? Without Dan? I wonder if I am good enough to play this new senior role.

I feel like Mary without Peter and Paul. And then I remember with a bit of optimism that Mary Travers had a solid solo career after the group broke up. I'm used to singing by myself too.

Wait. Will Hana and Tali still want to come to services? Or will they want to avoid seeing Dan's empty chair, his quiet lectern?

My bit of optimism evaporates. I'm scared about this new cast of characters, Gershon and me. Will we be able to lead effectively as a team?

Robert, increasingly preoccupied with preparations to leave for Chicago, mentions to me that Scott Balaban is slated to become the next president of the congregation. By this I am not surprised.

Scott takes office in July, and soon after I hear that he and Mary are getting divorced.

In his new role, Scott sits on the bima at Friday evening services and sometimes attends our senior staff meetings. His younger son, Joshua, has begun weekly Bar Mitzvah lessons with me, so our paths cross frequently, and we talk a lot.

Scott seems a bit bewildered, as anyone might be with all the changes going on in his life, but our conversation is easy.

We begin to step in on each other's sentences, anticipating the next line of dialogue in a nervous little dance.

In conversation I am not prim.

"At first I assumed you were a Republican," I reveal. "The day-in-day-out dark suit and red tie getup. That and your precision haircut. I can see the comb marks!"

Scott answers, smiling. "And you didn't assume that it was my lawyer uniform? That I was in disguise for a reason? That I was enhancing my effectiveness via subterfuge?"

"No, I thought you were unimaginative in your haberdashery and conservative in your ideology."

Scott laughs. I respond with a giggle. I hope my giggle is soft enough, soft and refined.

In January we go out on a date. Tali and Hana will be staying home alone with Jasper and a pizza. They are very quiet when Scott picks me up. He is awkward, and they withhold their charms.

Once out the door, my charms, however, are on display. I feel sparkly, all dressed up for the theater.

As we walk back to Scott's car after the play, I feel my back and neck lengthen a bit. Following suit, my shoulders adjust themselves into a new alignment. Mom would be proud of this good posture.

It's my turn, I think. *My turn to get the leading role in my own romantic play.*

Mother Abbess exits stage left.

A Sour Note

"Hi, Helen! What have you heard from Yoni recently?"

"He's great, thanks. Was the service especially long tonight?"

I'm going from group to group, chatting at the oneg Shabbat after services.

"Cantor, you sang a different tune tonight! What was it?"

During the service, I had looked out from the bima and met various blank stares. I had watched the congregation expectantly as I began refrains, indicating by leaning forward that they should sing with me.

They did sing, but their singing was lukewarm. There was no hand clapping, no swaying.

With Rabbi Robert and Cantor Dan gone, the congregation seems confused. People are newly uncertain about singing along. Where are the guitars? Where are the harmonies?

Temple members want to like the new rabbi, but I hear them saying that he's so young and so serious and his wife seems aloof. That's what people always say about rabbis' wives who are smarter than they are. Is the new rabbi himself too smart?

I take a short break and look for something to drink. I survey the tables set up along the back wall under the high window. The pastries are a bit limp. Yesterday's? I try some coffee that tastes like tea. I pour myself some tea, and it tastes like coffee. Not for the first time I notice that the social hall blinds are warping. I hear someone ask if the cream is off. I observe people tasting the punch, examining their cut glass cups, and grimacing. It's not sweet enough and too pink.

And of course I overhear bits of gossip. I've heard most of it before.

Some say that I've long been Dan's "beard." Some say that I'm a secret lesbian and take my own lovers. ("Her hair is so severe, so short.") Some say that we had to adopt Hana and Tali not because we were infertile but because we had a "white marriage." Some say that because they've always known Dan to be gay, it's inconceivable that I didn't know, so my shock over his arrest was an act.

The newest rumors began after people saw me with Scott, or Scott with me, downtown at the theater in January. Tonight some whisper that I broke up Scott's marriage. Others say that he broke up mine.

I take a sip of whatever lukewarm beverage is in my cup.

Congregants often say that they want their clergy to be real people. That's not entirely true. They actually want their clergy to be unimpeachable. Normal, but not libidinous; attractive, even photogenic, but not alluring. Serious, but not too serious.

Tonight, at this oneg, it's time for me to stop hearing whispers, to start a few new conversations, and to do what cantors do on Shabbat.

During the service and after, the cantor is supposed to make shabbat real.

I take a last swallow from my cup and dive back into the oneg crowd. I clasp the arm of a friend, lean in to kiss him on the cheek and straighten back up. I shake a few more hands, squeezing lightly. I tell a little girl that I heard her singing from her seat and that her voice was like candy. I put a few pastries on a plate and walk toward an elderly woman perched on her walker's folding seat, balancing her cup of punch and chatting with her friends. Extending the plate, I greet them.

"Something sweet!" I say.

They smile politely.

Romance

Scott and teenagers meet
And blend in their time
Full Gray Thistle Drive

Little Red Riding Wolf

I spread a flimsy paper napkin across my lap. Battered by the gossip about us, Scott and I are hiding from view. Sometimes we eat bagel sandwiches in his car.

I can't tell whether I'm justifiably protective of our new relation-ship or rightfully ashamed of its proximity to our divorces. We're both divorced, but no matter how I contemplate this situation, I can't escape feeling disgraced. I want so much to feel loved, but by dating Scott, I'm exposing us and all of our children to feelings of shame from all of the gossip. And I'm disturbed by a profound, constant wish: that Scott would spirit me away, with a ring on my finger, in a coach with four horses, never again to face confusion or embarrassment.

He does take me to Toronto to do some clothes shopping.

It's thrilling to have a man pay enough attention to me to want to dress me, and yet I worry, for obvious reasons, that I won't like his choices. At least I've stopped worrying about how much these clothes will cost. Scott is paying for them. So I feel rich.

My personal clothing money goes mostly to Tali and Hana. I know I need new clothes, though. My stuff isn't musty or ancient, but each article has lost whatever appeal it originally had, and noth-ing looks right. I've lost weight and everything hangs on me. And styles have changed, but all of my dresses retain their original shoulder pads. All of my sweaters have self-ties.

We go to Eaton Centre, and I begin trying on the clothes that he holds up in front of me. This is not easy. I look at myself in the dressing room mirror and think, *Yes, this one is good.* But the woman who is working with us laughs and says, "Let's measure you. All these things are way too big." I tell her no, that I know what size I am, and she goes to help another customer. But I don't really know what size I am. I persist in choosing things that might be two sizes too big.

It's as I feared: Scott and I don't share the same tastes. He likes blue in the way that Henry Ford liked black. Blue doesn't do anything for me. He likes wool blazers. I feel like a goddamn Young Republican in wool blazers. Yet he's so delighted that I agree to try on a fucking blazer. We argue further about sizes and wind up compromising. He's frustrated with me, and I feel uneasy. At least he didn't recommend a scarf.

At my next appointment, I talk to Arlene about these feelings.

"Why do you prefer clothing that is too big?" she asks.

"I like the way it looks."

"Really? You think oversized clothing looks good on you?"

"Yes," I say stubbornly. But this is a therapy session, so I do think about it. "No. With all that fabric, I can't see much of me. There's a lot of material and not so much of me."

"And why does that appeal to you these days?"

I almost say it. *If I hide, no one can touch me. If I hide, no one can grab me.*

But I switch gears and cover myself with words that reveal only a sliver of the truth.

"Because I'm hiding."

"Hiding part of yourself or hiding from something?" asks Arlene.

"I don't want anything of mine to show. I don't want to be seen, except undercover."

"Why don't you want anyone to see you?"

I spill a bit more truth. "They'll know the truth! I feel like a fake! I'm faking niceness like the wolf in *Little Red Riding Hood* is faking being a grandmother. I don't deserve new clothes or a new relationship. I guess I don't feel as bad about the new clothes because they aren't flattering. I can keep hiding inside them. Like the wolf. But it's not just the new clothes—I'm getting a new relationship. I feel like a fraud, and I'm ashamed."

Arlene persists. "Is that really why you're ashamed?"

And then I remember the old man who grabbed me at the Lincoln Tomb.

Slowly I describe to Arlene the shame I felt about my new floral dress back in Springfield, Illinois. I assumed, no small thanks to my father, that the dress made me look like I had breasts. As if wearing that dress had caused the man to touch me.

I tell her about the blast of mortification that hit me as soon as I closed my bathroom door on the naked rabbinical student. As if arranging to have a Hebrew tutor had caused him to take off his clothes.

I tell her about the husbands who didn't desire me as I am. The disgrace I felt. Feeling dowdy in my first marriage and undesirable in my second. As if I had fashioned myself into a repellant woman.

And then, I remember it. In quick bursts: *Dog-shit-scented humiliation. Missing my stop. Going without my bra. As if getting lost or not wearing a bra caused me to be raped.*

But these last memories are patchy and fleeting. I push them away before I can reflect out loud, before I actually retain them.

I remind myself to breathe in, then out. Slowly.

I reset my thoughts.

I say, "I am ashamed of all this history! It feels like I made all the dirty things happen. I want to hide!"

I've told the truth, but I've left things out. Apparently I have a lot more to consider than which number tells my true size. Like how to burn off misallocated guilt. Or how to stop hiding from my own secret.

Magic Wands

Browsing in shops is a respite from ruminating about failure, past or projected. To soothe myself, I still troll for indulgences, but no longer at Fannie May and no longer for the chocolate kind. I head for the cosmetics section of Lord & Taylor.

I pick up a smoky purple eye shadow and read that it's recommended for green eyes. But because I've studied this subject for many years, I already have a purple shadow.

Next to the eye shadow is eye shadow base. Base? I pick up the adorable square box that contains eye shadow base. I squint at the application instructions.

"Apply under eye shadow with the tip of your dominant ring finger."

A weak-ish finger, so as not to damage the delicate skin around the eye, but not so weak as to impede proper application. Sensing bullshit and feeling savvy, I place the box back in its pretty row.

Here I am on my day off looking for a formula that will transform me into something I am not: confident.

In my mind's eye, I see Snow White's evil stepmother speaking to her magic mirror, plotting to eliminate her competition for Fairest in the Land.

I glance at one of the many overlit mirrors on the glass counter. I wonder, as I observe the hegemony of my nose: *If I deploy every level of top-drawer makeup, will I become a strong fair maid? Like the ones in fairy tales and even in the Torah? Like the ones in ballads? Like the ones in Renaissance paintings?*

I return to the eye shadow base and ponder further. Would it indeed make my purple eye shadow adhere more effectively? Last longer? Cause my greenish eyes to pop?

I think not, but if I'm going to apply eye shadow, I'm going to do it right: according to the directions.

I pick up the same adorable little box again and continue my leisurely search for elixirs.

An hour later, I'm in line juggling my seven items, including mascara and mascara primer, and lipstick and lip pencil, one of which is also a lip exfoliant. Stacked near the register, I notice a miniature legion of celadon sample-size vials containing foundation primer. The wands are especially cute. I adjust my glasses in order to make out the directions on the slim cylinder. "Apply after moisturizer and before foundation." Heavens! I didn't realize that I needed a primer in addition to a moisturizer! I add the five-dollar sample to my shopping basket, reasoning that I could benefit from the powerful placebo effect of bullshit.

And that it's always possible that this will be the final ingredient in a potion that will render me worthy.

Driving to Chautauqua

In late winter, Scott and I drove to Chautauqua. I was crying. We were picking up a kind of alternative cancer drug that someone had quietly brought down from Canada for my niece Miriam, Sarah's and my brother-in-law Gavin's daughter. I don't think anyone had any hope for it or for Miriam by then, but this errand was the only thing we could do for her.

The ride seemed so long. As we drove, I thought, *No first kiss for her, no caresses, no soulful gazes. No one to tell her, as Scott tells me, "You're perfect. You're beautiful."*

It was hard to find the address. Chautauqua is full of winding streets with picturesque cottages and small front gardens, then waiting to turn green. Scott found the house, a plain one, and went in. He came back out carrying a heavy box, inside which were smaller boxes. He wouldn't tell me how much he paid. That's how he is when circumstances are ominous.

Now, about a month later, we're at our Seder table. Gavin, Sarah, Miriam, and Miriam's younger sister, Shoshana, have managed to make the three-hour trip to be with us. Miriam is determined to make it to the final "Who Knows One" song. It looks good until just before the maror blessing, but then Miriam feels too sick to stay any longer. Sarah and Gavin prepare to take her to Strong Memorial Hospital in Rochester. Gavin fiddles angrily with their car's back seat until it folds into a reclining position. Sarah fusses helplessly. In their wake, Shoshana, looking stunned and sad, barely says goodbye.

From that Passover night on, Miriam mostly stays in the hospital. A few weeks after the Seder, we visit her there. By then she is

maror: bitter herbs

puffy and quiet. But she grabs my hand to see my engagement ring up close. "I want you to be happy, you know," she says.

Maybe she means only that, just the words themselves, but I startle in this moment, thinking, *She knows she's dying. She wants me to be happy after she's dead.*

I hate these visits. It's just so hard to see, so sad. We try to be the entertainment and to be chatty about the news, but we're only a sideshow—a momentary distraction from an inescapable reality. Gavin massages Miriam's feet for hours. I can't wait to leave, and as soon as I do, I cringe at the extent of my relief.

I know—because Sarah has told me—that when the time comes, the doctors will give Miriam enough morphine that she will simply let go and die. Sarah couldn't say all those words, but she said enough of them. I also know that it won't be long now. Weeks maybe.

I think about the fact that Miriam missed the blessing of the bitter herbs at the Seder. It's strange that there is such a blessing. We bless the bitter. Year after year the unmitigated bitterness presents itself for blessing.

And of the four cups, Miriam has barely tasted the first.

Scott and I Get Married

Scott and I sit at the kitchen table at his house, finalizing some details for our simple wedding. He's lived here almost a year. I don't like the house much, but I hope it will be neutral ground for our four children. Scott is talking to Tom, the wine guy from Windsor Vineyards. They talk about the wedding menu and which reds will work. Then they talk about whites.

Never having done more than hold a glass of wine in my pre-Scott life, I now drink Chardonnay, unoaked, and like it. Yes, I am now a wine drinker, although a beginner. I recognize a few labels, but what I really like is taking small sips of something that pings on my tongue. I particularly like the warm fuzz that seems to sprout on my brain after half a glass.

Scott and Tom discuss personalized wedding labels for the selected wines. I come up with the winning idea: "Banfeld Wed-

four cups: the amount of wine to be ritually consumed by adults during the Passover Seder

ding." That's what the labels will say. Balaban plus Ostfeld. I am mellow AND clever!

Even as we sit and work, I repress this knowledge: The kids, mine and his, need another year. An entire year. In our newfound romance, our respective neediness, loneliness, and pain, Scott and I feel as if we've already waited a long time to get married. So we manage not to register what our kids need. We look only at each other—rejecting the knowledge, even as the children act out.

Hana slams the door to my garage and leaves a crack in the drywall. Tali commits petty household crimes, turning up the thermostat and leaving lights blazing.

Scott's sons, Adam and Josh, won't talk to him, and neither agrees to attend the wedding.

Even in the face of this, as the wedding approaches, I am feeling happy—the best I've felt in a long time. I am no longer rail thin. I am no longer hungry. My now-red hair is chin-length with tidy curls. I don't need flowers in my hair for this wedding.

I buy a lavender silk dress with a form-fitting, pin-tucked bodice at Lord & Taylor. It's slightly damaged and costs under ninety dollars. I have it repaired and feel virtuous, knowing that Scott will be pleased with the economics.

Our June wedding day dawns rainy. The morning sky emerges in shades of Buffalo gray.

But the middle-aged bride and groom look bright against the gloom.

Scott is wearing a new double-breasted navy suit. Our wedding was sufficiently important to warrant the purchase of a new suit! And he's paid extra attention to his Einstein brows. Being Scott, he's a little awkward in his finery.

I know he's also mourning the absence of his sons today.

My arms and neck are bare, and I'm wearing a strapless bra under my strapless lilac dress. I haven't worn a strapless dress since the Steinhart wedding twenty years ago. I look just right, and I predict that our wedding pictures will reveal my confidence and not my nipples.

After the ceremony at Beth Am, our reception at Rue Franklin begins. We stand in the courtyard for pictures. The camera snaps rhythmically, and with each flash I feel more relaxed—in a dress that fits, not a period costume.

I can't wait to tell Arlene. My next session is this week.

Extreme Unction

It's pretty quiet at the temple. Blessedly, it's summer, and most people, including the rabbi, are on vacation. Everyone is outside, and all living things seem to breathe a sigh of relief. As I do obsessively each summer, I go over my High Holiday Torah reading. Year after year, I make the same mistakes in the same places. The only solution is repetition. Over and over the problematic phrases I go. Suddenly the phone rings, and I startle. It's been so quiet.

"We have a patient here at Millard Suburban. He's a member of your congregation. Harold Schulman. He's just been in a car accident and is unconscious. His wife is with him now. Can you come over here?"

"Uh, yes. Yes, of course—I'll be right there."

My stomach drops. I don't know Harold Schulman or his wife. At least I don't think I do. I'm embarrassed to catch myself hoping that they're old and that the accident hasn't left marks on Harold. I am praying that Mrs. Harold is the calm type and will just cry softly while I try to appear like I know what to do. I look up her name in the membership directory. It's Muriel. Score one for me: No woman in my age group is named Muriel. I get my *Rabbi's Manual* and look up the section on the gravely ill. The pages crackle—I've never opened these before.

I drive to the hospital, park in the clergy spot, and put on my ID badge as I get out of the car. I've made many a call here, just none like this one. The badge is old and doesn't look much like me anymore. My hair was shorter then. I hope that I can be counted on and that I will do well whatever I am supposed to be doing. The woman on my badge looks competent, anyway.

I'm directed to a cubicle off of the ER. Muriel is very calm and greets me familiarly. I've never seen her before in my life. Harold looks dead but apparently is not. Fortunately for me, he is unscathed—at least above the shoulders. The nurse points out softly that his ears are turning blue. This I interpret as a signal that I'd better get moving.

I draw Muriel close and put my arm around her. I say the words. "Be with Harold now. . . . Please heal him," I chant quietly. I quietly ask Muriel to recite the Sh'ma with me. The ceremony is over so quickly. I feel tears gathering in my eyes. I compose myself. Muriel will need me to be a calming presence. It's just that I haven't done this before, and it feels so momentous, and I feel so unequal to it.

It's so quiet in this cubicle. Suddenly Muriel turns to me and says, "You have such a beautiful . . ."

During her pause, I fill in the blank: *voice*. I've heard this compliment so many times. Enough times that I no longer register it as a compliment. It's just what people say to their cantor in solemn, heavy moments when they can't find other words.

". . . complexion."

And I'm wrong. Muriel likes my skin tone.

Small Steps

Hana has turned sixteen, and Scott takes over as her driving teacher. Sometimes I sit in the back seat watching him as he insists that Hana make minute adjustments to the rear- and side-view mirrors. Listening as he lectures about appropriate driving footwear. Observing his teachings about the ritual locking of the car doors, and which wiper setting must be deployed to suit which kind of precipitation. He has a patient air about him, but my guess is that he hasn't caught Hana rolling her eyes. Ritually rolling her eyes. Or maybe he has, and he's smiling at her encouragingly nevertheless.

All the Balaban men are persnickety. Some about cars, some about balance sheets, all about healthful diets, and some about sleep hours. Scott, for instance, can't sleep unless our bedroom is cool. I'm happy about this because it suits me too. Of course Tali and Hana begin to freeze even at the thought of the targeted temperature.

Predictably, we discover that one or the other has turned the thermostat up to 80 after we've gone to bed. Scott suggests that the girls layer their pajamas. I put Post-its on the thermostat.

I don't like wasting anything, but Scott absolutely cannot abide it. Also, his definition of waste is a bit more inclusive than mine. For him, throwing out the last sliver of bath soap is just wrong. That flake should be affixed to the new bar of soap, extending its life by at least the length of another shower.

My girls leave all lights on in empty rooms. They abandon the TV to entertain no one. They put open containers in the refrigerator without affixing their caps.

I'm well known for tidiness, for clean counters and smudge-free surfaces. Scott has a higher tolerance for stickiness but NONE for sloppiness. When trash doesn't quite make it into the interior of the wastebasket, he turns beet red. When the toilet goes unflushed, he turns purple.

And I am the coward in the middle. I am both frustrated by the girls' waywardness and angered by Scott's intractability. I add Post-its to the fridge and to the light switches. To the flush handles and to the rims of garbage cans. I find these torn and lying lifeless on their battlefields.

The Columbine massacre is in the news every day, so I'm sheepish as I describe the Gray Thistle Drive Post-it Wars to Arlene. How is it possible that I can distance myself from the shocking reality of high school students shooting up their school but not from the basically run-of-the-mill sniping in my kitchen? I tell Arlene that it's just as scary for me to side with Scott as it is to side with Tali and Hana. She says that Scott must explain himself and his reasoning to Hana and Tali. I pass this along when I get home.

After dinner he begins, awkwardly. "I don't sleep well. I'm a light sleeper, and I'm a guy who really needs his sleep. Actually, I think I need more sleep than most people. So if it's hot in our room, all I can think about is how hot I am. I can't relax and go to sleep."

Hana, who stopped listening after hearing the word "sleep," advocates for her sister and on her own behalf.

"But WE can't sleep if we're freezing to death! We need our sleep too! We have SCHOOL!"

Her wisely chosen reference to scholastic achievement hits its mark.

Scott turns the thermostat up to 68. The girls start wearing socks and hoodies to bed.

Hana joins a soccer team, and Scott teaches her how to dribble, pass, and shoot.

I hear Tali and Scott comparing GI symptoms after meals.

We laugh a bit more often, even if briefly.

I breathe a bit more easily, and gratefully report the progress to Arlene.

Locker Room at the JCC

I place my book on the reading rack of my favorite treadmill and my water bottle in its cup holder. There is no reason why I prefer this machine, but it's become mine through regular use.

I haven't inhabited the world of the locker room since high school. Back then we had to wear yellow snap-up bloomers for gym. I remember shaving my teenage thighs nightly so that all areas exposed by my bloomers would be hairless. I swore I'd never again impose fitness on my body or push it against its will.

Having been so doctrinaire about resisting exercise for the intervening decades embarrasses me now, although I haven't given up worrying about body hair.

I open my book to the page with the folded corner. My feet straddle the belt so I won't lose my footing when it begins to move. I fiddle with the settings on the control panel, debating with myself about how fast I should walk (not fast!) and whether or not to add an incline (not!). Finally I fasten the safety clip to my sleeveless T-shirt. Sleeveless. Wait! Did I shave? Before I lose myself in my book, I perform a discreet check. All clear, and I take a little hop onto the belt as it revs up.

I admit it. With a spot of shame, I admit it: I'm a feminist who shaves under her arms and all over her legs.

In my twenties, I dated a rabbinics professor who pronounced me the hirsute member of my family. I've never stopped wondering how much time he spent looking at my forearms. I was pretty meticulous about everywhere else. Or maybe not.

Greater than the shame of being a depilating feminist is the shame that I would encounter were I to be seen in my native, fully sprouted state. Plus, given my nearsightedness, I'm never confident that I've shaved wherever the sun might shine.

So the risk of being seen naked and perhaps also hairy is one reason I don't like locker rooms. But these days only Neanderthals can get away without exercising. It's the 1990s, and for women like me, privileged and liberal, avoiding exercise is like chain smoking around children or cooking with lard, heaven forbid.

I make it a practice to change behind the shower curtains or in a stall. The few times I've tried to imitate other women my age by changing matter-of-factly, efficiently, at my locker, some temple member two lockers over has started a conversation about her son's Bar Mitzvah study habits or about another congregation's new rabbi. Being trapped by politesse in a state of (hairy) undress is torture for me.

Still, I submit to light exercise at the JCC several times a week. I walk on a treadmill, diligently hooked up to the safety cord, or I ride a stationary bike. I do not push myself. I do not sweat. I don't think I'm experiencing anything beneficial. Well, except for feeling virtuous. And that's hardly worth it. There must be some benefit in literally going through the motions though, I suppose.

Also Scott exercises with gusto and makes free with the word *wimp*.

Slow Take in a Therapy Session

I open my email to find a long message from Tali. Its length surprises me because she is famous for short, impulsive, ungrammatical email bombs that convey her outrage-of-the-moment. "Mr. Holmes is a DICK!!! He calls me Lolly in class!!!"

This message is different. It's addressed only to me, as far as I can tell. There are some capital letters and a few punctuation marks. It's phrased carefully and strikes its target. Me. Me, the bad mom.

The end reads: "It seems like you only care about Scott. You never say 'I'm proud of you.' I miss when you used to put little things on my pillow for me to find. I still love you I guess, but do you love me?"

Tearfully I print Tali's message. Will I have the guts to read this to Arlene at my next session? Arlene is Jewish. She knows me as a cantor. Am I going to reveal the WHOLE ugly truth about myself to Arlene? Can I show her how bad a mother I really am? How bad things are that my daughter bares her soul via email?

Yes. I'm all in. I'm going to spill, to spew out my ugly insides. Arlene may be intimidatingly beautiful and evidently perfect, but she's also sharp as hell.

Her sharpness whets my own.

Seated in her office, I inhale very deeply, preparing to read Tali's email out loud. As my rib cage expands, I feel the fabric of my blouse against it. My attention suddenly turns to the sensation, and I'm taken aback—my blouse! My white blouse!

Between one moment and the next, I realize that despite the progress I've begun to make, my default outfit is still a Choraleer uniform. It comes to me that disguising myself as a choirgirl keeps me safe from being touched by perverts in museums, safe from nude tutors, safe from . . . worse things.

I want to have perfect eye makeup, to be attractive, but not ever in the way that an adult woman can be attractive. Or SEXY. Sexy, as in going braless. Babysitting while braless. Being photographed braless. Sexy as in drawing unfamiliar rabbinic hands to my blouse.

This realization has nothing to do with Tali's email. And yet it's dawning now, as I'm here to talk about Tali's email!

I struggle to put these new thoughts into words for Arlene. She nods, clearly understanding my faltering translation. But I don't talk about babysitting, the subway, or the alley. I'm saying enough without those words, aren't I?

Yes. I am a good psychology client. To prove it, I tell Arlene that I'm ready to read Tali's email to her.

But Arlene tells me not to read Tali's email out loud. She tells me to summarize it, keeping my insight about my blouse in mind. Has she guessed the words I've hidden? I don't know, but I escape. I reveal the bad thing that I AM willing to reveal. Which, after all, is pretty bad.

"She hates me. I'm the bad guy."

Arlene laughs, and I do too.

She turns serious and asks me what my sudden awareness about wardrobe might have to do with Tali's email. I think hard. I think Arlene is telling me that it's time for me to examine the practices I've been using to ensure security at the expense of growth. That I need to start seeing my behavior for what it is.

And so I face it.

I've desperately coveted Scott's attention since the mushroom cloud that arose from my marriage to Dan began to dominate my existence. I've been so intent on keeping myself in Scott's sights, on being a desirable woman again—desirable in a safe, married way— that I haven't attended to my own daughters.

Tali's email calls the question. Until now I haven't looked to my children. I see them now, Hana and Tali, waiting for me to come back to them from behind the now-dissipating cloud.

Ah, I have words for this! I start to cry.

"Tali only wants to know that I put her first. I don't remember the last time I put a mini lip gloss or a perfume sample on her bed. I don't remember the last time I tucked her in or kissed her cheek."

Arlene waits for me to take a tissue from her Art Deco side table. Then she says softly that Tali is asking for something that every child needs from her mother.

I try to keep my eye makeup from running. As I examine the spidery black blots on my tissue, it comes to me in a rush that THIS is what the Arlene sessions are all about. By talking to her, I'm learning to listen to my own voice too. *I can have revelations by paying attention to my own voice.*

It is a revelation this time. About how I'm behaving. About who I am, in this case, as a mother.

But I think, *I will change this. I can shift my focus from Scott, from my choirgirl reflection in his eyes, to my daughters.*

On my way home from therapy, I hit Wegmans for microwave popcorn and rent *The Wedding Singer.* I will do better for my girls. And maybe, someday, I will tell the last secret.

Naming Sophie

Today, in a colorful, perfectly appointed living room, a father— a single gay man—stands next to me holding his baby, brand-new Sophie. I gesture for Logan and Jaden, her brothers, to join us. I give them both a corner of their grandfather's tallit.

As they wrap all four corners around little Sophie, her grand- mother recites:

> Shelter her under your wings, Shechina.
> Wrap her in light like a raiment.
> Give her to creation and creation to her.
> Be her shield and her music, asleep and awake.
> Guide her coming and going both now
> > and always.

Sophie squirms, crinkles her face, and emits a distinct com- plaint. Quickly I unwrap her, and I thank Jaden and Logan, not remembering which is which.

I sing a Ladino lullaby and translate it, looking at Sophie, who is now calm.

As always at a baby-naming, I am falling in love. How I love Sophie in her little olive-green and ivory smocked dress. *Her eyes will stay black*, I think as I sing.

I dip my finger in white wine from the kiddush cup and chant the blessing, translating: "Let us bless the wellspring of life that ripens her fruit on the vine."

Her mouth opens. I feel her lips pull at my finger, tasting some- thing new. She screws up her face but does not cry at the sharp

Shechina: God's feminine name and female presence ~ *Ladino: Judeo-Spanish*

taste. Her face relaxes, and she sucks again. I withdraw my finger. We regard each other.

I have given her this moment, this first taste of something other than milk. Her first kiddush, her first blessing. I said the words, and she fulfilled the mitzvah. *For a moment, she was my baby,* I think.

Sophie falls asleep. I read. "Find blessing, find words, find air and song. Find joy, find peace, find wonder and light."

Fleetingly, I think of the good fairies in *Sleeping Beauty.*

"This little child, Dara Daughter of David, may she become strong. As she enters into the covenant, may she feel the first of many loves. And may worthy deeds soon fill her hands like so many grains of sand."

I have given Sophie the Hebrew name Dara.

I bless her, as a temple priest would have done. And then I touch her head and stroke her fine, fine hair. For these few moments, we are bound together in ritual and text and song.

But I also just want to hold her.

The Evolution of Barbi's Shorts

I have a hate-hate relationship with shorts.

I page through the new summer issue of the Eddie Bauer catalog. Shorts are everywhere. I'm aware that, in hot weather, normal people wear them for comfort.

Not me.

Childhood pictures of me in shorts reveal that my lower legs are average looking. But from the knees up, my legs are dented here and puffed out there, looking as if they prefer not to be seen. It's almost as if my upper legs are Orthodox, loving the Jewish laws governing modesty.

Ordinarily I want nothing more than comfort. I love my chenille sweaters and (lined) wool pants when it's cold, and I love short sleeves, open necklines, and linen when it's hot. But even when it's hot, it is the fate of my upper legs to swelter in confinement. My garment of choice is long shorts—known to others as capris.

Scott teases me about this. I laugh along but enjoy knowing that my unsightly legs are hidden from view. One less thing for me to worry about.

But summer is coming, it's warm out, and I keep leafing through the catalog.

Here on page 37 is a pair I might wear. They're midway between pedal pushers and shorts, but they're not culottes. They'll cover my knees. I fill out the order form. With my neatest printing. These may be okay.

I've told Scott that the "shorts" I wore during my thirties were all made of heavy denim and fell to just above my ankles. In my thirties I was even primmer than I am now! I didn't want to reveal my calves! Aren't today's capris a sign of progress? They show three additional inches of leg!

I explain to Scott that I abandoned the ankle-length "shorts" years ago for two reasons: Hana wouldn't walk next to me at any shopping mall, and I tended to faint from the heat.

It's possible that the length of my shorts will shrink even more as time goes on. Maybe my shorts will gradually look less like gauchos and more like Bermudas. But I'm in no rush. It took me a decade to give up the first three inches of fabric.

A Pratfall for the Team

Scott and I take three of the four newly minted stepchildren to Hawaii. Adam has already returned to college for the fall. We hope that the sun and sea will dispel the heavy atmosphere that's been choking our kids during the transition from their former intact family homes to Gray Thistle Drive, the house Scott bought when he separated from Mary. Joshua and Adam have hated it since that day. Occasionally they visit, but under duress. Who can blame them? This is also the house I moved into after I married their father, bringing my girls with me. Tali and Hana have hated it since their first day, too. Hatred for Gray Thistle Drive is the one thing the four kids have in common.

On this our first stepfamily vacation, Scott sleeps in Joshua's room and I sleep with the girls. We're trying hard to be parental in the aftermath of two very bad divorces.

The kids are not enjoying each other's company, and they've made a show of mild disdain for everything we've attempted to do or see in Hawaii. Scott is angry about this, thinking that their divorce-related anger should melt in the island sunlight. I am sympathetic, but I'm overcompensating too, by making a show of egalitarian motherhood/stepmotherhood, encouraging Josh but chiding the girls.

We take Tali, Josh, and Hana to visit Black Sand Beach on the Big Island. We learn that the sand was formed by lava flowing into the ocean and exploding. So the sand is basalt. It's quite coarse and also quite shiny.

Scott—in his signature black work socks, sneakers double-knotted—stays well up on the beach, but I decide to attempt to play. I remove my sandals. In my below-the-knee shorts, I wade into the water with the reluctant kids.

My objective, with three recalcitrant kids looking on, is to cavort in the shallows. Ordinarily I do not cavort.

I see a green turtle on the beach in the distance. I'm excited by the lone turtle, flat on the sand. Before I can point it out, a wave knocks me off my feet and covers me with igneous tea. I lie in the sand for a moment, wet and filthy. I am royally pissed off by the gratuitous slap from these foreign gods, who apparently have no respect for primness.

While I stumble to my feet and raise my eyebrows in an effort to reconfigure my expression, I hear all three kids laughing.

I learn that a well-timed pratfall has its place in blending families.

Pissed Off about Religion

I dress as if I were going to officiate at a funeral and then undress. I am the designated Jew in a women's interfaith dialogue. Why would I go for somber?

I put on an olive-green knit dress and some carnelian earrings. I choose a lipstick by the name of Carmen. That's better.

Driving to the church, I repeatedly glance at the passenger seat, checking over and over that my notes are on board in their manila folder.

This noon four women will discuss whether religion is a way to peace or an instrument of war. The Jewish woman is a cantor (me). The other speakers will be a Muslim Ph.D. candidate who is the wife of a local imam, a Catholic nun from St. Joseph's, and a Protestant minister from Kenmore Presbyterian.

I'm good at reading verbatim from my text while sounding as if I'm speaking off the cuff. (I add in some ums and pause frequently.) This is how I get around my dread of fucking up in public.

I'm going to talk about the perspective of the ancient rabbis on what they called the good inclination and the evil inclination. Without the evil inclination, people would just hang out eating manna, drinking dew, and masturbating. The rabbis taught that the urges to procreate, to build, to strive all have origins in evil. Without the good inclination, people would behave like terrible two-year-olds, pursuing their immediate desires and throwing dangerous tantrums. The rabbis believed that education and hard thinking would give people the tools to balance innate drive with principle, holding the evil inclination at bay.

Here's my take: Because people are free to act as they choose, religion can either be a peace manual or a war manual. It's up to us. Judaism teaches that study is the highest value because study itself leads to right conduct.

We three clergywomen and my newest acquaintance, Bisma Badat, sit at a long table on a platform. We speak in the designated order, passing the squawking microphone from one to another. Then it's Q and A.

"I have a question for Cantor Ostfeld."

"Sure! Hi!"

"You don't sound religious. You sound like a science person. What about God? Are you religious?"

I am suddenly furious. Almost but not quite out of control.

"What kind of miracle is human intelligence? I'm a believer in *Something* with a capital *S*. And I'm, um— I'm a science geek. Charles Darwin wondered, 'Why are deep ocean plankton so beautiful if no eye can ever see them?' The questioning itself is divine! God is not about revelation or about a single pathway to truth!"

Whoa. I'm good. I remember to straighten my posture.

My evil inclination has prompted me to teach Torah.

Dybbuk in My Throat

I keep thinking of ideal opening lines for today's therapy session. I erase them as they pop into my head because I know very well that scripting myself isn't therapeutic. But if I can come up with a way to start my session, a perfect sentence, then Arlene will cure me and I will go forward.

And here it is: "Arlene, given that I've been told that my cough is all in my head, I guess I'll have to work on my cough in YOUR office!"

I walk into her waiting room, with its slightly moldering rug, and Arlene says, as always, that she will just go and get me a glass of water. She steps out into the corridor that leads to a makeshift kitchen. She returns and presents me with a glass.

I drink this water only when I cough, but I'm coughing all the time these days.

I don't remember exactly when it started. My singing hasn't been a concern since I learned to open my mouth back in cantorial school. And it had been improving, because although I don't practice on a daily basis, I do force myself to take weekly voice lessons. So boring. So necessary.

But I am regressing. At first, after Dan's arrest, I would feel a little tightening in my throat while singing any poignant liturgical phrase during a service. Back then I could swallow and continue. Over time the tightening became a catch. Still later the catch became audible, and now sometimes the very act of inhaling makes me cough—often convulsively.

I don't cough during voice lessons. I don't cough when I'm teaching. I only cough on the bima, where it matters.

I persist in thinking of the cough as a dybbuk in my throat, but that's not where the dybbuk was born. He was born behind my right eye, at brow level. Years ago, he gave me migraines, several a week some weeks. Now my dybbuk has outgrown my forehead and moved into my throat. He knows that a cantor needs an unobstructed larynx, so he has planted himself in my vocal chords.

Presto: the cough.

I could live without singing if I absolutely had to. But my voice is me, so this cough "of unknown origin" is a thief.

I drink glass after glass of water. I keep several under my lectern. I blow my nose constantly in case the cough results from dreaded phlegm.

There's never any warning, either. I'll be singing in synagogue, focusing on my prayer text, and the dybbuk will grab me by the throat, making a little choking sound. I cough and prayer stops.

Who can think of great peace pouring down like honey on the earth's inhabitants when the cantor is coughing? Who can call to mind the fact that the Torah's paths are fragrant if the cantor is stopped in her tracks by an inhalation gone wrong?

I've just returned from Denver's National Jewish Health facility after a week of testing. I test negative for every possible cause of coughing except a dybbuk. Although the test for the presence of a dislocated, clinging soul remains inconclusive.

When I was being examined and questioned by, of course, Jewish physicians in Denver, the word *cough* would cause me to cough.

Psychogenic. Of course. I have known this all along. My cough is psychogenic. All in my head. The doctors suggest this to me in an undertone.

I take my next glass of water from Arlene's manicured hand, sit in my corner of the couch, and wail, "Cure me, Arlene! I can't be a cantor if I am possessed by a dybbuk!"

This was not my intended opener, and I remark on this to Arlene. "Where did that come from? Wow! It's as if I believe that you, Arlene, are a wonder-working rabbi and as if I myself believe in the ability of dybbuks to latch onto a soul! I had a completely different opening line all planned!"

So many things are swirling around my brain that I pause to catch my threatened breath. Instantly I begin to cough.

Oh, I think. And then say, "This is exactly it, isn't it? It's me. My overwhelmed brain choking me. Getting in the way of my favorite means of expression."

Arlene smiles.

"I guess I had better figure out how to exorcise my cough."

And it comes to me that I will stop coughing once I dismantle the fears that stick to me. I can't start off with the biggest fear—that I will again lose my way and be pulled into an alley. I will begin with this one: the fear that I can't sing cleanly because I've become a pariah; that I'm not worthy of a place on the bima, like true cantors; that I actually have nothing but a croak to send upward. What good is an open mouth if all it does is croak?

One note at a time, one unencumbered breath at a time, I will relearn how to hear myself sing.

Inching through Injury

"Mom! I need you to drive me to school! I don't want to go with Scott! You and I never get to talk anymore!"

I tell Tali for the millionth time that since her school is minutes away from Scott's downtown office and since we live in the suburbs, I am not going to drive her. I tell her that it's a waste of gas and that I need to be in my temple office. Driving her into the city would reduce the amount of time I can spend at my desk.

Tali cries.

Scott is happy about driving her. It saves gas and time. Plus, he hopes to improve his relationship with Tali.

I'm just so tired. When I feel like this, I'm always going to opt for the path of least resistance. Why be harangued by Tali when I can work in peace at my desk? Aren't we saving gas AND giving Scott and Tali the chance to improve their communication?

Scott calls me from work to say that Tali's stomach seems to be bothering her.

"What do you mean 'bothering'?"

He tells me that she often has to scramble to get into the nearest public bathroom in order to avoid throwing up in his car.

"How often?"

"More often than not."

We agree to discuss this further in the evening.

I hang up and lower my forehead to my desk. So this is the condition of my Tali—angry, weepy, and now symptomatic.

Well, she has to learn about time management and conserving energy, I tell myself. I leaf through my messages and go back to returning phone calls.

Are things getting any better at the Banfeld house? I'm not sure. Hana would say no. But isn't there a bit more table talk at dinner? Tali and Josh are almost getting along these days. On weekends, they hang out together in the rec room and jointly plot against Scott and me. These plots involve ordering Chinese take-out and then feigning food poisoning. That's a good sign, right?

Okay, it's still true that when Tali and Hana fight, usually over clothes, Josh looks like he wants to die. It seems to me, though, that the tension between the girls lifts a bit on the nights that Josh stays with us. Maybe that's because the kids are united in hating us.

Dan and I aren't constantly scrapping anymore. We discuss the girls' progress in therapy and in school. Together, almost in harmony, we lament their late homework assignments and questionable friends whose grammar is faulty. Isn't this divorce detente?

Dan's new partner, Gary, is kind, funny, and smart. He and I have found that we can laugh together when we very occasionally see each other.

It's 2:45. Time to drive to see Arlene for therapy. In the car, I think about our household. I miss a left turn on Main Street and wind up near the airport. I turn around.

I'm a bit thrown off when I arrive at Arlene's Main Street office and find that my first AND second choice parking spots are taken.

This dampens my mood further, but when I take my ritual glass of water from Arlene's hand, I refocus.

I tell her about our dinner table progress—maybe overstating the progress. I say that a few small things—here and there—might be improving.

Then I have a flash of memory. I'm fifteen and Dad is crashing and burning. I tell Arlene about the nighttime phone call from the airport police. An officer had found Dad's Mustang parked diagonally across two spaces, with its engine running. Dad made his flight to Washington. And I started cutting myself in secret that night.

So I'm proud, I report, that Tali and Hana yell and slam doors—that they aren't wielding razor blades. And they're agreeing to go their therapy sessions.

Arlene interrupts my description of pie-in-the-sky.

"How are you coping with their sadness?"

I tell her that I'll never stop wishing that Scott and I had taken more time before getting married. Our kids are injured, I tell her.

Arlene asks why I used the word *injured*, not *hurting* or *grieving*.

"Because injuries are permanent," I answer. I cough and take a sip of water.

Picking Up My Feet

When I was little, Mom always told me to pick up my feet.

"You're ruining your shoes that way, Barbi. Pick up your feet! Put a spring in your step!"

Her reference to a spring always made me think of a Slinky. I liked Slinkys. But they didn't move with alacrity; they lazed or oozed from point A to point B. I still like Slinkys, the sound they make snaking forward or down stairs. I wish I moved like a Slinky, seamlessly and effortlessly. Walking has been a chore for me since grade school. These days I'm trying to like walking. For several reasons, I am not yet a fan.

Scott and I take lots of evening walks. We pretend that both of us want to take them. In reality, Scott wants to take them and I would rather remain seated, novel in hand. Still, I know it's good for me, good for us as a couple, and counts toward my secret short list of daily accomplishments.

While we walk, we talk—or, to be more accurate, I either perform a fascinating monologue or try to get Scott to talk. We hold hands and it's good—the walking and talking and listening.

If I'm feeling generous, I tell Scott that I'm pretty close to liking the walks. If I'm feeling stingy on a given night, I beg for the short route.

As we stroll through our pet-friendly neighborhood, I try to conquer my fear of dogs. This means that when a nearby dog barks, instead of jumping out of my skin and into Scott's arms, I manage to look over at it and say, "Hi, cute doggy." I'm lying, of course. I do not find dogs cute. They've always terrified me.

Between the walking itself and the inevitable canine encounter, I make slow progress.

My fear of dogs is usually dormant since I'm a lover of the indoors. I don't even discuss it in therapy with Arlene. She's devoutly pro-dog, and I'm just slightly embarrassed by my groundless fear.

Beau, Tali and Hana's new dog, lives with Dan in Buffalo's Elmwood neighborhood. Beau is a genuinely sweet dog—a happy, bumbling Lab mix. I've conquered my fear of Beau by making ample use of dog treats.

I should probably carry dog treats on our neighborhood walks.

I'm glad that Tali and Hana have a dog to cuddle and to care for. I know it's a good institution, the post-divorce guilt dog. Adam and Josh have one too, at Mary's house. Their dog, Red, is also a Lab mix and sweet.

On one quiet evening walk, thus far dog-free, it occurs to me that Beau and Red may not be guilt dogs as much as they are freedom dogs. I say to Scott, "When my girls are with Dan, they're free of my fears and my obsession with cleanliness. They're free to love a dog."

A few steps later, I venture further. "When Josh and Adam are at Mary's, they're free of your infallibility and exacting standards. They're also free to love a dog."

Scott is quiet. Half a block later, he says, "You're right. I think you're right about that."

Abruptly we're hailed with a series of shrill yaps.

"Hi, cute doggy!" I say, followed by a hard swallow.

Scott and I walk on. He laughs, and I have a little spring in my step.

Putting My Foot Down

Another Martin Luther King Jr. Shabbat. Ruefully I think, *This one's going to be completely forgettable.*

I think back to combining my youth and adult temple choirs with local AME (African Methodist Episcopal) and Baptist churches when I was in Great Neck. I remember how much work and how exciting that was. The Baptist and AME preachers rocked the house, and the singing was something to envy. I remember smiling throughout those services while trying to keep still. But I often wondered about the effect on my Sing for Fun Club. Most of the kids looked a bit shell-shocked by the raucousness of a service that was ordinarily pretty sedate. I couldn't tell if they enjoyed it. Larry ate it up, though. Memorable.

There's not much interest in that kind of thing here at Temple Beth Am, although the resources are available. Gershon Fishman left the temple for a position in Washington, and the new rabbi isn't motivated in the slightest. He seems to think that if he shaves, suits up, and spews hearty greetings, his job is done.

Nor is he my friend. He's not a worker. In fact, I've never known another like him. I can't say that I trust him. I remember the services marking 9/11. I waited for a wave of rabbinic leadership to follow the horror of that day. But there was nothing. A weak, derivative sermon, a few lazy, trite analogies. A lot of posing.

Since then he's continued to fake his way through this position. Cutting corners on adult ed, B'nei Mitzvah speeches, social action programming, confirmation projects. I'm depressed and burdened. I actually shudder when he passes by.

His pulpit manner is cheesy. He says, *"Please* be seated," like he's imploring us. It sounds as though he thinks that if he can just get us to sit, our souls will be saved. This cheesiness makes it impossible for me to pray when he leads a service. The words won't come. It's hard enough under ordinary circumstances, but when I'm being begged to turn pages or beseeched to rise, I can't summon the focus.

Not all the rabbis I've worked with have been stellar service leaders. Larry read the service in an understated, elegant way in his normal speaking voice. Robert was upbeat but sincere. Krasner's voice had a sweetness to it. Gershon was emphatic. Judy caressed the text. The timbre of Aaron's voice deepened the meaning. But this guy is smarmy, and my skin just crawls. Yes, yes, I'm judgmental.

And it's sermon time. I take my seat and turn my head toward the rabbi, as I've always done—as I was trained to do, actually. I assume a neutral yet interested expression, even though I'm already despondent.

"Fahve score yeahs a-GO, a great Americ'n, in whose symbahlic shadoe we stan' t'day, sahhgned de EmansuPAYsh'n PrahclaMAYsh'n. Dis moMENtous d'cree . . ."

NO! Yes, the rabbi is actually reading the "I Have a Dream" speech in an imitation African American accent. My head snaps down, and I look at my lap, examining my black wool skirt. Damn fine material. I don't even know what I'm trying to control. Disgust? Rage? Laughter? Should I quit tonight? Because I know for sure that I won't be able to stand next to him on the bima for much longer.

I hear the familiar words, which, even in this debased iteration, retain great power. Has my time come?

I botched mothering my daughters when they walked through the valley of family trauma, yes. But I have not lost my integrity. I am able to stand up. Me—a woman, a cantor, an American Jew. It's time for me to leave the side of this rabbi, to refuse his derivative script for the congregation and to find a better place for my convictions, my voice, and the work of my hands.

So I was wrong. It's not a forgettable Martin Luther King Jr. Shabbat. It is my last as a pulpit cantor.

Idyll

Much recognition
A pioneer now guides
For others' career paths

No, I Will NOT Be Seated

I will not work with a man who thinks that Martin Luther King Jr. Shabbat is an excuse to skip the writing of a sermon and to trot out his racist imitation of an American hero.

I say this to the Temple Beth Am leaders. And after serving this congregation for twelve years, it cuts me to the quick that these officers decide to retain the rabbi rather than me. I give six months' notice.

So that's that. I won't be retiring from the pulpit in a blaze of glory surrounded by generations of former B'nei Mitzvah students. I will not hear the singing of a huge intergenerational chorus of junior choir alumni. I will not be achieving my lifelong goal of being so well liked by so many people that I can bask for a few moments in my own reflected splendor.

Nope. I'm going to end up walking out quietly, with no one behind me, as I did at my high school graduation. I may be Barbi Prim, but Barbi Prim is Class Arguer—now and perhaps forever.

Kol Nidre, the Finale

It's sunset, and the service is about to begin. There's a sacred kind of quiet in synagogues right before Yom Kippur. I think about how this must be the same sacred silence shared by people in churches and mosques just before Good Friday and Eid-al-Adha services too.

At this holy gathering, we Jews are conducting a rehearsal of our deaths. The Torah scrolls are removed from the ark so that we are compelled to stare straight ahead into an empty box, to look into our own caskets.

Next, the Torah scrolls are held up in front of the worshippers, and everyone stands, in awe of death—out of reverence for the forgiveness we seek before dying.

The people who have come to pray are all dressed up. The scrolls are also dressed up, in silver crowns ringed with bells, in breastplates, and in velvet dresses. They wear necklaces with hand-shaped pendants. The scrolls and the people are poised to hear the cantor chant Kol Nidre.

I stand at my lectern, holding still. Behind me I hear the tinkling of bells as the scroll carriers shift the heavy Torah scrolls from arm to arm. From the congregation I hear muffled coughs. Somewhere a child is shushed. The organ begins its personal invitation. I check that my atarah is aligned, unable to resist reconfirming that it hangs evenly on both sides. I look down at the Aramaic words in my prayer book and then look up. It's time.

I inhale and imagine the first notes, praying that they will be clear and sweet. I send them out, but they fall short. Calmly I decide to fix the sound. So I will it out and up. I shape it and spin it and polish it and remind it of the words. I feed air into the sound and then pull back the volume according to those words. Louder on "the vows are no longer vows." Softer on "we regret them all."

In this moment, with my mouth open, I wield Kol Nidre power. I use that power to link my song with its close cousins, those other Kol Nidre prayers that echo now around the planet from one time zone to another, from one key to another. If all of today's Kol Nidre prayers were strung together, the sound would live for an entire day and miracles might happen.

And as I taper the last of the sound, I wonder for the final time in my career how high it went.

Sephora

Arlene likes my makeup today. She indicates this with the two-word comment "Nice makeup." I tell her that I recently bought

Aramaic: an ancient Semitic language, an ancestor of both Hebrew and Arabic

some new products at the Sephora store near the HUC building in Manhattan.

When I think of Sephora, I remember the doll section of Marshall Field's in Chicago. As a kid, I would look at all of the glass-encased dolls of different sizes and imagine playing with each one, each with her separate costume. It's as if I can still see the taffeta and lace, the pinafores and bonnets of those dolls. Today, at Sephora, I imagine instead my eyes being transformed by a new mascara or a different shade of eyeliner. Maybe my skin will be illuminated by an imported foundation or my lips by a new formulation of gloss!

Popping into Sephora during my occasional New York City trips always reminds me of another childhood scene—stopping at Fannie May for chocolate on the Saturdays when I rode the 'L' into Chicago. I still want treats to mitigate anxiety, in this case travel anxiety. Tangible little rewards in addition to the occasional Arlene-suggested Ativan, for when I start to panic on airplanes.

It's gratifying that Arlene, older than me and eternally stylish, approves of my cosmetics today. Week in, week out, she looks flawless.

On these rare visits to HUC, I want to look elegant and accomplished, if not flawless. As aware as I am that no one in the HUC community is giving all that much thought to my appearance, I persist in the fantasy that HUC folks think, "Ostfeld is looking good." Therefore I make it a priority to leave no styling act unperformed. I am a symphony of details. Eyebrows plucked and powdered. Lashes curled and thickened. Lips exfoliated and polished. Hair shining with fresh color and the requisite amount of pomade.

Arlene tells me that a Sephora will be opening in Buffalo, and I sigh with pleasure. Imagine! Then Arlene asks me about the word *sephora*, and I laugh! I hadn't given it any thought, but it's Hebrew for "bird," and it's the name of Moses's Midianite wife, Tziporah. It comes to me that the ancient rabbis described her as beautiful.

Arlene and I go back and forth about the fact that nearly every female protagonist in nearly every book or fable or tradition is beautiful. Then I think about the biblical matriarch Leah. The Torah comments that her eyes were weak, which may have been a way of indicating that she was not beautiful.

Letting the session continue in this vein, I ruminate aloud about the use of powdered malachite as eyeliner in ancient Egypt and about how many powders, oils, and paints it would have taken for Leah to look as good as Tziporah to a bunch of old rabbis.

Arlene asks me to speculate about how the matriarchs might have regarded themselves, their roles. I begin by saying that it seems certain that beauty has always been valued and that mates have likely always been chosen for their symmetrical features, height, and an appearance of health.

Thinking more about it, I wager that Sarah, the matriarch who spent a long life overseeing an enormous and productive herding compound, probably didn't take time to rub scented oils into the delicate area around her eyes every night. She may have worn color-fully dyed fabrics of the best quality to indicate her status, and her sandals may have had bling, but none of that actually belonged to her—property as she was herself. I doubt that she outlined her eyes in kohl.

Entertaining Arlene, I pantomime the application of liquid eye-liner, dipping an imaginary narrow stick into an imaginary ceramic jar. But since Sarah's power and authority meant that she had to carefully supervise the women and young men so as to maximize the efficiency of Abraham's extensive holdings, my guess is that on festive occasions, she brushed a bit of honeyed ochre onto her lips and left it at that.

Arlene and I are enjoying this bullshit, but I stop us.

I say, "It's one thing to dress up and fasten a diadem to your brow, don your most powerful pendants, and anoint yourself for festivals and celebrations, and yet another to do what Queen Eliza-beth I did."

Arlene asks me to elaborate. I tell her that Elizabeth died with layers and layers of white, lead-based paint on her face. It wasn't removed between daily applications! She'd had smallpox as a young woman and was obsessed thereafter with displaying smooth pale skin. The lead in her foundation probably hastened her death.

"How do we navigate the whole makeup thing? Is it about covering up our God-given faces so as to appear godlike? Is it about getting fancy for fun? Is it about deceiving those around us? Is it about wearing a demure mask of feminine submission? What the fuck is it about?"

Arlene asks me if I think that it might be a bit of all those things.

I do, but this is a therapy session, so I guess that the next logical question to answer is, why do I personally use makeup? Am I drawn to the perfectly stacked pastel boxes only because of my OCD? It's that, but not just that. I love the ritual of application, the exactitude of my own array of cunning little containers, and the way I feel when I'm wearing just the right amount and combination. Dressy, powerful, noteworthy, and in control.

I'm not giving that up anytime soon.

A Fete, and an Ode to Barbi Prim

My fifty-first year approaches. Am I actually turning fifty? What does that mean?

Dad writes a little ode to me on my fiftieth birthday, for which we all gather. Of course he holds court by reading it aloud. Of course we all listen.

> By the time she was fourteen months old, the handwriting was on the wall. She had two commands for her parents. "Sing Amy! Sing it again! Again!" And "Smoo' it out."
>
> That music was to dominate her life was clear. If only we had just listened.
>
> But less obvious was the second phrase, although its pragmatic strength was equal to the first in the long run.

"Smoo' it out" meant that there must be no wrinkles in her crib or on our bed.

Her parents joked and, at that time impressed by Freudian theory, wondered how she could be compulsive before she was toilet trained. But she was.

Now, there were detours on her road to compulsivity. She shared my glee in tilting pictures a millimeter or two and watching with pretend innocence her mother's distress. By the way, is that compulsive stuff hereditary? She didn't get it from me. I'm sure of that.

And for a time Barbara abandoned compulsivity completely. I remember the time her bedroom door was closed and I needed her for a phone call. I opened it— something I never should have done—and there, in a pile in the center of her room, were clothes. Nightgowns, socks, blankets, towels, washcloths, and some items I couldn't identify. Nor did I even try. For a moment, I thought of a photograph and a well-disciplined letter to *The Guinness Book World Records*, but I discarded the thought.

No one was meant to see that room. Her shame was so obvious. I tried to remember Holden Caulfield's problem with his slob of a roommate and scanned the episode to see if I could recall some comforting words. But Barb wanted me out. That was plain. And so I stepped out and closed the door.

Well, it wasn't long before Barbara left for the School of Sacred Music, and I was spared further evidence of the problem. When she lived in an upholstered broom closet on the Upper West Side for which she paid something like $100 per square foot, I—if I had been more deliberate—would have seen that the malady was back. But my mind was usually occupied with what we ought to purchase at Zabar's. And so I didn't pay enough attention.

Well, the malady persisted and then started to turn sinister. There was that ugly evening in Barbara's kitchen when, unsuspecting, I was overcome with ammonia fumes and had to dial 911. Fortunately the problem was self-limited. My problem with ammonia fumes, that is. Not hers with compulsivity.

I understand that she now uses something less lethal, but I will never again barge into her kitchen without a few precautionary sniffs first.

Is there hope? Is she flexible enough at her advanced age to lighten up a little? I don't know. Her intensity may be as intractable as her love of music. We'll just have to wait and see.

To close his tribute, Dad sings the following in his better-than-average voice to the tune of "My Favorite Things."

Grapefruit at breakfasts and grapefruit at suppers
Starts to dissolve out your lowers and uppers.
Most careful brushing and flossing with strings—
These are a few of my favorite things.

Citrus fruits inside dissolve your enamels.
Think how they'll cut dirt on tables and panels.
Sponge off those surfaces, clean one and all.
Keep them quite spotless with more CitruSol.

When the tooth snaps,
When the mouth hurts,
And I feel remorse,
I simply remember the large dental bill,
And then I feel much worse.

Of course I laugh raucously, as we all do, as is expected. Inside though, I'm stung, even as I ask myself why I can't just laugh at my own foibles. I always wanted Dad to pay attention, and here he's

written an ode to me, for heaven's sake! Well, not precisely an ode—
more like a roast. But I'm so roastable! I know I am!

Well, finally my own dad participated in a barbecue. Maybe he
IS like other fathers after all. No. He's not, and it's just up to me to
move beyond that.

Cantorial Placement Director

I see a job listing for placement director of the American Conference of Cantors, my professional organization. My brain lights
up. I call Scott, and we agree to talk over dinner, our accustomed
time for lingering, discussing the day, sipping wine.

As I do every night, I put a small glass bowl of carefully rinsed
radishes and olives in front of him. No dinner of Scott's ever starts
without this first course. My supper ritual is different, but just as
immutable. I eat the protein first, followed by the vegetable. If the
scale-god has been kind, I end my meal with a bit of starch. Our
nighttime routines never change. Okay, sometimes I make a salad.
With avocado and feta and pistachios.

I plunge into the career talk. "It's perfect. I don't think it's
full-time. I obviously can't move, and I won't have to. I don't want
another pulpit anyway. You and I will have weekends, Shabbatot, for
the first time! I'll be able to sit next to you when we go to temple!
The pressure will be off—no rushing around, no evening meetings. The executive director, Todd, is an old friend, and he'll be my
supervisor. I know there'll be a learning curve, but—"

"You realize that there will still be politics," he points out.
"It's not like you'll leave temple politics, never to deal with politics
again."

"Yeah, but ACC politics can't be as lethal as synagogue politics."
"Probably not."

So I write a letter to the executive director of the ACC.

I interview. I write an essay. I'm up against seven cantors for
this position. Still, I get the job.

So, with Scott's help, I perfect my computer skills. Thank
goodness Mom insisted that I take touch typing in summer school.

Shabbatot: plural of Shabbat

I like this new work. I get to impose order from my own Buffalo desk. I smooth things out, line things up, neaten edges. This is for me! And I am queen of my realm. Other women have served the ACC as placement director; I am neither the first nor the best, but I persist in a regal vision of myself as I affix my virtual seal to all kinds of documents. I savor the regimented precision of this work.

Two years pass while I juggle my phone, answer my email, and create Word documents. Two years of lunches at my desk, sponging off my work surface, and throwing out the cold coffee that daily develops a grayish skin.

The carry-on bag I bought before my first official trip to HUC looks ancient. The scuff marks make me proud. I am the new kind of placement director. The kind that regularly catches the early-morning JetBlue flight from BUF to JFK. I wheel my bag into a tunnel at Gate 7 at the Buffalo airport and wheel it out of what looks like the same tunnel, at Gate 6, Terminal 5, in Queens.

I pretend I'm time traveling because of that magic, and also because time speeds up when I enter the current HUC building, on West 4th Street. I meet with the current batch of cantorial ordinees and with next year's candidates. In double classrooms, I click from PowerPoint slide to PowerPoint slide, outlining the placement process, its rules and regulations. I am showing them a relief map that will help them navigate the synagogue world. The students click along on their laptops, taking notes. The fifth-year students are nervous and have lots of questions. The fourth-years are zoned out.

I have individual meetings with many of the students. We sit together in the student lounge while I gather information about their strengths and goals, and how their theses are progressing. I ask about their senior recitals. I work diligently to capture their answers on paper as they talk.

There are faculty meetings to attend and, during the winter, auditions and interviews for prospective students. Meals are served when we go late. I long for wine at these meals, but I wait until I hit the JetBlue terminal, where I sip my wine and read before heading to the departure gate.

Going in and out of tunnels, I've completed two entire placement cycles! I note with pride that I've updated and streamlined the placement process. I've done a lot of listening, and not only to students. Rabbis, cantors, and lay leaders talk to me. I hear about prayer and engagement. I hear about congregational mission statements and about the ways a cantor can welcome unaffiliated Jews and their partners and families into the kind of synagogue that keeps its doors open.

I read my evaluations and note with a little more pride that cantors have appreciated my support and counsel. Rabbis say that I've helped them find good clergy partners. Lay leaders indicate their satisfaction with the efficiency of the search process.

I, too, am satisfied. Cantorial placement is like a monochrome puzzle. I have to imagine the whole in order to start to solve it: Can I ascertain the borders and the magnitude of this congregation's needs? What are the contours of the gap that the retiring cantor will leave in the congregation? How will this new cantor fill those gaps? What are the dimensions of the gap left when she in turn retires?

Sometimes my brain aches with the effort of theoretical placement geometry. But the ache is soothed by the satisfaction that comes from doing something I'm good at—and the sound of pieces clicking together.

Counting Time Again

The pieces of the annual cantorial placement budget do not click. The numbers go wonky, and I consider giving up. The budget moves into my brain and occupies it as an enemy. In my dreams, spreadsheets move wildly in and out of focus. I feel exactly as I did in childhood when trying in vain to remember whether twelve comes before or after eleven. It's embarrassing to be a placement director who is unable to count.

I take the brain clog to Arlene. I tell her that I'm supposed to fill in a projected annual budget for the placement department and that even though I understand last year's budget numbers when I'm looking at them, I can't seem to keep them in my head.

I describe the way that the numbers and categories disintegrate, digit by digit, letter by letter, and disperse. I can't keep hold of a line of numbers, which makes me feel slow and dull. Why is it, I ask Arlene, that I can remember all the words to my elementary school fight song but not a short string of numbers? It's as if they appear and then immediately ricochet off each other. I tell her that I am actually afraid of numerals. I feel like they're teasing me, tricking me.

Arlene asks if my fear might have more to do with something else.

Yes, definitely. I think back to my dad's disapproval of my inability to count, of the fact that HIS CHILD couldn't keep her numbers in line.

Arlene reminds me that I have the ability to apply reason to this budget anxiety.

AHA! How did I not realize before that I can simply ask for help? I can easily get help from someone who works with budgets and knows her way around them!

My head is swirling with the crystal clear simplicity of this solution when I hear Arlene asking me why I haven't already asked for help.

"I, uh, I'm still stuck between eleven and twelve. I'm still acting like the helpless preschooler I was in the fifties. A kid who, without her dad's approval and attention, was worthless. Helpless."

My ears have just heard my mouth reveal me to myself. Another revelation!

Arlene says, "I think you have your answer."

And so I do. I need to see the budget as a project with which I need help—step-by-step instructions. The budget does not have to be the stuff of nightmares. It just has to be logically tackled. I even know who to call first.

I feel lighter already.

I Fail at Yom Kippur

It's Yom Kippur, but after years on the bima, I'm no good at being a congregant. I ready myself to be inspired but cannot be budged. The soloist here in nearby Longtail, Pennsylvania has not mastered her melismas. I grit my teeth and silently fill in the missing notes. The cellist hasn't tuned to the organ. I clench my fists.

This year Tali has joined us, and she's sitting next to me. I reach for her hand, hoping that her warm, plump hand will do the trick, that I will focus on the sweetness of her nearness and find myself stirred. Her hand feels much as it did in childhood, and my attention begins to turn. But then she whispers in my ear that the soloist sucks, and I lose whatever hope I had. She's right.

I try to engage with the service again, though, listening to the force of the congregational voice reading aloud. "Whither can I go from Your spirit?" I wait for an answer.

The soloist goes for a high note, barely holds on to it, and releases it too early. It is stillborn. I grieve for it, wishing that a real cantor were standing in her shoes.

I tell myself to rise above my melodramatic grief. I pray, *Let this be the year you overcome your pettiness*. But I know that my petition will be denied.

A young Torah reader attempts to read from Leviticus 19. He stammers over every third word and has not mastered the trope, although he soldiers on.

Had I taught him, I would have told him, "Either perfect it now or work on it for next year."

It's not fair to the congregation to have such an exalted text rendered without regard for its meaning or for the ear of the congregation or for the solemnity of the day.

I keep my jaw clamped shut. I concentrate on sitting with Scott. I lean against Scott.

We break for a Yom Kippur study session. I revive, and it seems that others do too.

Back in the sanctuary for the closing services, I sit with my family and focus. Focus, focus. As we read aloud, I am busy changing the printed words—*Lord* to *Eternal One* and *Kingdom* to *Realm*. Futility, and yet I persist, getting in my own way.

The service is coming to a close, and there has been no majesty.

Only lackluster chanting with missed notes, the wrong nusach, empty spots where liturgical masterpieces should have lit up the sanctuary. I droop. We end early, and I am mournful.

I've turned out to be a judgmental congregant, a nitpicking liturgist, a rigid pitch pipe of a worshipper. And I have 317 days until the beginning of next Elul, when I can really get down to introspection and self-correction once more.

Clearly I'm going to need every hour.

"Unassuming"? Nice. "Pioneer"? Eeek.

An old friend of mine, now director of the School of Sacred Music, calls on the phone. Bruce Levy is a cantor of my vintage and also a Ph.D. in Jewish history. We reminisce about cantorial conventions gone by and review our cache of insider jokes.

After we stop laughing, Bruce segues into business.

"I'd like to write an article about you for the *Journal of American Synagogue Music.* An issue about women cantors is in the planning stages."

I think this over in a moment. Yes, it's time for a new article! Women cantors have outnumbered men for years now! I register a jolt of pride.

"I'd be honored! Are you going to interview me and everything? Will there be footnotes?"

Bruce laughs and says, "When I'm not imitating Groucho, I write a mean article."

Who could forget his Groucho imitation? If drowsiness threatened a lengthy meeting, Bruce could be relied upon to say, "I've had a perfectly wonderful evening. But this wasn't it." (Groucho himself denied saying it.)

Weeks later, our interview is concluded. Several months pass— months during which I forget everything about our conversation and anything about an article.

Consequently I startle when I open my email and see Bruce's draft for my review.

Its title is "Barbara Ostfeld: An Unassuming Pioneer."

After reading it in disbelief, with my heart in my throat, I reassure myself. *It's not me tooting my own horn. It's what Bruce says, not me.* Then I stop myself from repeating this tired old refrain. *What the fuck would be wrong with blowing the shofar for myself?* The word *NOTHING* comes to my waking ear.

I resquare my round shoulders and, with an immodest click, forward the draft to Scott and my girls.

A Clutch of Cantors

My fourth ACC convention as placement director approaches. While most of my cantorial colleagues are anticipating being caught up in the convention whirlwind of workshops, master classes, text study, prayer, plenary sessions, and concerts, I am girding my loins and holding my breath.

Long before the travel date, my first preparatory step is revising the Word file titled "ACC Convention Packing List." What if I forget my tallit, my PowerPoint presentation, concert clothes, or budget reports? I back up my documents to my iPad for safety. What shoes should I bring? Do I need to schlep the curly hair diffuser? It's as if I think that by ticking things off an actual list, I will not only be provisioned, but somehow also prepped for the substance.

And here I am in Dallas. Tomorrow morning is the first board meeting, which will be followed by appointments with cantors. I send emails to each of them, reiterating the location of the coffee shop and confirming the time we will meet.

I go to the hotel café and order a broiled fish dinner with a glass of Sauv blanc, my new favorite wine. I eat while reading my book, taking my time, loving the calm that precedes tomorrow's storm.

Morning begins with the infernal chirping of the crickets. Why did I select crickets as my ringtone? I get out of bed and straighten the sheets, knowing that the hotel staff will make the bed. I am a model guest, as if anyone cares.

I wash my hair and dry it using the diffuser attachment, scrunching as I go. Dressed, made-up, and armed with my iPad, I head for the elevator, turning, as always, in the wrong direction. I find the elevator, get inside, and pause. Where do the L, G, and M buttons take you? The board meeting is on 3. I push the numeral and wait. The elevator remains in place. I sigh—I make this mistake all the time. Then I push the actual button, NEXT TO the number, and feel the elevator respond. I still have trouble with numbers. Oh well.

Oh! Here are my friends! We hug and kiss, and then with our Starbucks cups, we assume our places around the L-shaped table. Everyone opens a laptop or an iPad. Everyone deftly clicks or taps, and twenty-odd machines come to order. The cantors drink half-caff skinny lattés.

I doodle on my agenda. Eyes, flowers, a Hebrew word.

When the meeting ends, I ask several uniformed people for directions to the coffee shop even though I have a pretty good idea of where it is. I don't want to get lost or be late.

The succession of cantors I'll meet on the half hour for the next few days will consume all my attention. They're choosing to move on from their current pulpits or thinking about it—or wishing they could leave their pulpits or being forced to leave their pulpits.

"Barbara, I'm constantly being harangued to get our worship numbers up. I've reached out to friends whose sanctuaries are packed, but their methods don't work for me! I've tried everything, and all I am is exhausted. The rows are still half empty."

"Barbara, I feel like I'm the little ball in the pinball machine. I'm ricocheting from rehearsal to classroom to bima to graveside. I never see my wife or kids!"

"Barbara, I know membership numbers are dropping. My board is rethinking our dues structure, but in the meantime, all the clergy salaries have been slashed! Life at the temple is one cliff-hanger after another!"

I order many skim no-whip mocha drinks (an upgrade from lattés), only to watch them grow cold, because these conversations are hard on me. I overidentify. My colleagues are mired in atmospheres of congregational angst or even gloom, and I feel the muck between my own toes.

I can't fix the demographics of their Jewish communities. I can't restore their membership numbers or grow their preschools. I can't add thousands to their declining salaries. I can't teach the occasional congregational board how to treat a cantor more fairly.

But I can adjust their perspectives by drawing triumphs out of them and emphasizing quality rather than attendance. I can discuss options ranging from mediation to resignation. No one leaves my table laughing with relief, but some are heartened or ready to launch.

At the very least, no one will have to wait long before we reassemble for prayer.

When cantors gather, we ditch our personal baggage and enter a temporary sanctuary. We open our mouths, and no matter what, singing happens. During our twice daily services, held in the round, usually in airless meeting rooms, we find our collective sound. We make up harmonies. We whisper certain prayers and shout others. We beat out rhythms. Those of us who can, execute lip trills when the mood strikes. There are guitars and variously pitched drums. Often a flute. We hold prayer books or we read from a hanging screen. Sometimes the instruments cut off and we are left in the space with our own voices, scores of them, sounding in all registers. We move together too, sometimes dancing, sometimes swaying.

I don't let my primness keep me from joining the cantors who dance and sway. I can be one of the cantors who grow and evolve, as people are meant to do, as Judaism is meant to do, as even the Eternal One does, by moving beyond the divine requirement to burn animals on an altar, for example.

These days, singing is only a tiny fraction of my work. Instead I am choreographing dances between congregations and cantors. I use my music in new ways, but to the same end—connection to a Jewish path through melody. This melody is one in which cantors can dance their ways into the hearts of millions.

I still love the nuclear unity of the Vienna Boys Choir sound. I will always love their regimented choral formation and singers' posture. But today I think that the Eternal One prefers an earthy, variegated sound to an undifferentiated preadolescent falsetto, and drums and tapping to unpunctuated streams of tone.

"Eternal God, open my lips that my mouth may sing Your praise." All Jews sing, but we cantors disappear into our own sound. All Jews dance, but we cantors do it with Miriam and her timbrels. I know each time my mouth opens or my feet move that I am called to this work.

Shopping at Wegmans

I wake up. Among my first thoughts is one about Wegmans. Wegmans isn't just any grocery store. It's a state-of-the-art grocery store.

The stacks of toilet paper in the Banfeld basement are destined to be used over time, but our fish must be fresh and our produce dewy.

Wegmans' produce section features the variety that I came to expect from the storefront shops on Middleneck Road in Great Neck. Sprayers mist the rows of vegetables at regular intervals. The contents of the cases at the fish counter are odor-free.

Predictably, I have a love-hate relationship with Wegmans. Do I need to go to Wegmans today, or can I put it off until tomorrow?

I hate driving into its parking lot because each time it feels like mere moments have passed since I last left. But I love perusing its aisles for funky items like persimmons, fresh figs, raw pistachios, and kefir. And there's an entire section dedicated to artisanal chocolate.

I get out of bed and ask Scott to turn on "THIS—is CNN." That's what I call it.

While Scott prepares our breakfast, I conduct a mental inventory of our refrigerator. Yes, there's salmon. I bought it yesterday. Yes, green beans. White wine for me. Uh-oh! No radishes or olives? I'm going to have to hit Wegmans.

Was grocery shopping easier for my mom than it is for me? I think back on the quotidian piece of meat and frozen broccoli of my childhood. Yup—I decide that it was. Mom could get by with shopping once a week since freshness was defined more loosely back then.

I wash my face at the bathroom sink. In my mind's eye, I see the unending pastel yogurts of my early adult years.

I open a new toothbrush, toss the old, and shudder.

Was I really the mom who assembled a bunch of highly processed foods for my family every night? Can I cite pulpit life as the excuse?

Last night I marinated halibut in sriracha and teriyaki sauce and roasted spiralized beet noodles in olive oil and pink Himalayan sea salt.

Do I think about food and Wegmans this intensely every morning? Maybe.

I go down to the kitchen and write, "toothbrushes, soft," on the shopping list, knowing that I will purchase several multipacks.

In the Wegmans parking lot, I find a spot blessedly close to the entrance. My boots crunch over salted ice, and the heat of the entrance blasts me a welcome.

Wegmans' carts are sleek and ergonomic—perfectly designed to accommodate the shopper and the shopper's child, no matter how plump. The sharp metal grocery carts that pinched my thighs in childhood are only a memory. These new carts are squeakless and have wheels that swivel smoothly in any direction. I grab a cart-sanitizing wipe and go over the handle with it—attentively, but not exactly edge to edge.

Shopping list in hand, purse slung across my body, parka unzipped, I guide my cart up and down the aisles in a mild trance. I greet people as I go.

A former congregant openly assesses my cart. Is he looking for an appropriate balance of fruits and vegetables or searching its contents for kosher items? Is he counting the chocolate-themed foods? *Whatever*, I think, smiling at him.

Is that "The Christmas Song" I hear playing overhead? It is— it's Nat King Cole, with his velvet voice. I quietly join him.

I browse the extensive Chanukah aisles. Their fullness reminds me that it's time to get candles. I choose from four kinds of Chanukah candles. I like the hand-rolled honeycomb beeswax variety, even though I'm nostalgic for the orange, blue, and white assortment that came in old-fashioned blue boxes.

I pick out some fair trade chocolate coins while I'm at it.

And now it's time to conduct a search for the shortest checkout line. No logic ever applies to this search, even at Wegmans.

I unload heaps of mesh-bagged chocolate coins and three multipacks of soft toothbrushes.

After the cashier asks me if I found everything I needed, she and I discuss the snow as if we were meteorologists. She refers to the squall line, and I follow up with an update about flash freezes.

We are resigned and ironic when we wish each other nice days.

Well trained by Wegmans, she also calls after me: "Happy Holidays!"

I remember being little and sitting uncomfortably in a cold grocery cart. I remember Mom's twisted smile after my radio-voiced announcement about not having Christmas.

Today's carts are better, and so are the farewells.

"Happy Holidays!" I answer in my radio voice.

Cantorial Fledglings and Their Plumage

Maybe the thing I like best about being the American Conference of Cantors placement director is the chance to spend time with cantorial students.

I take a seat in the chapel at Hebrew Union College and put on my reading glasses. I don't know the woman student whose practicum is about to take place. These practica are so different from the pro forma recitals of my day. Today's students have vocal ensembles and instruments, including percussion, and programs with citations. It's a new world. I'm sitting next to an assistant dean who became a friend after we served on a search committee together. We whisper comments to each other between pieces.

A second young woman joins the first on the bima, and they begin to sing a Ben Steinberg composition, a duet. The piece sounds familiar. The young voices are so perfect together, sweet and clear. When they're through, the students and faculty breathe a sigh together. Really together. Our collective sigh means this is perfect.

I look at my program and recognize the piece. Nearly thirty years before, my friend Lanie and I sang it together at an ACC convention. Tears come to my eyes. It's been so long since I was a young cantor starting out, making people sigh with a perfect duet. Now I'm fifty-six. When this practicum is over, I'll go to class and prepare my senior students to enter the profession. I blink back the tears.

It's not that I'm struck by my advancing age. Not in this moment, anyway. It's that such spritely music-making exists here and gives me hope. On my own I'm so jaded. The worship music I usually encounter is so flaccid and lackluster that I have to PRETEND to be engaged whenever I occupy a pew.

I think of a book of Greek myths that we had as kids. On the last page of the Pandora's box story was a picture of Hope climbing timidly out of the chest. She looked forlorn—not a bit optimistic. The word *hope* has made me afraid ever since. But with these students, I'm not afraid to hope. The way they sing is different from the way we did all those years ago. Then, we were testing our voices or following instructions. But these students are experimenting with worship while they study it. They're not afraid to put wings on prayer words, their fresh voices reviving the old melodies.

I want to be like them, but all I can do is be with them.

Well, I can teach them too. From the lectern, I remind them: In your interviews remember who you are and what you aim to do in the Jewish community. Speak up. Talk about God, talk about Torah, and don't skip over the Jewish people. Don't tell search committees that you've applied to their congregations because you want to live near the ocean or in the mountains—keep your geographical lust to yourself. Focus on what you have to offer adult Jews—not just little kids or B'nei Mitzvah. Articulate your ideas about teaching new melodies.

Now we go over some questions.

And Leigh asks, "How am I supposed to explain that I will officiate at a same-sex wedding if both partners are Jews but not at an intermarriage?"

Samantha asks, "When do I tell them that I'm due to give birth between Rosh Hashanah and Yom Kippur?"

Shira asks, "At what point should I come out to them?"

I become fond of them. In truth, I fall in love with them. This process starts on our first day of class in November, and my love is cemented by the time they're ordained in June. At that point, most of them have found their first cantorial positions, and I've helped them through the steps. By that point, we've talked for hours.

Rabbi Judah the Prince famously said that he'd learned a lot from his teachers, more from his colleagues, and the most from his students. I used to try to apply that to my B'nai Mitzvah students. Their questions about Torah, posed in soon-to-reach-the-age-of-thirteen unworldliness, had a sacred quality. Questions like this: Is God a terrorist?

In the give-and-take that followed that question, my brain lit up! Aha! I need to discuss Torah in terms of its human authorship and to chat about God as a human construct. Long life to the grandson of Betty Friedan, the Bar Mitzvah boy who asked me that question!

I think about the hours I spend with my cantorial students and what I'm learning from them.

My female students dress with verve. Their clothes fit their bodies and suit their temperaments. They dress in ways that enable them to curl up to study, squat to talk to a homeless person eye to eye, or run to catch a subway. They don't spend a lot of time, as I used to, standing before an imaginary Religious Fashion Jury that assesses their wardrobe for primness, piety, and a splash of gloom. Their hair is long or short or untamed or elaborately braided. They wear makeup, or they don't. They don't listen to a voice that says, "Without lipstick, your mouth disappears on the bima, but with too much, you look like a strumpet." If a student's blouse sports an open

Rabbi Judah the Prince: a second-century editor of rabbinic literature

neck, she thinks nothing of it! After all she is a woman, and women have breasts!

I inhale unevenly. *Why does this idea make me so anxious?*

As if it were happening now, my stomach knots up the way it did when Joyce the Congregant handed me that unretouched wedding photo. Again I see my nipples shining through the fancy fabric of my party dress.

I hold my breath as my brain, unbidden, surfaces an older memory, a memory lurking beneath this one. The one featuring my wet bra. Wet bra? No—no bra.

That evening, almost forty years ago, I rushed home from the laundromat near my 79th Street apartment. The Clothes Spin was just around the block on 80th. There wasn't enough time for me to use the dryer because I needed to catch the subway to babysit the Nagy baby. My only other bra was dirty, so I went without one. Then I missed my stop.

I was not raped because I wasn't wearing a bra.

How long have I almost known that? Is this what I've been trying to grasp? Is this the part I couldn't tell Arlene about my Choraleer uniform?

I was no more responsible for being raped than those glass bottles were for shattering when they were thrown against the walls of that alley. It wasn't my fault, and I don't need to hide.

Can I now finally fly up, past the Choraleer uniforms and out of the dog shit and broken glass? Now that I can see these shackles, can I break loose from them?

And maybe now I can exhale. Slowly I let out my breath. There.

My stomach expands, and I start to itch in both shoulders. Are those nascent wings, iridescent green wings? To match my eyes?

Opening My Mouth in Therapy

I sit down across from Arlene and immediately pull a tissue from her stash. The words won't come, but I know I'm going to cry. My head is full of red-hot gibberish that won't translate into English.

Arlene says softly, "It looks like you're very sad, but is it sadness or something else?"

Then the single perfect word flies out.

"NO!" I scream. "I'm angry!"

Arlene waits while I cry aloud. I wait too, while the words form.

I tell Arlene brusquely that my dad was supposed to save Miriam, his own granddaughter—not merely comment about the nature of her diagnosis, which is all he did back then. As I talk, I feel both the power and the childishness of my present-day conviction: Daddy with his MD is omnipotent. Clinging to irrationality, I declare to Arlene that Dad is now supposed to save Sarah, his daughter, my sister—my little sister. Sarah has breast cancer, and it has metastasized.

"It's his fault," I weep.

Arlene asks, "Your father's? Your father's fault? That Sarah has cancer?"

"YES!" I cry.

And a notion comes to me. Shaking me with its enormity.

"I thought he could do ANYTHING!"

And again Arlene is quiet in her chair, but I feel her lean forward.

I hear a sound of my own making and recognize it as keening. I've never heard it before, except on TV. *Keening* is the perfect name for this sound.

". . . I can't fix ANYTHING!"

"Your father can't, or you can't?"

My mind spins. The Almighty Father, the Omnipotent God, the Fixer of All Things, the Loving Parent, the brokenhearted cantor. We align ourselves, we the good guys, only to lose. Death wins every contest, and I see things lining up. God, Dad, me, modern medicine, science, the synagogue, HUC on one side. On the other side, death. Death and evil. Evil and despair.

I wipe my eyes and look directly at Arlene for the first time in today's session.

I say to her that Hebrew prayers have no power. I say that my sister will die before my eyes and that I will have to endure it. I say that she will die before my MOTHER dies, and that I will have to watch my mother endure it too! In the quiet, more things line up inside my brain, and I tell Arlene that I'm angry and then that I'll scream if I want to.

Arlene says, "Who is keeping you from screaming?"

Crying again, I tell her that my dad is keeping me from screaming. That he told me that I was a loudmouth and that my trap needs to be kept shut.

Wow. I can hear him saying it. Such an ugly word for mouth, *trap*. I didn't want to be a little girl with an open TRAP. I wanted to be a little girl who was quiet, demure. But a quiet girl can't do anything with her anger.

"It hurts so much to be this angry and to shut the fuck up about it! So fuck him and his golden silence, and fuck God and fuck all those bleeding psalms! Instead of praising God, I call FOUL!"

Arlene tells me gently that our session is almost over and, reminding me that there's nothing good about keeping silent, asks me to say more.

Here goes. "I always knew Dad was wrong, but I desperately needed to believe that he had all the answers. Dad, my first god. I kept my mouth shut to please him from the time I learned to talk until now! He's in his eighties, and my mouth is open! And as for the God of my people, She is somewhere in our back-and-forth, Arlene."

"God is in our session?"

"Yes. Crying with me."

Mom's Box of Photos

Sarah gathers up boxes of old photographs when she and Gavin visit Mom on the memory care floor at Whitney Center. I've promised to go through these boxes, which are old themselves, with broken metal clasps and some faded scrollwork on their borders. Since I'm the oldest child, it feels right that I should organize their contents. It's also a good idea to do it sooner rather than later. After she dies, looking through her keepsakes will be much harder.

So there have been several of these large boxes in my basement for weeks now. On a Sunday I ask Scott to bring them up. The cold basement is no place to do this job.

The boxed items are in no particular order. There are snapshots of Mom's cousins, aunts, and uncles who were gassed at Auschwitz, and some letters and postcards in Hungarian dated mostly in the early forties. I'm afraid to have these translated. One letter is in pencil. The handwriting is an uneven scrawl, light and dark, wandering, disconnected.

I scan everything into my computer, including the postcards, and put all the files on a disk. Now I can look at the images on my screen and avoid damaging the family artifacts.

The most important image is a black-and-white postcard from Vienna dated 1933. In it four Speigler cousins, ranging in age from five to nine, are seated close together. All three girls are wearing sleeveless white dresses and smiling politely. The boy is wearing a sailor suit and a smirk. Paul looks like a mischievous little devil. His arms are wrapped tightly around his chest, but it looks like he's about to burst out laughing. On the far left is my mother, age eight, looking calm, and next to her is her sister Lil, whose eyes are a bit shadowed underneath. On the other side of impish Paul is Alice. Alice is the one I've stared at since childhood. Why was I more riveted by Alice's fate than Paul's?

Mom and Lil are cute, with dark eyes and huge white ribbons tying their dark hair back. But Alice is strikingly different, with light blonde hair and pale eyes. Even though the postcard is black and white, it's obvious that her eyes were bright blue. Alice's hair appears to be floating around her face.

I see now why I fixated on her when I was a little girl in the fifties. She looked like storybook girls did then, like the little girls in midcentury TV commercials.

I remember asking when I was a child, "Where are your cousins now, Mom?"

"They were killed in the Holocaust."

As a kid I used to wonder if "Holocaust" was a place. I used to think that my mother was lying. I was sure that they'd escaped death. I looked at Paul and thought, *There's no way that Paul didn't escape, like in the Hardy Boys. You can tell that he would escape.*

And I looked at Alice and thought, *No one would kill Alice.*

I close the postcard file and proceed to click on photo after photo.

A picture from the thirties shows another young Spiegler cousin on an outing wearing a trench coat, white ankle socks, and Mary Janes. I suppose that was the style for little boys in Vienna.

Two unidentified little Vogels sit side by side in matching sailor suits. The photos are black-and-white, taken in Budapest in the twenties, and it's clear that these children, too, had blonde hair and blue eyes. It's difficult to click on the arrow to continue past them. Who were they, and did they escape?

The next one is of my omama, Olga Spiegler, wearing a dark-hued turn-of-the-century bathing costume trimmed with white piping, plus bathing shoes with intricately crossed ties, knee socks, and a puffy bonnet. In this wonderful getup, she lounges on the sand, head on hand. Had Omama lived longer, I wonder if she would have taught me how to wear makeup, style my hair, and pick out clothes.

And here is my grandmother Margaret Ostfeld shaking hands with the sister she hadn't seen for fifty years. Yes, shaking hands, as if she were in a congregational greeting line—not embracing. Gramballs never took our hands when we crossed the street or kissed our cheeks or stroked our hair. In the absence of her touch, I had to infer that she loved me.

In this one, my beautiful aunt Jenka wears a coronet of dark braids, a lace high-collared blouse, and a heart-shaped locket.

Next appears my mother's confirmation class picture at Temple Beth-El in South Bend, Indiana. Mom is fourteen and looking quite serious—much older, too. She's wearing peep-toe heels and clutching a large bouquet of white flowers, her floral offering for Shavuot. The bima is covered in greenery. The boys, smaller than the girls, are all wearing tweed suits.

I pick out my father in a photo of Naval Air Technical Training Center trainees.

Shavuot: Weeks—a harvest festival that occurs seven weeks after Passover and commemorates the giving of the Torah; often an occasion for a confirmation ceremony

After this is a thank-you note to my father from John Emerson for speaking to the youth group at the Unitarian church in Elmhurst on the topic of hallucinogenic drugs.

And here is one of me. Over the years I've destroyed as many of the pictures of my young self as I could find. The ones in which I was thick and oily-haired and bespectacled. The ones featuring a dark upper lip that competes for attention with an ill-placed hair ribbon. The ones with the evidence that I went to junior high wearing my Maria dirndl because I had been asked to sing for the school board at noon. Even the class photos, because they showed a child who didn't know she had a choice about how to look and feel.

I lean in toward the computer screen and examine the few junior high photos that escaped liquidation. What if this ungainly, earnest girl had been swept into a tight embrace by her parents or her grandmother? What if she had known consistent, easy affection? Would she have become a different woman? A woman who allows herself to move beyond her earlier shame? A woman who is confident of her right to exist? Maybe even of her stature?

And here's another one of me—one I'm forcing myself to keep. I'm performing a scene from a children's theater play alongside a girl in blackface. She's making her eyes bug out, just as she was no doubt instructed to do. It's hard to look at the racism that I didn't recognize at the time.

And now another. I'm second in line, posed with the other tap-dancing third graders and wearing the same tights, tutu, and sequined bodice. My thighs are larger than all of the others. I am attempting a smile.

Here's one of Sarah and me. Mom had cut our hair very short and very unevenly. We have bald spots. I know I should be able to laugh at it, but I still can't. I'm still ashamed.

And two more pictures of me, after my voice recital in 1965. I was twelve or thirteen, standing awkwardly in front of Mom's camera. We were on our way to a modest concert hall that Miss Taylor rented for student recitals. Miss Taylor had instructed Mom to find me an aqua silk shift dress with a fancy collar. Of course

Mom made one instead. An ill-fitting white slip, all bunched up on top, is visible underneath the dress. I wasn't allowed to wear pantyhose, so I'm wearing ankle socks and ordinary shoes. My hair is slicked down with water and pulled back by a headband for the occasion. I'm wearing the shiny pink lip gloss that Miss Taylor required.

I remember the blocking for my song. I was supposed to enter from behind the curtain and twirl around until I reached center stage. But my glasses were taken from me, and so, slightly disoriented, I got briefly tangled in the curtains. But I twirled on, winding up too far back and a bit off center. Also mussed and winded.

For a laugh, I email Sarah, her daughter Shoshana, Hana, and Tali the least flattering photos of me, adding appropriate self-deprecating captions.

A few days later, Tali emails back: "Mom, you were so cute. What great pix! Love, Tali."

An hour or so thereafter, Hana texts: "Mama, so sweet! What a cutie! I love you, H."

Late that night I realize that my daughters had conferred. They discussed the images and decided not to go along with my jokes.

They know about my Shame Demons. I conjured them via email this time, but they're easy to recognize in any medium. Every time I make a comment about my nose or my hair or my butt, a Shame Demon steps forward.

Hana and Tali simply refuse to shake their hands.

Squaring My Shoulders

I'm only a few months from retirement. Temple Beth Zion here in Buffalo is going to celebrate my career by holding a cantorial concert. The religion reporter from the *Buffalo News* comes to our house to interview me. His photographer colleague thinks that the best spot for the photo is our front porch. The morning light is perfect just outside our door, and now the camera is in position. I remember my mother's advice about doorways and stand up straight.

A week later, the proof arrives in the mail. I tear open the envelope.

I see that my facial expression is stiff but true. I've always had a hard time looking natural in pictures. I've always been anxious about how they'll turn out, and my face has reflected that worry. This photo is a little different. I look deliberate and focused. There's nothing apologetic in my stance. My expression says, "I've got this." Maybe even, "Take your shot. I'm ready for my close-up."

I note with satisfaction that my tallit is correctly aligned, and I register my own gravitas. The word *gravitas* actually pops into my mind. Before I critique my hair or note the new slackness in my neck, I pick out my own trustworthy, kind face. This is the face of someone who's got it down, who isn't pretending, who's come into her own.

So before I'm tempted to look more closely at my nose, I make a little check mark on the accompanying form, approving the photo for publication.

A Prim Queen's Happy Dance

From childhood on I've read about Queen Elizabeth I. She was the kind of woman I wanted to be when I grew up: a queen. Her red hair was natural, and she loved to set it off with green velvet. She played the keyboard skillfully. Her handwriting was flowery, and her signature featured an outsized capital *E*. She was also a graceful dancer and favored a particular dance called "la volta," which involved twisting, leaping, and touching thighs—a stately lewdness. I like to imagine that the volta was Her Majesty's happy dance.

I still want to be like her.

As a child, I started out by reading *The Story of Good Queen Bess* and claiming green as my favorite color. Lately I finished *Elizabeth I: The Novel* by Margaret George. And when I write letters to my cantor friends, I use Florentine patterned paper and a green pen with a very fine tip. I begin with the date at the top, take time over my best handwriting, and finish with a signature that features an ornate capital *B*.

I open an email from one of my recipient cantor friends. She tells me that when she opened my letter, she felt as if she had received a missive from the queen! I laugh out loud with delight.

What aspect was she referring to, though? Was it royal handwriting? Nah. My handwriting is nice, but it isn't calligraphic. Was the letter stiffly worded? Oh I hope not, but it might have been. Was it the very formality of a letter, now that everyone texts back and forth?

I actually call this friend and ask. "What do you mean: 'the queen'?"

She says, "Barbara! Come. On. You're the queen of the cantorate."

I laugh again. I don't know what to call the feeling, but immediately tears come to my eyes and I imagine dancing the volta to the accompaniment of pipe and drum.

Shoe Shopping with My Inner Therapist

It's so satisfying to have shoes that really enhance an outfit. I'm not referring to matching shoes, which are passé according to Shoshana. Certainly it's been years since I thought about shoes that go with my purse.

But I do love the thought of leather lace-ups paired with pleated skirts, or of pumps with discreet bows to complement sheath dresses.

The shoe problem is complicated for me, though.

For one thing, despite having worn sensible shoes forever, I've developed bunions. So although I'm sufficiently liberated from severe primness to wear heels, now I can't walk in them without saying "fuck" audibly. Brownies accused of having potty mouths grow up to say it like it is.

Also, I've internalized the therapeutic process. When I shop, my desires and I take part in silent therapy together.

On a department store shoe rack, I see a brown leather, thick-heeled brogue with perforations and a fringed tie. I lust for these shoes. I imagine that wearing them, I will be graceful, willowy, and British—prim, and amusing.

My inner therapist says, *Do you not recognize that your desire for these shoes has more to do with your wish for an instant, magical transformation than it does with the actual purchase of footwear?*

I turn the shoes over, looking for a price, and perhaps a reprieve from the question. Sighing at what I see, I put them back.

Pale beige-pink ballet flats, soft as flannel, with cunning little string ties catch my eye next.

I hear the nonjudgmental but pointed question: *Are these the shoes for an authentic woman, or do you imagine that they will erase your childhood clumsiness?*

There is nothing pink in my closet, so I walk on without doing a price check.

Then I see them—the right pair. Black patent leather, a round toe with a subtle grosgrain ribbon. Bima shoes, and appropriate for evening. Suitable for a concert or a lecture.

Yes. These will indulge your fancy without calling attention to your everlasting attraction to regalia.

It's good to know that my inner therapist has a sense of humor.

Singing in the Original Key

Our new TV must have come from the future. It's an LCD, whatever that is, and now we need something called an HD cable box to make it work right. Scott spent about three hours picking it out at Stereo Advantage while I died of boredom. I don't know or want to know the details, but it's currently being installed in our family room.

The self-proclaimed geek who hooks it up gives us instructions. He seems very proud of the TV, as if it were his baby. It comes with lots of colorful wires, many cables, and two gray remotes. The geek shows me how to change channels with the arrows on one of the remotes. But how will I know which remote to use after he leaves?

I will never learn how to use this TV, even if I actually develop a desire to watch the cartoon he plays to demonstrate it to us, which features the Grim Reaper. No rabbits, ducks, or mice. Today's kids watch cartoons about Death?

And how can there be this many channels? I ask the geek. He

tells me that there are over two hundred channels but doesn't go into why. I tell him, feeling old, that when I was a kid, there were three channels. The geek is incredulous, just as I intended.

When he leaves, I turn off the TV, which was way too loud the whole time it was on.

I ask Scott if he remembers adjusting the horizontal and vertical holds on the back of 1960-era televisions. He does and asks me if I remember fiddling with rabbit-ear antennas. I do. We laugh, and I proceed to dust the new set with a microfiber cloth.

Everyone at Edison School watched the same TV shows because there really were only three channels then. My schoolmates and I had all seen the cartoon featuring Bugs Bunny styled as Wagner's Brünnhilde, with fake eyelashes and fake armored breasts, singing operatically to a horn-helmeted Elmer Fudd.

At age seven or eight, when I realized that I sounded exactly like Bugs-as-Brünnhilde to my classmates, I stopped singing loudly and began to soft-pedal my voice. After being made fun of by other kids, mostly boys, I sang in an undertone, with my mouth demurely opened just a little, staying far away from any operatically high keys. I wanted to be a Vienna Choir Boy, or a kid who sang on Mickey Mouse's talent roundup, not Bugs Bunny in drag.

When I was seventeen and new to HUC, my favorite cantorial teacher tried to cure me of that. "Open your mouth," he said. "Let the sound come out. Sing the music as it's intended to be sung." But I couldn't get all the way there. Not until now.

Until now, I never sang fortissimo. I also never risked singing concert pieces in their original keys. I always sang them in lower keys, unwilling to hazard cracking on a high note. So I never did crack on a high note. I avoided the power that higher, brighter keys impart to synagogue music and performance pieces. I was afraid that someone, maybe the Almighty even, might find it too crackly or too loud.

Power does have its risks. But after all these years of therapy, I'm finally willing to risk fortissimo in treble keys, open-mouthed and standing up straight. My inner Barbi-Bugs-Brünnhilde has returned to me in my fifties. The early, reactive primness—the primness that pursed my lips and inspired my unalterable rules—is giving way.

I loved my formality, though. Parts of it do live on—mostly in my knees, which I press together when I sit. And in my hands, which are usually clasped. But I am newly in love with the power I can wield. The radio speaking voice, the brighter keys, the higher truths.

Recapitulation

Time to travel
As her retirement has arrived
Grandbaby spells joy

Tap-Dancing My Way into Retirement

It's been a lazy Sunday and I'm rolling up socks. This is the most work I've done all day. I wind up with one extra sock, as usual. I look in the washer for its mate. I look in the dryer for its mate. I think about ditching it, knowing that it will always be a loner. This makes me sad.

I bring the bundled socks up from the laundry room to our bedroom and open up my sock drawer. It's full because I like socks. Striped socks, the kind with narrow stripes. Socks with a bit of lace around the ankles for fun. Socks with dots so tiny that you have to look for them. I squeeze the plump, newly laundered sock rolls into the drawer. I force it shut and turn to my closet, not knowing why exactly. I pull back its door and look at my clothes.

Now that age sixty approaches, will I buy some elastic-waist pants and a transparent origami rain hat? Will I still be a cantor? Will anyone still call me "Cantor"? Does the title matter to me? Is there such a thing as a cantor who doesn't lead worship? Will I be a former cantor, a late cantor? What will happen to my skills if I no longer sit daily at a keyboard or speak diplomatically and strategically on the phone?

When I was growing up I heard talk of women who had "let themselves go." I assumed they were no longer dying their hair, wearing heels, or bothering with lipstick. Whatever it meant, it was clearly a bad thing to let oneself go.

What will my days be like once I'm not answering to a job description? Will every day be like this lazy Sunday?

Wait. No.

I'll set up an art table and buy little tubes of cerulean-blue and cadmium-yellow paint!

I'll study voice and learn nonliturgical music!

And I'll come up with a cool way to describe my retirement status too. Wait. I've already found one! It's the title of a book by a former nun, Maria Harris. *Jubilee Time*. It's perfect.

Am I overthinking this because I'm a woman cantor? Other women cantors have retired before me. They're chaplains, and they sing with Alzheimer's patients. They've established vocal ensembles and relearned the piano.

Sometimes overthinking is actually a good practice. Like now when I'm wondering what I'm going to do after I retire. My brain is firing, and I see images of myself in the middle of a chorus line. No. A line of tap dancers! That's it! I'll take my place in a line of women who dance with relaxed precision and humor—and wear tulle! We will fine-tune our choreography and laugh with pleasure.

I can hear us chanting with focused abandon, "Shuffle ball change, shuffle step heel, shuffle brush, ball change, ball change and slide!"

I'll have to find tap shoes. What kind of socks does the well-dressed retired cantor wear with tap shoes?

I step from the closet back to the sock drawer. Nothing's quite suitable in here. I guess I'll have to launch a search for tap-dancing socks for the older woman. Fun!

Can a retired cantor maintain the dignity of her calling while executing shuffle-ball-change in funky dotted socks?

Does she even care about dignity as she taps away? I answer myself—*She does not*—and head downstairs to my desk to begin sketching out some jubilee plans using my skinniest green pen.

Oma and the Merry-Go-Round

My fifteen-month-old grandson knows me as Oma. This afternoon I settle him on the bright red merry-go-round at the elementary school playground. The molded plastic kid twirler has a number of larger and smaller seats. I place Jonathan on a small seat so I can hold him firmly in place as I walk him around and around in circles.

With gleeful shrieks, two ten-year-old girls, one in a pink tutu, race toward the twirler. The taller girl whips it into high gear and whoops. Faster than lightning, her hands grasp and turn the wheel on top that makes it go. Instantly I feel like I'm a cartoon version of myself, my legs spinning around an anatomically impossible axis.

There's no way my feet can perform at this pace—not in these black tooled Dansko clogs. There's no time to complete my *What am I, an idiot?* thought. I make a grab for Jonathan's opposite underarm and clutch him to myself, flinging us away from the whirligig. Oma takes flight with her nestling!

We land on my left foot, then on my hip—or hip then foot. I'm not sure which or how. Still, I'm not complaining: We land on 100 percent recycled styrene-butadiene rubber, a two-layer safety surface. I register that this is because Heim Elementary School is in a largely white, affluent suburb of Buffalo.

Oh yeah, my foot is definitely fucked up.

I hoist us up, and Jonathan chuckles briefly. Leaping into the air and then bouncing on the ground with Oma is fun!

Standing again, I exhale, whispering, "We're okay, we're okay, we're okay." Until I realize that I'm soothing myself alone.

We need to go home. My foot—ow!

Jonathan spots a school bus and makes a run for it. I cut him off and wrestle him into my car. I sing what I always sing when fastening him into his car seat. "Oma's gonna let you blow the horn, Oma's gonna let you blow the horn."

Once we're inside the house, I step with no small measure of relief out of my clogs. Wincing, I carry Jonathan down the stairs and into the rec room. We sit down on the carpet and begin to play.

Abruptly he becomes fragrant in that baby way, and I start to lift him to take him upstairs to change him. And no. No, there is no way I can walk. None. My left foot won't bear any weight.

I call Scott. His meeting has just ended, and he can come right home. Little Jonathan crows with delight to see him. The diaper gets changed.

Two series of X-rays and one CT scan later, I learn that I have broken my foot in two places.

For the next six weeks, I'll be wearing a black Frankenstein boot. Instead of decorative tooling, it has a functional blue button that, when pressed, inflates the boot, squeezing my foot nicely.

I've always been deathly afraid of losing my balance. I walk on ice as if I were ninety instead of sixty. I don't jump under any circumstances, for any reason. Why risk anything? I won't take an overly long step over snow, water, even filth. What if I were to fall?

But today I learned that nothing, not even my deepest fears (dirt and pain, pain and dirt) will ever keep me from shielding my grandson.

Barbi's Shorts Revisited

I go directly from my dresser drawer to my computer screen. I need shorts. It's too fucking hot to wear cropped pants or capris. Climate change calls for genuine shorts, linen shorts.

EddieBauer.com, here I come.

Online shopping has liberated me from dressing rooms, with their carnival mirrors, ominous hooks, and flimsy curtains.

And because I can order clothes today, right now, and return them via mail next week, it's easy to take fashion risks.

I click on Clothing and then on Women and then on Shorts. Ooh! So many choices! Now that I allow myself to look beyond black and khaki.

Plum? Or maybe russet? If I looked good in scarlet, damn, I'd order shorts in scarlet.

I click on Tops. A sleeveless ribbed tee in champagne. Nice with plum.

It seems strange to me now that I invented and then slavishly followed so many wardrobe laws. It's almost hard to remember why, but I do remember. I had no female cantorial role models, so

I reverted to my white-blouse-black-skirt Choraleer uniform. The rules I made up about female clergy attire kept me feeling safe. I thought they would protect me from letting bad fashion choices derail my career, but now I understand that they were an attempt to protect myself from more than that.

Slowly but happily, I've been repealing these laws, even if I need a little therapy push to continue sometimes. When I scroll through my recent online purchase history, I see a spectrum from carnelian to jade.

Back to Shorts, and here they are. The third pair in the second row. These are called Women's Ripstop Bermuda Shorts, Slightly Curvy. Perfect.

This cut and length will suit my body and feel good.

I used to like the feel of drapey clothing and the look of layers of eyelet, velvet trim, and touches of lace. I wore lots of Laura Ashley, and long Gunne Sax dresses. I imagined that I was modestly covered and adorned, but instead I was posing. I was posing as a properly reared, well-mannered girl (that's right, girl, not woman) of the Victorian era.

Therapy with Arlene has helped me embrace myself as a whole woman. Hana and Tali have helped me make parallel progress in my actual wardrobe. Sometimes this means that one of my girls will look me up and down with a popish expression on her face, shake her head slowly, and say, "No. Mom. What. Were. You. Thinking?"

So I've learned that if I buy an A-line dress or a waisted dress— one that zips neatly up the back, one whose hem hits my knees— and if I shy away from pastels (aqua, peach—been there), I win my daughters' approval. Add a string of pearls and black or pale beige flats and I earn a gold star. My earrings should not match my pearls. I know this from my niece Shoshana. She may be in med school now, but her wisdom is not confined to idiopathic thrombocytopenic purpura.

My girls don't like me in short hair, nor does Scott. I agree. I see now that chin-length hair does suit the shape of my face. It looks good.

And I do major consulting before choosing a pair of glasses. Do the frames obscure my eyebrows? Does the bridge make my nose look bigger? Do the stems make my eyes look wider? And importantly, do they look great?

Inevitably, every year the time comes to get back or down to the very important question of shorts. In no way do I resemble the stunning, superfit black woman with spiky bangs who is modeling item number TA30177.

But I look perfectly fine in shorts.

My girls think so too.

Elephant

What am I doing in Botswana? As fortunate as I am to be on safari, as comfortable as I am riding high in an upscale jeep, as relieved as I am to find our accommodations rather grand, I am struggling to feel clean enough. I have nowhere near the control over my physical being or its cleanliness that I so carefully maintain at home. On safari, I have to pee from a squat behind giant termite mounds, and then I have to use a tissue to wipe myself, and then I have to pack that tissue out. My only salvation is my hand sanitizer.

Is there any aspect of this incredible experience so exalted that it can lessen my fear? A newborn giraffe finding its footing? A leopard sinking its teeth into a gazelle? The lavender and turquoise feathers of a lilac-breasted roller?

The answer is in my camera. I snap photo after photo, deleting 96.5 percent of them and gasping at the beauty of the 3.5 percent that remain. Seeing these intoxicating images allows me to cope. The camera is my teacher. I have the power to adjust not only camera settings but also my own settings. I congratulate myself on my well-earned self-awareness.

That is, until I hear what I take to be the blast of life's final trumpet inches from my face. In the ensuing silence, time slows and the air around me grows still.

Slowly I begin to identify the sound. It's neither the final trumpet nor the wail of the shofar. The sound is not from an instrument.

It comes from somewhere in the vicinity of the tusks. Yes, I see tusks and heavily lashed red eyes. A trunk. Very close. The sound came from somewhere below the eyes of what I know to be an elephant. A charging elephant. He is making that sound with his trunk and announcing my death. UUuuHhheeerrrruuhhRRRRR!

I do not even think the word *Sh'ma*.

Our guide shoves me away, ripping off his jacket at the same time. He snaps it ferociously in the elephant's face, causing him to turn his mighty head away. And to snort wetly.

I am rescued from death-by-elephant and from the *Wild Kingdom* soundtrack that would have accompanied it.

Now, hours later, showered and seated with our travel companions on the deck of our high-end tent camp, I grab a cold copper wine cup and request a Sauvignon blanc. Scott is laughing with our friends, both of whom also look scrubbed and relaxed. The lounge is open to the river, and yellow lanterns hang here and there. I lower myself into a padded armchair and remind myself to loosen up.

Drummers assemble on high stools nearby. They begin to drum at the same instant, without any apparent nod or cue. So many pitches! My ears follow them as I sip my wine, enjoying the scents of spice and citrus in my cup.

But before the wine and the drums relax me entirely, I log a note to myself: The next time I hear anything like UUuuHhheeerrrruuhhRRRRR, it might be advisable to invoke God's name.

The Supermoon and Adonai

An electronic harp arpeggio comes from the depths of my purse, and I dig out my phone. It's 7:30, my phone reminds me. It's time to call Mom. Just a few months ago I was calling her at 8:00. Now by 8:00 she's asleep.

I tap "Mom, Whitney Center" in my Favorites list and wait. Mom's aide, Wanda, picks up. While she's handing the phone to Mom, I hear her say, "Ruthy, it's your daughter, Barbara!" Wanda's voice is sweet, even at the volume she needs to use so Mom will hear her.

Sh'ma: Listen—this prayer affirms God's oneness and is to be said when death is at hand

I walk over to the sliding doors leading to our deck. It's a clear November evening, and I can see the supermoon, which has been heralded in the *Buffalo News*. It's spectacular, worth the hype.

When I was little and went outside at night, seeing the moon was exciting. Observing the moon's phase is still important to me, even sacred. What else comes out at night, but not every night, changes shapes and colors, and is surrounded by glitter? It also moves from one place in the sky to another, but not if you watch every second—only if you forget about it for a little while. Mom used to sing a moon song to me on the outside nights.

Hana's first word was *moon*. On the nights that I was home, when the weather was good, I would take her out to the front walk during our bedtime ritual. Excitedly I would point out the moon and name it. One night around the time of her first birthday, Hana pointed to the moon herself and proclaimed, "Moo." Her decree was a sacred amen for me. My baby spoke a word.

Tonight I hear my mother's rasp over the phone.

"Barb?" she asks hopefully.

The hope in her voice is evidence of her enduring love.

I coo, "Hi, Mom! It's BARB. How ARE you, Mom?"

"I'm fine," croaks my mother, "How are you, Barb?"

I ask her about dinner, about her day, about any crafts she's doing. Her answers are uncertain. She doesn't remember and can't tell me anything, really.

I change gears.

"Mom, it's a full moon tonight! SO bright and beautiful!"

"Moon?" asks my mother. "Oh, the MOON!"

I hear the sound of her wheelchair being moved. Wanda heard her say "moon" and is moving her to the window in her room. I love Wanda. I hope she senses that in this very moment.

I hear her say, "Look, Ruthy! See it?"

Mom says to one of us, "I SEE it!"

This is a good night, a good conversation. Mom seems happy.

I know it's time to wind down our talk so she can get to bed.

"Are you in your NIGHTGOWN, Mom?" I ask.

"YES!" she says with gusto.

"So are you ready to sing, Mom?"

"OF COURSE!" she shouts.

In old age Mom loves to sing—and loudly. I admit to being embarrassed by this, while at the same time delighting in her pleasure. Her raucous voice next to my ear in temple in recent years often made me squirm. But she can no longer attend services. Not since Dad's death a few years ago. I know that her death is not far off.

I hear a soft bump and then some rustling. She's dropped the phone.

While Wanda is picking it up for her, I think about how Mom used to keep a pair of stainless steel travel chopsticks with her. She would never eat an Asian dish without chopsticks, and boasted that she could easily grab a single grain of rice with them. She never used disposable chopsticks and constantly reminded us, when we took her for sushi or dim sum as we used to do, that chopsticks are the product of slave labor and that 200 million trees are wasted to make them each year.

Mom can't hold chopsticks at all anymore. Some nights Wanda has to feed her. She doesn't remember that she played the cello. The music is still with her, though. If a staff member plays a recording at mealtime, Mom sings and sings, remembering every lyric. I'm proud that she remembers song lyrics.

I quiet my mind and muffle my sadness. It's time to put Mom to bed. As I always do before we sing, I wish her pleasant dreams. I say, "Goodnight, sleep tight, don't let the bedbugs bite." Usually Mom will say the last two words with me. Sometimes she gets stuck wishing me only pleasant dreams and will say, "Only pleasant dreams to you, too, Barb," four or five times. I reply, "You, too, Mom," as many times as it takes. Also, just before we sing, I tell Mom that I love her. Invariably she replies, "I love you, too, Barb. So much. For always." Occasionally we get caught here, too, in a cycle of exchanging love words.

To help her to the next phase of our routine, I say once more, "Should we sing now, Mom?" She always says, "Of course!"

Each time I start to sing, Mom goes with my key. Mom's voice in old age is very low, and her range is limited, but I know just where to pitch our duet.

> I see the moon and the moon sees me,
> The moon sees the one that I'd like to see.
> God bless the moon and God bless me,
> And God bless the one that I'd like to see.

Then I segue into the Sh'ma, and we sing the Sh'ma together too.

I know just where her voice will crack, where her passagio falls—the place where her voice transitions between her head and her chest. I've always known precisely where it is. In the key I set for the Sh'ma, it's on the last syllable of "Adonai."

This strikes me as a holy note, every night.

Defined Curls and Pencil Skirts

The phone rings and it's Tali's childhood friend Frannie, looking for her. This means that Tali's phone is off or out of juice. Frannie would text her directly otherwise.

I greet Frannie fondly.

She is very cheery when she hears my voice and tells me that she saw me walking past her mother's house with Scott only a few days ago.

Frannie says, "Wow, you were looking good, um . . ."

"Barbara," I say. "You're thirty now! For heaven's sake, call me Barbara!"

"Barbara," she says, continuing, "You have such style now! I loved that skirt, and your hair looked great! Oh yeah, and your makeup too!"

"Thank you, Frannie! That makes me feel fantastic, especially coming from you!"

I tell her that Tali is in town here in Buffalo for her Grandmother Balaban's funeral, but that I assume her phone, as usual, needs charging. I assure her that I'll alert Tali so they can get together in the next few days. Frannie offers her condolences and we say goodbye.

Last week, when Scott and his brothers were planning their mom's funeral, they were asked if she'd had a favorite song that might fit into the service.

Scott's mom, Gloria, was an ardent feminist who fought against the grip of any man who attempted to restrain her. Recalling that, I suggested "I'm Gonna Wash That Man Right Outta My Hair" from *South Pacific*. Fortunately for me, her sons reacted only with laughter.

Gloria's hair was always just so. My hair has always had a mind of its own. But in recent years, the frizzy curse of my teenage years has become a crown that thrives in humidity. Frannie is right; my hair looks great. When I look in the mirror, I no longer see helmet-haired Mrs. Dean, my first-grade teacher, looking back at me.

These days I have my hair cut by a stylist who knows his curls. I use tried-and-true curl-enhancing products in my graying hair. And I've perfected my hair-drying technique, which involves patting it with a microfiber towel first and then scrunching it under the diffuser. My curls respond by coiling up and looking lively and full. My curly-headed friends and I swap hair stories with a kind of bravado.

Women don't talk as much about their makeup techniques. I was always careful with my makeup. Women like Gloria look great with a little bit of color here and there. I never thought in terms of touches or hints. I used to approach line and pigment with the concentration and painterly technique of a nearsighted Renaissance master. Today I'm more of an Impressionist. A streak of honey-colored powder on my lids, a coppery liner, spikeless mascara, and a bit of russet on my delineated lips.

When I look in the mirror, I see a woman with a good haircut who dresses with flair and has healthy color in her face. I've learned that superfluous fabric and excessive draping work for swimsuit cover-ups but not for daily life, where they're tedious and cumbersome. I cringe remembering the aqua floor-length dress that Mom spent months crocheting for my ordination, with its ill-fitting lining in almost the same color.

My current closet is a thing of beauty—to me, anyway. The blouses hang on top and to the right. Some are flowered and some have tiny triangles. The sweaters, olive and cream, are folded in perfect stacks below, alongside the British pencil skirts that hit at or slightly below my knees. On the extreme left and hanging evenly are my pants, and in the center are my dresses—black or green or black and green. On the end, at the back, is a magenta tee, an aubergine jacket, and a hanger draped with belts of all widths. Beneath them sits a shoe organizer containing a variety of cute flats that accommodate my aging feet with grace. Two pairs of Mephisto sandals, tan and black, live next door to each other on the floor.

And ah, the body that wears them. I see it in the closet's mirror. For so long it was my enemy. I thought of it as a burden, with its fleshy excesses, its perpetual demand for attention, its unpredictable bloodiness, its refusal to make babies. Now we are sisters, albeit sisters who don't always get along.

I talk to myself when I try on bathing suits. *You are not fat. And cellulite used to be the sign of a healthy Renaissance woman.* This isn't the Renaissance, though. So in our era (Late Capitalism?) I like to think that my cellulite signifies my refusal to buy bullshit creams or shock my flesh with bullshit electronic flab busters. That almost sounds like I'm proud of my cellulite. Maybe I am, in an intellectual way. But I'm definitely not yet above wondering why some women's thighs and upper arms never ripple.

We hold hands in aging, my body and me. I keep schlepping it to gyms and yoga studios. It's often slightly sore. But it carries me around playgrounds in the footsteps of my grandchildren, and for that I appreciate every inch of it.

Painting Flowers

That's it for this morning's cappuccino. When Scott presented it to me, its surfeit of chocolate shavings made me laugh out loud. I think about the day ahead. It's a watercolor day. I feel like painting.

The breakfast dishes have already been taken care of—again by Scott—minus my cup. I rinse it (why?) and put it into the dishwasher right next to its mate.

All I need to do today is exercise and grill or steam dinner. That's it.

Well, maybe not quite. I tense as I remember unfinished work. I do need to send out the minutes of yesterday's ACC Internal Membership committee meeting. I revise that thought: I can send those minutes out any day this week and still be timely, efficient, and responsive. I relax my shoulders.

So painting is how I'm going to use my jubilee time today. I write when I feel like writing and paint when I feel like painting. I walk outside, holding Scott's hand, when the air is crisp and the day is clear. All those school and work years, I did what I was told when I was told. I wanted to please anyone in authority. I used to long for report cards of any kind—concrete validation of achievement and gauges of progress. I needed to feel reassured that I was a good student, a good cantor.

Today I want to feel a brush in my hand.

I head downstairs to my art table under the glass block window in the basement. It's chilly down here, but there's a space heater at my feet. I straddle my stool, the kind of high stool that can spin and tilt. This is comfortable. I exhale.

A memory pings in my knees and my breath catches a little. All those years spent sitting stiffly on the bima with my knees pressed together. I used to think that crossing my legs would have been inappropriate—too informal a posture and too revealing of my lower thigh. Ha! Such bullshit. I exhale again.

Perched on my stool, I shift my legs slightly, finding the ideal spots for my slippers on the foot ring.

Since retiring I feel such relief. It's wonderful to be free of constant assessment and to be allowed—to allow myself—to make all my own decisions. Unlike in kindergarten and first grade, in retirement, I can go to art when I decide to go to art, without having to stage a fit to get there.

With a palette knife that still bears its label, I separate a single cold-pressed sheet from its bound block. I position the paper and hop down from the stool. I fill my water containers at the utility sink and set my can of brushes on the table. A rag is at the ready, for blotting brushes and mopping spills. Wait! I need a model. I head back upstairs for one of the African violets on the family room windowsill. I pick the one with the most buds. I like painting buds.

Down we go, the plant and I. I set it on the storage shelves in front of my desk and watch as the light hits it.

I uncap my watercolors, the six or so colors I use over and over. Today they don't need replenishing, only a bit more water.

I start with the clay pot. I dip a square brush in a raw sienna and join one curving line to another. I pat the wet paint here and there with a little square of steel wool. I twist the wires a bit, and the pot sports a little mildew. I smile.

Playing with paints and fiddling with various materials is satisfying in a way that filling out assignment sheets for student after student was not. I wanted parents and rabbis to look at the students' sheets and KNOW that I deliberated about each kids' homework. I wanted the multicolored, painstakingly written notes to show that I tailored every assignment to each kid's abilities and to our joint learning goals. I used my many skinny colored pens to specify study methods. It never occurred to me to use the colors for pleasure.

But it occurs to me now. I think about what I want.

I want flowers.

My omama loved the flower patch behind the family dry goods store in Indiana. My mother's garden was wild and sprawling. My sister, an organic farmer, had flowers springing up at her feet! My ancestral and familial flower growers are all dead, and they took their green thumbs with them. I myself am slowing down a little. But my flowers still sprout endlessly.

This violet has single white flowers—only a few—and lots of fat green buds in clusters. I paint the leaves first. I do each leaf with two conjoined strokes in a green that has nothing to do with reality. I take a stylus, the narrow end, and dip it into dryish white paint.

Lightly I dot each leaf with almost invisible pricks of white. Now the leaves appear fuzzy. Just what I want.

I mix an altogether different green with lots of white, so that the flowers will stand out, slightly tinged, on the white paper. Petal after petal. Thick yellow dots here and there for anthers. When the paint is dry, I uncap a Micron pen—black, .005—and barely outline the petals.

This is how I paint, making up techniques. If things go well, the results are as satisfying as biblical poetry—say the Song of Solomon, which is mostly written from a woman's perspective and full of flowers.

I call up to Scott from the foot of the stairs. I want to show off my creation.

He politely takes his time looking over the painting, which is small.

"I like this one," he tells me. He has learned not to say, "Very nice."

If I liked sweating and getting dirty, if I liked physical work, I would garden. Like my sister, my mother, and my omama. Instead I paint. Some of my flowers sing for me. When they do, I photograph them and post them on Facebook. Some of these flowers sing for others, too, accruing many "likes."

I don't have Sarah's knowledge of horticulture. I don't cultivate bed after bed. But I do know about caring for orchids and African violets. I do cultivate bloom after bloom in my field, during my jubilee.

And I grow rows of small paintings that Scott strings together for me with clasps on a wire.

A Cappella in a Brewery

On Sunday evenings, Scott and I routinely head for Buffalo Brew Pub, not far from our house. We consider this a treat night, and we sit in one of our several regular booths and order pub fries with our meals. We eat our separate orders one fry at a time. With salt. And ketchup. I always order an avocado on the side, and Scott asks for two thick slices of tomato, which he then seeds and puts on his grilled chicken sandwich. The seed removal process takes about half an hour. Without exception, Scott orders a hoppy beer and I order the house Sauv blanc. We crack the free peanuts and swipe the shells onto the floor with gusto. We know all the servers by name, and we ask about their academic progress or their babies.

Tonight it's mid-December and we're seated near a series of linked tables occupied by men of all ages wearing tights. Green tights à la Robin Hood. Many pitchers of beer and many sweating mugs weigh down their tables, which appear to be set up on a beach of peanut shells. I watch them as if they were the entertainment.

One among them, in a clear, bright tenor, begins: "Good King Wenceslas looked out on the Feast of Stephen." A strong male chorus, balanced and disciplined, continues: "When the snow lay round about, deep and crisp and even."

Now I know that these are my people—these men, these madrigal carolers. With a wink, I leave Scott in our booth, seeding away, and join the men at their tankards. We look each other over while they sing, and nod slightly. They assume the risk—the look plus nod means that I will take the next verse, though I might be a drunken wench who can't carry a tune or who doesn't know the words.

The song proceeds with the men singing the king's lines:

> "Hither, page, and stand by me,
> If thou know'st it, telling,
> Yonder footman, who is he?
> Where and what his dwelling?"

I become the page and answer the king, singing:

> "Sire, he lives a good league hence,
> Underneath the mountain;
> Right against the forest fence,
> By Saint Agnes' fountain."

Then the merry men and the merry wench finish the carol together.

. . . Ye who now will bless the poor,
Shall yourselves find blessing.

We singers take a slight ritardando at the end of the song, looking from one to another so that we stay together.

The brew pub is quiet for a long moment. Then it fills with
hearty applause followed by the glad and ordinary sound of boot-
clad feet on peanut shells.

Tonight I'm not bound up with worry about finding substitutes
for Jesus-words or compromising my beliefs by singing a Christmas
carol in public.

I'm just singing with some merry men in a peanut-strewn bar
on a December night, with my mouth wide open and tears in my
eyes for the beauty of it.

New Protest Songs

About eleven weeks ago, my country elected a reality show
host to its highest office. Like some other Americans, I lost sleep
for several nights thereafter. Since then I've begun to realize that
although I rose happily for the national anthem during the eight
years of Barack Obama's presidency, it's going to be at least another
four until I will again feel proud rising for "The Star Spangled
Banner."

I haven't marched since college, back in the early seventies. But
I will be marching tomorrow morning, should daylight ever arrive.
People here will be walking in solidarity with the Women's March
in Washington on this, the day after Donald Trump's inauguration.

My stomach plunges with excitement and apprehension when it
crosses my mind that I will likely be motivated to lead some protest
singing.

At some point sleep comes, followed quickly by daylight.

I put on my new Black Lives Matter T-shirt and pick up my
equally bleary-eyed friend. We drive to the march and finally find
parking. Taking our places in a very long line of people, I awkwardly hold up my handwritten sign. It says, "Jewish women will

never stop fighting for human rights." It takes me a while to remember how to properly wield a sign while walking. I look around at my sisters, many of whom are wearing hot pink caps with pointy ears. *Oh, THESE are the famous pussy hats!* Even though the pointy cat ears are clever-cute, I cringe for a moment at identifying myself as a pink vagina.

I remember the time I piously rejected the palm branch that was handed to me at a demonstration when I was a teenager. There's a lot I know now that I didn't know then, such as: It feels good to embrace, to kiss, to shout, to jump in with both feet, to grab the unfamiliar palm branch and march as a Jew with believing Christians and Muslims. Yup, I'm putting on a hat.

And it feels extra good to learn a new protest song. So what if I remember the words to all the old protest songs? (They're so *Kumbaya* now!) It's time to learn some new words and some new melodies.

I listen over and over to MILCK's song "Quiet." I'm increasingly jealous. I wish I'd written a song about refusing to shut the fuck up! I think about what it means that there is now a famous song about a woman who runs riot. How I wish I'd written a woman's protest song with the word "no" all over it! A Miriam's song for today, a woman's song on steroids!

I didn't write it, but I can sing the shit out of it.

Class Arguer Interjects

Scott and I are waiting for Dr. Prince, his cardiologist—the newest doctor in our lives. I note that I'm feeling something like breathless anticipation. Breathless? It's been two hours. I should be pissed!

I readily accept the challenge from my inner therapist and lift my eyes off the screen of my Kindle. After a close forty-year acquaintance, my inner therapist knows how to get my attention. I refocus, like the good patient I am, on doctors. Another doctor. *Another god*, I think. *Another disappointing father in his white coat.*

Scott, always anxious about his health, has been diagnosed with atrial fibrillation. We are awaiting his test results. He's so obviously anxious that if I didn't know better, I might attribute my breathlessness to his state of mind. Scott, who had the calm presence of mind to back up our computer files as the second tower collapsed on 9/11, is anything but calm about his prospects for making old bones. All of his doctors probably know him well enough to steel themselves ahead of his questions.

Dr. Prince comes in and presents us with good results. Scott asks the questions he prepared in advance.

The prince sighs heavily. "Mr. Balaban, we've been over this before. Why are you so worried about this?"

Scott maintains his cool and poses his questions once more.

"If I have to answer these redundant questions for you at each appointment, Mr. Balaban— You realize I have other patients!"

And suddenly I hear my cue in the voice of Dr. Glick, of blessed memory. *"Dr. Prince may be royalty, but does that justify his lack of empathy?"* Without the benefit of a phone booth, I don my Class Arguer cape. As I cast aside my mild-mannered Barbi Prim-ness, my lifelong desire to please all doctors everywhere shrinks away. I say, "I'm going to interject here, Dr. Prince. You're being abrupt and dismissive. Your tone of voice does not allow your patient to ask his questions or to achieve peace of mind around the matter of his test results. Perhaps you'll start over."

Dr. Prince swallows hard and proceeds to apologize. My inner therapist notes that the apology appears to be coming from a frog sporting a stethoscope.

Friends

My friends Janet, Jane, Lauren, and Sharon sit down for our annual reunion lunch.

The five of us are in constant daily contact not because we text frequently, not because we live in the same neighborhood, but because we all play the same word games on our phones. My friends consistently whip my ass in Words With Friends, but my scores are improving due to incessant practice.

Once a year the five of us women cantors, now all in our sixties, spend a few days together. Not that it's easy to arrange. One
has a wedding to perform on a weekend that works for the others.
Another, also still working, has a concert. Eventually we map out
place and date and do our best to keep costs low. We go back and
forth about who rooms with whom and about who fronts the ticket
costs and who makes the reservations.

My friends are increasingly important to me. All of them—not
only the cantorial friends.

I remember the days when family goings-on and home maintenance ate up half my waking minutes and synagogue life ate up the
other half. Friendships were less critical during those years. Now I
think about my friends all the time and imagine them going about
their days.

But now here we are, all five of us in one place.

My heart sinks, though, as the server approaches. I look at my
watch. Ordering lunch always seems to take us about an hour. One
of us can't eat gluten. Another turns green if watermelon is anywhere in her line of vision. A third is vegan. We each observe some
idiosyncratic version of the Jewish dietary laws.

"Do you have skim? What? Only 2 percent?"

"I like my fish cooked all the way through."

"Half decaf, half caffeinated, please. Leave room for milk."

"Is the broth vegetarian?"

So I tell the server, every time, that I want my lunch exactly as
described in the menu, trying to make things easier—trying to be
the good customer, the one whose order is easy, who gives the staff
no trouble.

Oh! Wait, why is it that I think I have to earn a gold star from
this lovely waiter? Won't I tip him according to his labors and
treat him appreciatively in the meantime? Why can't I order what I
would most like to eat?

So this time I say, "Just leave off the blue cheese. Oh, and the
onions. Can I have extra avocado?"

Reform Jews on the Reformer

Patti and I are supine on industrial-strength traction machines in a Pilates class with Ginny, our instructor. Although they called a machine like this "the rack" in the Middle Ages, I've learned that this one is called a "Reformer."

We brace ourselves against foot bars attached to sliding platforms. We breathe loudly, as instructed. We "send the carriages away," pushing the balls of our feet against the padded bars. We do our best to maintain neutral pelvises.

Pilates is the only kind of serious exercise that doesn't make me feel like I want to die. This is as close to liking a sport as I have ever come.

Ginny laughs at us with some regularity. Well, more at me than at Patti. She laughs now because we're changing position, and we aren't exactly mounting our machines like Olympic gymnasts.

I can't help but feel a twinge of shame when she laughs, but I quickly remind myself that such a reaction is ridiculous. Patti is a successful dentist and I am an accomplished cantor. And how could anyone observe our maneuvers and not find them a little bit funny?

Patti and I share not only a friendship that spans many years, but kyphosis—our curved spines and rounded backs. Our backs are our shared reason for attending Pilates classes. Round shoulders are the result of bad posture, gravity, and some genetic crap that no one needs to trace.

I look up at Ginny, who's standing over us, phone in hand. She has the toned body and military posture of an elite athlete. By contrast, my posture resembles that of Monty Burns from *The Simpsons*.

Oh yes, I still compare my body to the bodies of others, even though I know better. And I still remember all the ways I hated gym and could list them alphabetically.

I may never overcome my resentment of phys ed, but I've gotten myself to go to the gym—voluntarily. Almost every day, in fact. Afterward, Scott always asks me how my workout was, and I tell him the truth: I'm enjoying the book I'm reading on the treadmill.

And here I am, taking fucking Pilates by choice too! I persevere on the goddamn Reformer—while wearing colorful spandex costumes—because this can actually improve my posture. I knew for a long time that I SHOULD do these things, for the sake of my ongoing health, but now I'm actually DOING them instead of finding excuses not to.

At the end of class, Patti and I endeavor to get off our Reformers. Again Ginny laughs. This time it's because our techniques for dismounting involve grunting and tripping or, in my case, falling down.

Clutching my back as I arise, I say, "Ginny, didn't anyone ever tell you that derision is not an effective teaching tool?" Which makes her laugh again, along with Patti and me.

Smartphone, Emancipation

It's late May in Buffalo and fairly safe now to plant perennials. That's the good news. The bad news is that I never remember how to get to the garden center. As much as I want to buy flowering plants for all of my outdoor pots and hanging baskets, my stomach drops just to think of the drive. Will I get lost? Will I have to consult Scott's written directions at every stop sign along the way?

My brain lights up, though, calming my stomach, and I seize on a contradictory sensation. I would call the feeling "uplift." Because there on the shelf between the kitchen and the family room sits my iPhone, charging to the rescue. It's the big one.

"Mom! That's huge!" Tali said, laughing at its size the first time she saw it.

"Yup," I answered unapologetically. "It's much easier to operate and much easier to see!"

I'm even good with the phone's cute little lightning connector, which needs to be detached from its port with care. I used to be inclined to yank cords from outlets and jam connectors into ports. Scott used to cringe whenever I unplugged something or connected anything to anything else. Force always seemed like the best approach because anything mechanical is the enemy.

But no longer. This phone is my friend, my travel companion, and maybe my rock and my redeemer.

With a loving hand, I remove the connector from its port and unplug the charger. My phone, in her floral cover, lights up, happy to see me. I rest my thumb on the home button, and behold, colorful little squares beckon me from every corner of my screen.

Two of the apps are my constant companions: Google Maps and jTips.

For each of my regular driving destinations, I've memorized one route. No amount of traffic or conviction that another way is shorter or faster will alter my course. I think of these dependable paths as my buddies. I know them. Following their lead makes me feel happy. But when I have to drive to a new place, or to a semi-familiar place (like the garden center), my phone will tell me how to get there in a quiet, calm voice. I love being told, one step at a time, how to drive somewhere.

En route today, with a bit of sunshine in my eyes, I have to remind myself that the phone voice can't know about stop signs or the position of the car in front of me. Observing safety rules is up to me. But I rely on my phone for a sense of security. Even if I make a wrong turn, my phone will save me from getting lost, something I fear as much today as I did in childhood.

I treat my phone to changes of wardrobe from time to time, and I swab her often with glass cleaner. Spanking clean, she sits in my car's cup holder, chatting.

At the garden center, which smells of peat, I spend over an hour going aisle by aisle, selecting plants according to color wheel charts. Yellow and purple, orange and blue, pistachio green and red-violet. I love including miniature ivies in and among the blooms. I gather two carts' worth of flats and head to the cashier counter. Of course I have a loyal customer coupon, which allows me to imagine briefly that I'm economizing.

There are only two turns on my route home, so I'm confident enough to listen to WBFO while I'm driving.

After unloading my plants in the garage, I head for the shower.

I'll be meeting Patti for lunch in forty-five minutes. No time to wash my hair if I want to wear mascara.

Over our wine glasses an hour later, Patti and I talk. We describe our husbands' antics with absolutely no exaggeration. We quote our daughters and laugh. We tell each other what parts of our bodies are sore. We eat soup and split a salad. Postponing our departure, we order skim cappuccinos. Of course, I put sugar in mine.

The check arrives too soon, but I'm prepared for it. I no longer have stomachaches as I anticipate calculating the appropriate tip. No sweat prickles under my arms as I try to remember how to figure out 10 percent of my bill and then multiply that number by two. Nope. My jTips app is at the ready, on my phone's first screen, presenting itself with a bold green T icon.

There are no shortcuts that eliminate the need for therapy. I still spend a session here or there taking aim at my Number Monsters or at my fear of being lost. But it's reassuring and practical to have a dependable coping tool by my side, my trusty iPhone 6s Plus, guiding me on straight paths and performing my arithmetic.

I may resemble the five-year-old in her nightgown, standing up in bed, trying to count. I am certainly related to the teenager who missed her subway stop and got lost.

But I shall not fear because, here in Buffalo, I am a clear-eyed woman, emancipated by her smartphone.

Dad's Yahrzeit

It's February 16th in the sixth year after Dad's death. Dad always said that he'd be happy if he reached the year 2000. Well, he reached 2011, so he lived long enough to brag about Simon's well-regarded book on Lyme disease, but he wasn't happy.

I loved my father. Maybe it's taken me until now to understand that his espoused values were strong and that he walked gently on the planet. He did noble work, and, when he paid attention, he was careful with his three kids. He was good with words and with languages. He loved exotic cuisines. He hand-lettered stories for his grandchildren and illustrated them with colored pencils. Of course Mom addressed and mailed them.

On this, his sixth yahrzeit, I light a memorial candle and place it on my glass kitchen table. I remember how he teased me about the amount of Windex I used on that same table after every meal or snack. Or when he saw that a greasy fingerprint had caught my eye.

I stare at the match, remembering Dad. I wish he had tried harder and applied his considerable intellect to raising us. The candle sputters as if in response to my conflicting feelings about him. Will the flame catch or die? Will my memories of Dad warm or burn?

I sternly remind myself that the flickering is due only to a bit of moisture trapped in the wax.

Dad, I'm doing my best to remember the good things about you, but NOT for your sake. You're dead. I'm doing it for me.

The melting wax smells up my kitchen.

I remember a good thing now, Dad. Every once in a while, you "stayed a couple of minutes," pacing our bedroom floors in your hard-soled shoes. Those were good nights.

Visions

Celeste, the owner of MyFrames, had a cancellation and can see me this very afternoon! I'm excited. MyFrames is just like a candy store, except without the candy. It sells eyeglasses.

In 1959 I desperately wanted to wear glasses, but I didn't need them until the following year. Since then, though, I've been needing glasses or some kind of corrective lenses for fifty-seven years!

Until today. Today it's been six weeks since a multifocal lens was implanted in my left eye. One week later, I had the second implanted in my right eye.

My vision has officially stabilized, and I won't wait even one more day before ordering new glasses. This surgery is a goddamn miracle. It's not up there with postmenopausal childbirth, but my eyes have gone from 20/900 to 20/20, and that's fucking astonishing at the very least.

Six weeks ago, as I woke up from the first procedure and the recovery room came into focus, I recognized the features of my ophthalmologist! I recognized him without my glasses! Instantly I recited the Shehecheyanu, the Hebrew blessing for singular moments. Bless You for bringing me to this distinct split-second.

Perched on a high stool in front of a mirror at MyFrames, I proceed to tell my story to Celeste.

"The doctor says that I'll need a minor correction for reading and a negligible correction for computer work. Celeste! The top part of the lens can be clear!"

Celeste knows I want fancy specs—fancy specs that bring out my eyes. Without tinted contact lenses, my natural eye color is greenish. I want green frames from MyFrames.

If Shoshana knew that, she would archly remind me that we must avoid being all "matchy-matchy." It amuses her to ironically pass along fashion tips this way, as if they govern the essential self.

Celeste allows me to try on exactly four pairs of glasses, three of which are not green. She rules her shop and does not allow clients to randomly pull frames down from her displays. She considers the shape of my face, the position of my eyes, how the frames compliment my nose, and whether or not my eyebrows are obscured. Each pair she's chosen looks amazing.

While I'm trying them on, I think fondly of Gramballs, who complimented my eyes many times. Then the word *biblical* pops into my mind. Leonard Bernstein. The great Leonard Bernstein called my eyes "biblical." Since then I've read the book Max wrote about him. Maybe Bernstein wasn't just tossing me a nicety. Maybe he wasn't referring to Leah's plainness, either. Maybe today I can allow myself to reinterpret the words he chose—as a perceptive observation. I can think that he recognized an ancient, life-giving artistic spark.

I pick the pine-green ones, trimmed in gold. Queen Elizabeth I would have loved these—if, in her day, glasses had been more than horn and leather-bound crystal.

The Scale in the Master Bathroom

This morning, I declare that my battle with fat is over. I've always weighed myself like clockwork every morning. After I pee but before I eat breakfast.

My fucking weight has been stable for nearly twenty years, always registering in a healthy range for my height and body type.

Henceforth, although I will check the scale with some regularity, it will NOT be to determine what I can or cannot have for dinner on a given night.

It's time for me to realize that I've actually prevailed over my obsession with fatness. It's a fact that I will never again starve myself in the service of some notion of sleekness or purity. And it's a fact that fatness doesn't mean the same thing to me anymore.

I've been thinking about the idea of fatness a lot this morning.

I no longer think of fatness as state of being with a name and a metaphorical definition. When I allowed myself only a certain number of calories per day, I lost more than just pounds. I lost my heft as an individual. Sure I looked streamlined, but I was starving. When my padding faded away, so did the dimensions of my place in the world.

One of my grandson Jonah's JCC friends, a two-year-old named Sage, happened to be at the playground with us a few weeks ago. Jonah was delighted to see her. I'd been watching them play and admiring the little girl's adorable retro gingham romper when she loudly signaled that someone should now lift her off the giant ladybug. Strong and agile, Sage had climbed right up but had decided unequivocally that she would not be climbing down. Happy to do the hoisting, I registered that her weight must have been twice Jonah's.

And last week I had lunch with a woman I know from temple. Audrey is a few years my senior. I taught her kids many years ago. As we enjoyed our salads, Audrey told me that her mother had started putting her in a girdle for school every day when she was in fifth grade.

Over coffee, I studied Audrey's physique. She has large breasts and full legs and arms.

This morning, having made my own unequivocal declaration, I ask myself, *Do I see Audrey as fat?* Fresh from lifting Sage off the ladybug, I answer, *No.* Audrey is a picture of health. At seventy, she does weight resistance training at the JCC. She walks three miles every other morning in good weather. Audrey is Audrey, complete and uncorseted. Sage is Sage, nimble and decisive.

And I am Barbi Prim. Naked right now. 130 pounds. Strong enough to lift Sage, healthy enough to love playing at a playground, and smart enough to call an end to quantifying my flesh in order to judge it.

White Goats and Melting Chocolate

I watch as Scott's older son, Adam, and his wife, Louisa, move confidently in an unfamiliar kitchen, preparing the first dinner in the house we've rented together for a family vacation in Colorado.

I am unmoored, out of place with all the Balabans, wishing there were more Ostfelds here than just me.

Then I hear small noises coming from small babies in the next room. Scott and I position ourselves on the family room floor between the baby cousins, Phin and Olive. I trot out my baby songs for these new babies. Songs about white goats and melting chocolate, about riding to market and buzzing insects.

As an Ostfeld among Balabans, I have much to be thankful for: Two babies in particular—and their parents, who include me as one of their own, calling me Oma. Two babies who have songs to learn.

Honey, Aloe, and Cranberry Sauce

Tomorrow is Thanksgiving and I'm worrying the way that I always do before family gatherings. Nervously, I list the several items I forgot to get yesterday at Wegmans.

Tali, who's visiting from Atlanta, begins to grate orange peel for the cranberry sauce. While she works, she describes her course load to me. She's just begun a master's in social work program and is eagerly anticipating her first internship, at a maternity shelter. As I listen—still thinking about my shopping list and worrying about whether my sauce will measure up to the ones made long ago by better moms—I'm stopped short, fascinated. But it's more than fascination. Is it pride? It's more than that—it's admiration.

I'm proud of her for the career she's chosen. But I also admire the woman she has fashioned herself into—a woman capable of and willing to transform the hurt she endured during her adolescence into insights, and her insights into liniments.

The phone rings and it's Hana. She asks how she can help out.

"Sweetheart! Are you getting another cold?" I ask. I can hear that her voice is hoarse.

Hana spends her days in her fourth-grade classroom, its windows now shut against the November-in-Buffalo chill. Between her beloved students at school and her beloved little boys at home, she catches more than her share of colds. I've always marveled at the way she pushes past symptoms that would lay me out flat, but today I see this in even higher relief. Here she is, calling her mother—a healthy retiree who has all the time in the world to make the inevitable return trips to Wegmans—asking to help.

Again I feel it—the pride, the admiration. *This is lovely*, I think.

Tali gestures for me to go back to my list and takes over the phone, putting Hana on speaker so she can keep working on the cranberry sauce. The girls—no longer girls but adult sisters—quickly sort out what remains to be done and assign most of it to themselves and their husbands. Tali asserts that the mustering and delivery of her nephews to the gathering counts as not one but two tasks, and therefore reduces Hana's other tasks accordingly.

One shard of guilt works its way into my feelings of pride. I can take only so much credit for these kick-ass thirtysomethings.

The three of us are pretty far along in mending our relationship now. Therapy helped me to see myself more clearly, and to see how far I still needed to go to help them. I got so only far before they became adults, and we've continued working things out, together and on our own. Now I learn from the examples they set. The ugly things that seeped from my childhood into theirs are nearly frozen solid.

Hana and Tali have become my aloe and honey. Aloe for comfort and honey for healing.

I'll probably always worry about my mothering skills. But that's not a bad thing. It was back when I DIDN'T worry about them that I let my girls down.

I pause for a moment, listening to their voices.

Then I head into the dining room. Time to break out the good dishes.

Dolls in Storage

For some reason, I just had to look at my childhood dolls today. Standing over the Rubbermaid trunk I've retrieved from our crawl space, I observe that although they're almost ready for Medicare, most of them wear their ages lightly.

I unwrap a naked doll, about 20 inches in length with brown skin and straight jet-black hair that's still silky to the touch after all these years. A label falls out of the paper and identifies her. "Mädchen mit langen braunen Haaren." Her joints are rickety; I can see the metal springs that attach her limbs to her torso. They move haltingly, but her head nods and swivels as if she were new. I try to remember her long-lost dress. Was it a powder blue and white gingham? Like Dorothy's in *The Wizard of Oz*? I rewrap her in tissue.

Next to her is my Madam Alexander baby doll. She was labeled "Kitten" and billed as lifelike, and she still has a newborn's floppiness. "Lifelike" was an exaggeration. Her head was unconvincingly topped with a chin-length pageboy. Still I persisted in pretending that she was a baby version of me, just cuter and with better hair. I posed her, dressed her, and diapered her. I also "shielded her from the elements" many a time. I mothered her alone, not picturing a daddy. As much as I worshipped my own, he was one of the "elements" she needed to be shielded from.

When nuclear war broke out in the vacant fields behind our house in suburban Elmhurst, I ran to get her to safety. As I ran

Mädchen mit langen braunen Haaren: girl with long brown hair (German)

with her, I agonized over the jolting of her fragile infant neck. I excused my neglect in light of the exigencies of nuclear war.

I've learned a lot about babies since the infamous Battle of Elmhurst, which ended tragically for primary school kids in 1962.

Here's what I know now: All babies are just like me. Every baby can be easily wounded, first by the absence of focused love, and later by things like the rigidity of numbers, the flatness of mirrors, and the cruel mimicry of classmates. Every baby can be soothed by singing, rhyming words, gentle motions, eyes looking into eyes. Like the doll in my arms, every baby needs to be shielded from the elements.

And here's one more thing I know: The ones who call me Oma will reap the benefits of having a grandmother who remembers how hard it is to be a baby.

I wrap the baby doll back up in her bubble wrap swaddling and forage around for my Barbies, who have migrated to the bottom of the trunk. Their iconic facial features are fading. Here and there I can still pick out a line of sky-blue eyeliner or a carmine smudge of lipstick. Their high and perky ponytails are raggedy now—dusty too. I smile as I look at their toeless, improbably arched feet. Without stilettos, their feet are obscene, as if deformed by foot-binding.

Why did I need to see these dolls just now? I suppose I wanted to see my original babies, just for a moment. Kitten and Mädchen mit langen braunen Haaren have now been replaced twice over. Once by Hana and Tali and now by Jonathan, Jonah, Phin, and Olive. I want the dolls to know that I still love them.

I return my Barbies to their (eternal) repose, wrap up my baby-dolls one more time, and seal the doll trunk. I reposition it in the crawl space, next to Scott's old tennis rackets. In a few years, I will introduce Kitten and Mädchen to my flesh-and-blood babies. My Barbies can remain entombed.

Puzzle Pieces

Jumping down from the crawl space lands me in the Banfeld playroom. Two of the grandchildren visited yesterday, and now that

I've had a night's sleep, I start putting the toys back in order. I take my time over this task. I box the board games and disconnect the train tracks. I place the wooden fruits and vegetables back in their felt baskets. I dress the boys' anatomically correct baby dolls and place them in their strollers. I save the puzzles for last, putting the pieces back into the right boxes and then stacking the boxes, in order by size before shelving them. As I turn off the lights in the playroom, I wonder how someone came up with the notion of puzzles, and it occurs to me how good a metaphor puzzles are for my life now.

I climb the stairs from the basement to the kitchen, fleshing out the thought. The kitchen is clean and dinner is planned. My carefully chosen things all have places that are perfect to me. I pause to look around my pleasantly, precisely ordered kitchen, and it occurs to me that I've put a lot of work into my own puzzle. I've honed the edges of many pieces, and now most of them fit together comfortably.

And now it's time to head out to the gym. It's Tuesday, Pilates day. Having successfully mounted the Reformer, I proceed to extend and flex and pivot, and some of the body pieces of my puzzle remind me that they still have jagged edges. But then the hour is over, and, taking a sip from my water on my way to the locker room, I walk by the wall mirror. I look at myself in black spandex and I'm taken aback. Is this someone else? I note with a bit of shock that my shape is blessedly ordinary. Maybe these pieces of my puzzle fit together in their own way after all.

At my locker I check my phone, looking—hoping—for a last-minute summons from Hana. Maybe she needs me to watch the boys. I scroll past a photo of myself in a white eyelet summer dress. My lipstick is the right color, and I'm smiling. This photo isn't posed, meaning that I didn't preen, or even pat down my hair right before it was taken. I didn't intentionally or automatically point my nose directly at the lens to diminish its impact. My nose is what it is.

My nose. This big Ostfeld nose, strategically placed by the Almighty near the center of my face, has taught me finally how to love myself.

As I walk to my car, I feel the pull of my hamstrings and smile to myself. That tug is a salute from my tired butt and from the backs of my thighs. As I ease myself into the car, I anticipate the sigh I will breathe soon, when the butt puzzle piece clicks into place. There it will be, full and dimpled. Without the clerical conceit of a long black robe.

I love the light clicking sound puzzle pieces make when they come together. It's like my mother's cello pizzicato, adding impetus with nothing but sound.

When We Open Our Lips

The convention committee of the ACC has brought us to Las Vegas for our annual four-day conference. The title of this year's gathering is "Sing City."

In our assigned conference room, it is neither day nor night. There are no windows to orient us in time, but my phone tells me I'm a moment late. The morning service has already begun. I take my seat on the periphery, a bit behind because everyone ahead of me in the coffee line had at least seven adjectives modifying their order. Not me! Mine was only "skim." And "extra shot." And "extra foam." I pride myself on simplicity.

In prayer too. I walk in knowing I can sit anywhere because friends are everywhere—in every row. I see cantors clipping their kippot into place as they sit down.

My wiry hair, which has always rebelled against a kippah, is uncovered. I've experimented over and over with wearing a head covering (affixed by several clips), but it's always felt like an affectation to me. Perhaps if my grandfathers had worn them. My mom's dad, in Indiana, was a staunch Reform Jew who wouldn't have been caught dead in a yarmulke, like many liberal Jewish men of his generation. And my dad's dad, in St. Louis, attended Ethical Culture Society meetings rather than even the most liberal synagogue.

Many of the cantors here do have their heads covered.

On the makeshift bima I see two guitar-wearing women who turn to face each other. They are circled by a hundred of us cantors,

kippot: plural of kippah/yarmulke

some wrapped in prayer shawls and some whose arms are bare.
Some whose eyes are closed and some whose eyes are riveted to
the page in the prayer book. Some heads are covered, some aren't.
I see short curls, long braids, and some heads with no hair too. A
middle-aged cantor propels her wheelchair into the circle, prayer
book in her lap.

This morning, the Torah will not be read, so my tallit is in my
hotel room. Only on Torah reading days do I wear my tallit, the
last in a series made by my mother. It's ivory, somewhat lacy, and
edged with gold embroidery. The area around its neck is now a bit
discolored.

Both of the women on the bima, cantors of different vintages,
are wearing kippot. Gracefully they toss the prayer melodies
between them. In Hebrew and in English, quickly and slowly, leaning first this way and then that. There is something balletic about
the movement around me.

The tender prayer words are nearly inaudible, and we feel them
as much as we hear them. "How deeply You have loved us, Adonai,
our God, gracing us with surpassing compassion." Certain words
strike our ears awake. "When justice burns within us like a flam-
ing fire . . ." Other words pierce our ears with their concentrated
pitch alone. "My God, guard my speech from evil and my lips from
deception."

Underneath is a cantorial hum, to which we all contribute. It
feels like a warm blanket. The drone is earthy—primal and soothing at the same time. Drums of different sizes and the piano create
a kind of audible garland, tying every sound together.

But the prayer is more than sound. On my right is a young cantor who sings under her breath. I hear her humility. On my left is
an older cantor, his voice raspy with wear. I hear his weariness and
longing. Several rows in front of me is a cantor who is probably only
vaguely aware that he ornaments each long note with many small
ones in sequence. He runs his voice up and down the scale with the
nasal beauty of a muezzin's prayer call. And in the very back of the
room, I pick up a dark basso continuo. Dark like my coffee.

That rich voice—and the tickle on my lip of a crumb of caramel salt—remind me to take some last extra dark, extra foam sips.

In my ears is the sound of a hundred cantors—a sound so layered, so resonant that all our hearts spring open, and certainly Hers as well.

Song Words

My kitchen counters pass inspection, and I've hung the rag to dry. I hang the rag again—so its corners meet exactly. I have ten minutes before I have to leave for yoga. Time enough for Facebook, the perfect filler!

I see a post that marks the fifty-seventh anniversary of *The Fantasticks*. It ran in Greenwich Village for forty-two years and just closed after another fifteen at the Theatre Center.

The post transports me back to 1977, when as a twenty-four-year-old newish cantor, I was finally able to pay for tickets to the off-Broadway show.

Sitting in the Sullivan Street Playhouse, I felt like a kindergartner watching Shakespeare. Nothing about the words, the melody, or the choreography made any sense to me.

The performers were singing tra-la-la about rape. Tra-la-la, they were dancing a rape scene.

And the audience was laughing.

For five years I'd been practicing not thinking about being raped. If I didn't think about it, if I didn't tell about it, I could go on pretending it didn't belong to me. It hadn't been hard to let that shit-scented memory hide itself away. But surrounded by the laughing audience, I couldn't escape its nasty smell.

And so I'd doubled down on this practicing, burying the memory even more deeply.

Startled by my iPhone's chirp, I realize that it's time to go to yoga. Doing my best to shake free of *The Fantasticks*, I close Facebook, sling my lime-green yoga mat over my shoulder, grab my water, and head for the House of the Rising Sun. I love the name—so many possible meanings, all so divergent.

I take off my sandals, park them in a cubby, and check in to class using the touchscreen. I join the others in the studio, beginning the yoga class routine. First, I take a look at the instructor's mat so I can tell which items I'll need today. From the back shelves, I take two purple blocks (always purple ones), a turquoise Mexican blanket, a black bolster, and a fading khaki belt. Then I begin to set myself up, first arranging all the props around my mat. I like this process. It makes me feel like a real yoga student.

The music in the studio hasn't started yet, but I can already hear it in my mind. I quietly hum a note but then shut myself up, respecting the rule about maintaining silence in the studio. There are times for silence.

Now I prepare for shavasana (corpse pose), placing the bolster under my knees and one of the blocks under my head. I take a long, deep breath and read the word on the ceiling tile above me while slowly releasing it. *Focus.* I close my eyes. I try.

But I don't feel the usual descent into calm. Instead, I'm still thinking about the rape song, and about my personal Upper West Side story, although it's begun to play back differently.

As long as I can remember, it was always easy for me to sing stories, prayers, texts. They weren't my own. I was only a narrator.

But recently I sat at my desk and let my fingers press key after key, typing my rape story one word at a time. I let myself smell the dog shit as I began, and my fingers took it from there. While the words appeared in front of me, it registered that I'm old enough to be that babysitter's grandmother. And perhaps for the first time, I cast that nineteen-year-old in her rightful role: not as a rebellious daughter, not as a braless teenage temptress, but as a child victim.

Seeing the story in words helped me to take it in as an event. An actual scene from my life. One I had tried to cut. And once I recognized the girl in that story as me, I was able to stutter those words out in therapy. Naming it loosened its hold. And released, I was able to get to work on mending the tears it made in my story.

Continuing to breathe slowly, I exhale completely through my mouth and then close it. I inhale through my nostrils, counting to four. I hold my breath for a count of seven and release it over eight beats.

I hear light, gentle footsteps and open my eyes. The teacher is walking in, barefoot, her toes beautifully splayed.

So I sit up, rearrange my bolster, and assume a modified lotus position, anticipating the exact pitch of the singing bowl. I smile when it proves me right.

The teacher invites us to let the mmmmm sound in. For me this is effortless. I don't have to let it in—because it's always in. And now it's working away, ever so slowly, clearing my mind of broken glass with a perfectly circular sweep.

Breath and Life

I catch myself smiling in our bedroom mirror.

My carry-on is on the bed, ready to be unpacked. Since nothing needs dry-cleaning at this point, I hang up my dress and pants, and fold a sweater, setting it on top of a neat stack of sweaters. I dump my dirty laundry into the bin just inside the closet. My tallit bag goes back into the bottom drawer of my nightstand. I unzip the suitcase's waterproof sleeve and take out my plastic pill dispenser and toiletry bag. I walk these into the bathroom. Another mirror gets my attention. And again I find myself smiling. I top off my travel containers of shampoo and curling gel and refill my mini Q-tips container. I put the pill dispenser back into my medicine cabinet.

And just like that, I'm finished unpacking. The stuff, anyway. Now I can unpack the events of the weekend. I smile again, eager.

Scott and I have just returned from visiting Temple Beth-El of Great Neck, where I'd been invited to participate in a service marking the 90th anniversary of its founding. For the occasion, Larry Rappaport came out of retirement to preach. We once again shared the bima, alongside the man who is one of my successors as cantor and also several of Larry's rabbinical successors. I got to sing one more time in front of that stark white Nevelson ark.

As Larry stood up to give his sermon, my mind called up one of his eulogies, delivered a generation ago. In it he described the decedent, who had been a selfish ass-wipe, as "a man whose windows opened inward." That's truth-telling done with poetry.

Larry told the truth then, and he still does now. Unlike so many rabbis, Larry is willing to take even the president to task directly, calling him out by name. It's so satisfying to hear the truth from a rabbi's mouth again! How I've missed salty sermons!

Larry hasn't changed much since I last stood beside him, but I have.

During my twelve years of the temple's ninety, I lived according to innumerable rules—rules that I invented. I was certain that strictly following them would lead to rave reviews of my debut trouser role. But these negative commandments added up to just so many forms of self-confinement. Only recently have I been able to see them for the bullshit that they were.

As Beth-El's cantor, I could have eaten real food. I could have grown out my hair. I could have worn green shoes. I could have kissed my babies in public.

I've changed a lot since then. I knew I had, but visiting Great Neck showed me how much.

Heading back to the bima of Temple Beth-El after thirty years, I left my long black robe in the cedar closet. I wore a form-fitting knee-length brown dress—glen plaid with a deep V-neck. I left my hair down and untamed.

In the oversized pulpit chair, I allowed myself to cross my legs for comfort. I even allowed my spine to come into contact with its tall wooden back. I didn't fix my features at attention during the sermon. Instead, I simply listened.

This time around, when the congregation applauded one of the speakers, I clapped too. When someone made a little joke, I even laughed out loud with everyone else! And when I stood at my podium to sing, I took great, deep breaths, not the anxious catch-breaths that were all I could manage in my youth.

In the absence of worry, I laughed, clapped, and breathed deeply. I sang in my own full voice with all its overtones. I loved the vigorous, ringing sound.

trouser role: a part for a woman playing a man in a play or opera

And then it dawns on me, here in my bedroom in Buffalo: I sang like the cantor I've always wanted to be! And my singing went beyond the sound. It felt like rediscovering my original brand of certainty and joy.

I zip up all of the zippers on my carry-on and take it into Hana's old bedroom. I try to open her closet, but the sliding door slips out of its track. This door has always been quirky, and it hasn't aged well. After realigning it, I set my bag inside, leaving the door open—there's no need to grapple with it right now.

Before I leave the room, I take a deliberate long look in the mirror on the wall just inside the door. There I am again. Tears come to my eyes, and I smile one more time.

"America the . . . Alabaster"

I play with Shoshana's son, Ernest, holding both his hands as he runs. Ernest is attempting to catch a black cat in the backyard of Gavin's newly purchased Connecticut house. It's good that I do yoga. Otherwise my back would never allow me to walk this quickly while bending over a toddling eleven-month-old.

After the unsuccessful conclusion of the cat chase, Scott, Gavin, and I walk down New Haven's Chapel Street with Shoshana and her husband, Todd, looking for coffee. Todd has Ernest in a front pack.

We come to a popular outdoor café, and after I check my wrought iron chair for bird shit, I join my family on its terrace. It's late August in New Haven. The new crop of Yale students has arrived. Energetic swarms of them add a sense of anticipation to this bright, warm day.

Shoshana is a resident in internal medicine and pediatrics at Yale New Haven Hospital, where her grandfather detoxed in the late sixties. Dad would certainly have taken credit for her medical prowess. I reflect on this while Ernest dozes in his pouch and we grown-ups watch the New Haven foot traffic and sip very good coffee.

Four young people in khaki pants and black polo shirts assemble in front of our café and take instruments out of their cases. It's a string quartet—a racially diverse string quartet, the members of which have clearly played together many times. They are casual, laughing—but focused. I hear an A—the tuning begins. I wonder if this is how they always practice in good weather—outdoors and in public, near the New Haven Green. Ernest twitches in his sleep while I spoon extra sugar into my coffee. I'm caught up in envying the young players.

And here comes the music. "America the Beautiful." I hear them discuss changing the key and laughingly experiment a bit with the tempo. They find the starting pitch and begin, taking it slow, I think because they're improvising. No music stands or pages of sheet music are in sight. They play beautifully, and my envy of their youth and their talent and their open-air fun grows.

I'm not listening to Gavin and Scott as they chat with Todd and Shoshana. Shoshana adjusts Ernest's sun hat, but he remains soundly asleep. I hear nothing but the music, and I begin to sing an alto line softly at my seat, some distance away from the quartet.

Fuck it, I think. I rest my spoon on a saucer and get up. Without hesitating, I walk right up to the players and tell them that I've always dreamed of singing all the weird and archaic verses of "America the Beautiful," especially and ironically the verse about "alabaster cities . . . undimmed by human tears." They appreciate the subversive fun in the idea and reply, "Let's do it!"

There is no pause; we simply begin. I've already called up the lyrics on my phone. They key is perfect for me, and I play around between the melody and an alto line. One of the students begins to take the melody in a bluesy voice, which I then echo below him.

Why would I sit on a wrought iron chair, worrying about the possibility of bird shit, when I could gleefully mock hypocritical white people imagining white cities in song? Oh this is fun! Singing with a string quartet alfresco, ironically but tunefully, uninvited and bold as brass.

Sitting in the Catbird Seat

When we kids were little, our first pet was a vivid yellow if lethargic canary. Simon and I optimistically named him Sonny Boy.

We used to wedge pieces of fruit between the wires of his cage and wait eagerly while he ignored them. Once or twice Sonny Boy actually sang his canary aria, but after he started balding, due to feather mites, he became silent. Shortly after that, he wound up in a shoebox underground, not far from Simon's dinosaurs.

Sonny Boy sang out until he got sick. I sang with my whole voice until I was bullied.

I still pursued singing after that, and I sang sweetly enough, but no longer with my full voice. I worried so much about being mocked by the people around me that I began to sing in an undertone. And so I moved through the first twenty years of my professional singing career using half of my voice, walling off the rest along with my deepest and oldest fears.

Then those fears broke through my defenses, manifesting themselves as a dybbuk in my throat. I couldn't sing without coughing, and my mind pulsed with worry, with dread, with anger.

In the shtetls of Old Europe, wonder-workers exorcised demons by casting spells, by immersion, or by fumigation. If those methods failed, they could sometimes vanquish dybbuks by discovering and then speaking their hidden names.

At the turn of the twenty-first century in the city of Buffalo, I found my own wonder-worker—a therapist. In weekly or bi-weekly appointments over almost twenty years, she and I gradually figured out and pronounced the dybbuk's name: חֲרָדָה, charada. Anxiety, despair. Therapy made possible my liberation—hard-won, sweet as dark chocolate.

And life has become so good.

Standing in front of the Banfeld bulletin board and adding items to the grocery list, I feel the morning sun streaming in from our deck. It's hot on my left arm. Mourning doves are cooing in our backyard, and I can hear the hoarse cadenza of a red-winged blackbird. My allotted single mocha is half-consumed. A few of the blooms on my violets are sparkling in their little pots.

I pause to think about when we last had fish for dinner and wonder which would be a good choice for tonight. Unwilling to make an extra trip to Wegmans because I've forgotten one item, I recheck my list and begin to hum the first measures of Mozart's "Ridente la calma," which for me is a prayer for unruffled feathers. *"May calm rise up in my soul, casting out the fear and trembling. . . ."*

Catfish? Nope. Salmon will be good tonight.

Re-relaxed, my mind wanders, but not to the dark side. Canaries, catfish, catbirds . . .

During much of my life, like a catbird—expert mimic that she is—I sang a lot of melodies that weren't my own, melodies I didn't quite understand. I sang them the way I imagined a Proper Woman or a Proper Cantor would sing them. I took shallow breaths. I feared that if I breathed naturally, deeply, I would be too loud and too showy to be proper. But I can see now that for a cantor, man or woman, singing properly means singing with strength, in your own true voice.

It was James Thurber who coined the phrase "sitting in the catbird seat," which caught my attention the first time I heard someone use it. A character in his short story explains that it means "sitting pretty like a batter with three balls and no strikes." Even with the explanation, though, the meaning of the expression was lost on me. I didn't understand it even well into middle age. But now I do—because now I know what it feels like to be sitting in the catbird seat.

For Thurber's protagonist, it meant watching pieces fall into place—the result of his efforts and then a clever guess. And for me, it's watching the curtain open on act three and knowing that it's beginning happily—the result of my own hard work and ever-accumulating insights. And this time, I'm making my entrance as me, dressed and coiffed like me and singing my very own tune.

So much has changed! And so very much for the better!

Looking back, I can glimpse previews of how sitting in my catbird seat might feel.

When Mom would drop me off in the Oak Park Temple parking lot for junior choir, I would sigh with relief, anticipating opening the heavy door. I wasn't going to be worried or afraid once I went inside. At school, I couldn't catch a ball or fit into my gym clothes the way it seemed other girls did. My classmates saw my awkwardness and fear, and they taunted me.

Even getting good grades didn't help. They were just letters, and they didn't tell me what I needed to know—that I was likable, that I mattered.

But on the weekends, in temple, I felt likable. There, kids and adults listened to me first and THEN saw me. I got to sit in the middle of a group of people who were learning about important things, like doing justice and loving mercy. I liked knowing that I was soaking up what it took to be a Jewish kind of good girl. It felt a little bit like I was understudying Queen Esther. Like maybe I really could grow up to be a leading woman.

But it wasn't simply aging that got me from there to here. It was therapy. Session after session, I voiced my fears. Session after session, I named and dissected them. And I started to feel better.

It's as though therapy took away a sinister handheld mirror that I'd used since childhood. That mirror showed me only my weaknesses. When I looked into it, I was frightened. Over the years, therapy helped me let go of that mirror. And it helped me discover a succession of new mirrors, each one showing me fewer distortions and more facets of my whole self.

If there were a Hebrew blessing to recite before therapy sessions, it would be one of gratitude for the awesome capacity of the human mind to learn how to transform itself.

Gradually enlightened, I've come to understand why my good grades didn't add up to fulfillment and why achieving physical grace wouldn't have either. Like most kids, I simply craved open arms and the chance to lock eyes.

Now, when I hug a fortysomething former student and feel her reluctance to let me go, I feel the same way I did when the rabbi emeritus cupped my face in his hands and told me eye to eye that I would sing in the opera. I feel proud. Proud to matter, to be important in a moment of connection.

Fitting in and connecting in temple was a source of relief throughout my childhood. So was reading. I needed to read, especially late at night. NEEDED to. If I didn't read, I would think about death. Reading under the covers was risky—if Mom caught me reading after bedtime, she would take my book away. But I was a lot more worried about death than I was about losing my library book. So from under the covers, I would whisper, "I am calming myself with my brain." It was dark, and I was afraid, but I was able to concentrate on the magic story words until sleep took over.

Anxiety has continued to plague me, but I've relearned how to calm my mind. When threatened by one or another of my fears, I can defy it. I've found the words to use to talk myself all the way to feeling confident and secure again.

I've recovered something else, too—the way I felt in my body before I learned to compare myself to other little girls, both real and fictional.

I remember twirling around and around in front of my parents' bedroom mirror, my mother's tulle slip fanning out around my ankles. It was white, and it made me feel like a night-blooming flower. I patted Mom's Ma Griffe perfume on my cheeks, right near my nose.

I thought, *I AM a flower. A gardenia!*

The flower feeling has come back because I've remembered what I knew then—what young children know before they experience meanness: that pretty is a sensation. Pretty is not a verdict confirmed by a reflection in a glass or in someone else's eyes. Pretty is in the air. I can send out pretty like a gardenia sends out fragrance.

As the curtain goes up on my third act, the stage no longer looks to me like it's set for a tragedy. Maybe I did feel like a protagonist of some kind all along. But it took a lot of work—and a lot of help—for me to realize that I don't have to perpetually audition for the lead role in my own life.

Sitting in the catbird seat means directing my life based on what I know instead of what I fear.

These days, a bit late for a cantor, I'm composing a piyyut—improvising it loudly as I go along. Instead of singing like some

piyyut: poem—a liturgical work composed by a cantor

imaginary, idealized person, I've freed my own original hymn, its melody scored for my own voice, its words my own—nothing but my truth.

Although I've fucked up a lot of the standard repertoire along the way, doing the hard work of finding the truths in my story has let me become a better mother, a better cantor, and a better friend, even to myself.

The song I'm making up is a good song. It's got some counterpoint going on and a Janis Joplin throatiness. It sounds a little like haftarah chant and a little like Dixieland.

Adding the last item to my Wegman's grocery list—salmon rub—I think about how I'm going to sing my song once I've drawn the bold double bar line at its end.

I already know how I'll sign it. That's because I've reclaimed my nicknames. *Barbi* has become my favorite term of endearment for myself. And *Prim*. As a surname for Barbi, *Prim* means "self-styled."

Who I am is on the tip of my tongue.

Listen to me sing, here in my catbird seat, unafraid.

Coda

A High Note, Strong and Mighty

I stand up straight in front of the gilded full-length mirror in Nancy Townsend's voice studio. For the hundredth time, Nancy suggests gently that I look in the mirror as I breathe.

I see that my breath comes from below my waist. I see that my shoulders don't hitch. So far so good.

Then I look out the window, past one of Nancy's innumerable cats, this one a ginger tabby, and focus on the elaborate roof tiles of the tall house to the rear of her huge Victorian.

There, I think. *Go there, sound!*

Nancy says, "Release the breath, release the sound—with energy, with abandon! Ignore the tone quality!"

So I aim for the roof tiles and let go of the sound.

Oh my! Nancy and I look at each other. No crackle, no viper, nary a dybbuk anywhere. A high note, a clear high note, strong and mighty.

Vocal progress at sixty-five.

prim

adjective: feeling or showing disapproval
of anything regarded as improper;
stiffly correct ~ verb: purse (the mouth or lips)

— *Oxford English Dictionary*

adjective: inclined to be deliberately authentic
or to behave according to core values;
ethically self-styled ~ verb: articulate clearly
the words you determine to be right

—*Barbi Prim*

Acknowledgments

Sandie Feinman Antar, who told me years ago
to keep a journal. ~ Beloved members of the American
Conference of Cantors, who encouraged me to write down
my stories. ~ Rabbi Larry Rappaport, who taught me
that unsightly truths can be expressed harmoniously. ~
Jane Leyderman, formerly of the ACC office, who suggested
that I model my memoir on a graphic novel, proceeding
from snippet to snippet. ~ Beth Gaede, who arranged *Catbird's*
first feathers just so. ~ Rabbi Kerry Olitzky, who introduced me
to Beth. ~ Eric Vollen, a copyeditor with perfect pitch. ~
Ann Delgehausen, my editor at Vaerden & Co., who saw where
Catbird could go and mapped its flight. She heard my overtones—
and barely audible undertones—and with her queries, focused
my voice and brought out its color. ~ Lisa Braun Dubbels of
Catalyst Publicity & Promotion Group, for adding reverberation
to *Catbird's* song. ~ Dan, who stands proud, surrounded by
powerful affection. ~ Sarah, whose present to me on my sixtieth
birthday was a page of original haiku, which now open *Catbird's*
stanzas. ~ Scott, aka Barbi's Barista, who spent days and days
in front of either his or my computer, clicking away on revision
after revision of *Catbird*, demonstrating his love, constancy,
and language skill. ~ Psychotherapists Dr. Arlene Burrows and
Dr. Susan McDaniel, and psychiatrists Dr. Cynthia Pristach,
Dr. Linda Pessar, Dr. Stephen Glick, Dr. Zachary Puca,
and Dr. Eugene Kaplan, who helped me unshut my trap. ~
Cantors Roslyn Jhunever Barak, David Berger,
Galit Dadoun Cohen, Orna Green, Kim Harris,
and Alane Simons Katzew, for one-on-one Hebrew language
consulting. ~ Rita Kapoor Wojcik, author photo. ~
Patrick Higgins, HAIR!

Credits

Translations following Hebrew text are by the author.

Scripture quotations are from *A New Translation of the Holy Scriptures According to the Masoretic Text*, Jewish Publication Society of America:
The Torah – The Five Books of Moses, 1973, 1962
The Prophets – Nevi'im, 1978
The Writings – Kethubim, 1982

Translations of "Ma Tovu" are by the author and from *Mishkan T'filah: A Reform Siddur: Weekdays, Shabbat, Festivals, and Other Occasions of Public Worship*, Central Conference of American Rabbis, 2007

Prayer book quotations for the High Holy Days are from *Gates of Repentance: The New Union Prayer Book for the Days of Awe*, Central Conference of American Rabbis, 1978

All other prayer book quotations are from *Gates of Prayer: The New Union Prayerbook, Weekdays, Sabbaths, and Festivals Services and Prayers for Synagogue and Home*, Central Conference of American Rabbis, 1975, and *Mishkan T'filah: A Reform Siddur: Weekdays, Shabbat, Festivals, and Other Occasions of Public Worship*, Central Conference of American Rabbis, 2007

Rabbi's Manual, Central Conference of American Rabbis, 1988

"Hear My Prayer," *Union Songster: Songs and Prayers for Jewish Youth*, Central Conference of American Rabbis, 1960

"O Lord, open our eyes," *The Union Prayer Book for Jewish Worship*, Central Conference of American Rabbis, 1940

Reader's guides
for group discussions
are available at
catbirdbook.com.

CPSIA information can be obtained
at www.ICGtesting.com
Printed in the USA
FSHW021819031119
63672FS